JANE AUSTEN AND THE FRENCH REVOLUTION

JANE AUSTEN AND THE FRENCH REVOLUTION

Warren Roberts

Associate Professor of History
State University of New York at Albany

First published 1979 by
THE MACMILLAN PRESS LTD
London and Basingstoke
Associated companies in Delhi
Dublin Hong Kong Johannesburg Lagos
Melbourne New York Singapore Tokyo

Reproduced from copy supplied
printed and bound in Great Britain
by Billing and Sons Limited
Guildford, London, Oxford, Worcester

British Library Cataloguing in Publication Data

Roberts, Warren
Jane Austen and the French Revolution
1. Austen, Jane – Criticism and interpretation
I. Title
823'.7   PR4037
ISBN 0-333-26302-2

To Anne

Contents

Preface

Nothing would seem more unnecessary than another book on Jane Austen, particularly after the spate of articles and books that appeared as a result of the recent bicentennial. In fact, these publications are only part of a larger outpouring of studies that shows no signs of abating. One wonders what remains to be said about a novelist whose complete writings are contained in six volumes of modest size (in the Oxford edition of Austen's novels) plus a volume of correspondence. One particularly wonders about what can still be said about Austen when one contemplates the names that figure in the Austen criticism. Has any other English novelist attracted the interest of such a distinguished and varied group of writers as Lionel Trilling, E. M. Forster, C. S. Lewis, Edmund Wilson, Mark Schorer, Arnold Kettle, Kingsley Amis, F. R. and Q. D. Leavis, Malcolm Bradbury, Gilbert Ryle, Brigid Brophy, Geofrey Gorer, Lord David Cecil, Virginia Woolf, David Daiches, D. W. Harding, Raymond Williams, Tony Tanner and Ian Watt? The above list does not even include the Austen specialists, whose journal articles and full-length studies contain some of the finest twentieth-century criticism. The Austen criticism covers a vast range of topics, reflecting the disciplinary affiliations of those who have produced it, including literary scholars, novelists, psychologists, philosophers and anthropologists.

No historians are on the above list, and to my knowledge none have published separate studies on Austen. As varied and superb as the Austen criticism is, I believe that it can bear a historical study, and I am not alone in that belief. As B. C. Southam said to me, a preponderance of Austen criticism, something over ninety per cent in all probability, has been written basically without a historical framework, as if the novels were timeless. In Southam's opinion a historical study is precisely what is now needed. I hope that this book is an answer to that need.

Acknowledgements

As the idea for this book came to me while I was on sabbatical leave, it is only fitting that I should thank my university for making that leave possible. My colleagues, both in the History and English departments, have given timely and helpful criticism on the manuscript as it has passed through its various stages. That some of them will scarcely recognise what they find is in no small part the result of their probing and helpful comments. I should now like to thank Professors G. J. Barker-Benfield, Robert Hoffman, Thomas Barker, Kendall Birr, John Reilly, Robert Donovan, Deborah Dorfman, Walter Knotts, Edward Jennings and Walter Goldstein, all colleagues at The University at Albany, and James Sheehan, Alistair Duckworth, Marilyn Butler, Gina Luria and Frank Bradbrook for their invaluable help. Finally, I should particularly like to thank B. C. Southam for telling me that a historian could have something to say about Jane Austen and that I should go ahead and write the book.

Abbreviations

E	*Emma*
L	*Jane Austen's Letters to her Sister Cassandra and Others*
MP	*Mansfield Park*
NA	*Northanger Abbey*
P	*Persuasion*
PP	*Pride and Prejudice*
SS	*Sense and Sensibility*
MW	*Minor Works*

References to Jane Austen's works are to R. W. Chapman's editions:

The Novels of Jane Austen, ed. R. W. Chapman, 5 vols., 3rd ed. (London: Oxford University Press, 1932–4)

Minor Works, ed. R. W. Chapman (London: Oxford University Press, 1954)

Jane Austen's Letters to her Sister Cassandra and Others, ed. R. W. Chapman, 2nd ed. (London: Oxford University Press, 1952)

Introduction

Jane Austen was born at Steventon Rectory in rural Hampshire on 16 December, 1775, and died at Winchester on 18 July, 1817, at the age of forty-one. She spent all of her life in southern England, never travelling abroad, or for that matter into the Midlands or northern counties. She never married, living her entire life with her close and protective family. Along with her sister Cassandra she received a genteel education, spending several years at boarding school, first at Oxford and then at Abbey School, Reading. While the Austens belonged to the gentry, their modest income put them towards the bottom of that class in the economic sense, which helps to explain the limited schooling of the two sisters. But girls did not pursue higher education in the eighteenth century, and the learning of the Austen girls was by no means deficient for their sex. The Reverend George Austen and two of his sons, James and Henry, took a lively interest in the education of both Jane and Cassandra. The family read together, giving Jane an audience for the precocious writings that began to flow from her pen in 1788, when she was twelve. Like other girls of their class, she and her sister probably had visiting masters who taught the female accomplishments. Cassandra drew, Jane played the piano, and both of them sewed and embroidered. They attended Assembly Hall dances at nearby Basingstoke and at the homes of friends and relatives. Life for the two sisters and the entire Austen family was quiet and domestic, reflecting the values of a country village with its church and rectory.

The world of Steventon was insular and self-contained and its rhythms were agrarian. The Reverend Austen took an active interest in agricultural developments, and the home farm with its five Alderney cows provided the family table with much of its daily fare. The household had its own dairy, baked its own bread, and brewed its own ale. Sewing and darning was not a genteel pastime, but a necessity. The village of Steventon was but a row of cottages, most families in the parish living in farm houses scattered across the countryside. In all, the parish included something under two hundred households. The Rectory, which burned down in 1826, was situated on a lane alongside a few cottages and across from a large barn. It was a square Georgian house, plain both in design and construction, with walls free of ornamentation and floors covered with common-looking carpets. The road leading to the Rectory was unpaved and required periodic shovels of gravel to be passable. Behind the house there was a garden from which two hedgerows radiated, one of them running up a hill and ending half a mile away at St Nicholas's Church. To visit that church today is to have a sense of what Jane Austen's world, at Steventon, was like. Looking across the surrounding countryside one sees undulating fields that, after much attention—they are not particularly fertile—still yield their annual harvests. The church itself is on a scale with the village, its walls enclosing a space little larger than an ordinary room. Built in the thirteenth century, it would have been adequate for the village services given by Austen's father in the eighteenth century. Life at Steventon was rural, small of scale, and had about it a certain timelessness. The qualities and contours of this world left a permanent impression on Austen's thought and outlook. The twenty-five years that she lived at Steventon were what might be called the root part of her experience.

To reconstruct that experience, it is necessary to look at the larger eighteenth-century world that lay beyond Steventon. After the convulsions of the seventeenth century life in England became more settled and stable as political compromises were made, and as there was less willingness to spill blood over religious differences. Several generations of violence led to greater circumspection, and the lessons of science furthered rational modes of thought. The pomp and heroic grandeur of one age yielded to the propriety and correctness of another, just as metaphysical speculation gave way to the more careful probings of empirical investigation. The thinkers of the age were content to ask less in order to understand more clearly, and felt a flush of confidence over scientific achievements and the age of progress that followed therefrom. A tragic view of life was replaced by one that was benign and hopeful and regarded man not as a fallen creature but intrinsically generous and morally good. Social life became more refined and cultivated, furnishings more elegant, language more precise, houses more comfortable and commodious, and life within the family more intimate. While the distribution of wealth continued to favour the few at the expense of the many, there was an overall increase of wealth; life for the propertied classes was better than ever. The England of the eighteenth century was self-confident and proud of its achievement, proud of a political system that was admired and praised everywhere, proud of its overseas possessions, and proud of an economy and fiscal system that was second to none. The term 'civilised security', which so aptly has been used to characterise the age, applies not only to measurable, positive material conditions but to a collective state of mind. The stability of eighteenth-century England was more than political and economic; it was also psychological and emotional. Even the riots, which were endemic, were carefully controlled and did not threaten established relationships. Problems there were, problems aplenty, but they occurred within a framework that was stable and relatively impervious to such stresses and strains as welled up from within the social body. While England was hardly a macrocosm of Steventon, both worlds were orderly and subject to controls and limits that were fundamental to the age as a whole. If life at Steventon was not a reflection of the age it did blend into it.

Austen's outlook was influenced by her experience at Steventon, in the midst of her family and friends, but it was also shaped by the larger eighteenth-century world. Careful scholarship has identified the writers that she knew and judiciously considered their effect on her thought.[1] To go through a list of these authors is to encounter names that both mirrored the age and defined its outlines. Those authors helped Austen find her bearings inside her world. Her value system and special qualities of mind, her brittleness, refinement, precision, control and clarity all relate to the eighteenth-century civilisation from which she sprang.

Much of the Austen criticism views her fiction as a reflection of the quiet, rural life that she did in fact live, and much of it sees the mode of her thought and prose as eighteenth-century, as to a large extent it was. But Austen was not just of the eighteenth century, and her world was by no means completely calm. She was thirteen in the summer of 1789, when forces were unleashed in France that set that nation and every nation of the western world on a different course. Life was no longer the same and never would be again, so great were the transformations that flowed from this crucial historical moment. This was so in France and throughout the continent, and it was so in England. England was shaken politically by the French Revolution and drawn into a struggle for survival that lasted almost to the end of Austen's life. The years of international peace that followed

Napoleon's final defeat were years of profound uneasiness and political restiveness throughout Europe, and perhaps most acutely in England. So the clear outlines of Austen's world became blurred as she passed from youth into adolescence; the stability of the eighteenth century broke down dramatically before new and devastating forces that passed across the Channel from France. While Austen's root experience was provided by Steventon and conditioned by the larger characteristics of eighteenth-century life, she underwent a quite different experience as the stresses and strains of the Revolution entered the rural calm of her world and disrupted its accepted ways. The impact of the French Revolution on Austen's thinking and writing is the subject of this study.

It is a subject that has received but limited treatment. For this there are reasons. Austen never referred to the Revolution in any of her novels, at least directly, nor did she do so in any of her extant correspondence. In the second half of the nineteenth century the members of her own family assumed that she had lived outside the political storm that raged away during her lifetime. Her niece Caroline discussed this point after a visitor asked what Austen's 'opinion on the great public events of her time had been', and mentioned that, after all, she had been a 'young woman, able to *think*, at the time of French Revolution'. Reaching into her memory, this niece searched for clues about 'what part such a mind as her's had taken in the great strifes of war and policy which so disquieted Europe for more than 20 years'. Having retraced her 'steps on *this* track' she was able to find 'absolutely nothing'.[2]

The moment has arrived when literary critics have become more aware of the importance of viewing Austen against the historical background of her age. B. C. Southam has recently issued an appeal to historians 'to offer us a helping hand'. He adds that 'more and more critics are venturing into this (to them) strange territory, and Jane Austen studies seem set on a historical course for some years to come'.[3] Thus far historians have only added to the misunderstanding of Austen by perpetuating the myth of her remaining aloof from the great events of the day. In Volume XII of the *Oxford History of England* J. Steven Watson says that Austen seems to have been unaware 'of the events of the outside world'.[4] Elie Halévy writes in his authoritative *England in 1815* that Austen was 'ignorant of the brutal and unclean aspects of life' and, isolated from the outside world, she portrayed the 'petty jealousies and hatreds, the littleness and the meanness which characterized social relations in the country and the provincial town'.[5] G. M. Trevelyan refers to Austen's novels as evidence of English complacency during this time of turmoil.[6] Thinking of the tranquil world of Austen's novels, Winston Churchill wrote, 'what calm lives they had, those people! No worries about the French Revolution, or the Napoleonic Wars.'

Just as historians have contributed to a misunderstanding of Austen, so too have some of the literary critics who have looked for connections between Austen and the history of her time. Arnold Kettle has argued that 'the rise and development of the English novel, like any other phenomenon in literature, can only be understood as a part of history'.[7] Taking his cue from Georg Lukàcs he found 'an atmosphere of stablity and security and also a certain complacent shortsightedness' in the eighteenth-century novel that he feels Austen 'emphatically shares'. He infers that Austen should be seen not against the background of the Revolutionary Age in which she lived but as a representative of a stable order that had already, in 1688, experienced its revolution. Austen's class, the gentry, had come to power at the end of the seventeenth century and continued to reap the benefits of victory throughout the following century. These conditions contributed to a complacency within the gentry that Austen reflected in her fiction. This 'limitation must not be ignored or glossed over'. Arnold Hauser levels the same charge against Austen, regarding her as 'ill-informed' and unaware of the political issues of her day. In her novels 'social reality was the soil in which the characters were rooted, but in no sense a problem which the novelist made any attempt to solve or interpret'.[8]

This is a view that Lionel Trilling has rejected. In the Charles Eliot Norton Lectures, given in 1969–70, he said:

> The once common view was that, although her characters are rooted in social actuality, Jane Austen does not conceive of society as being in any sense problematical, as making issues by reason of the changes it was undergoing in her time. In the present state of opinion about the novelist there is little disposition to accept this. On the contrary, a large part of the interest of her work is now thought to lie exactly in the sensitivity of her response to social change.[9]

To examine Austen's response to social change inevitably means considering the impact of the French Revolution on her life and writing. Her lifetime exactly coincided with a decisive period of change, when the old, hierarchical society of England came under heavy attack, struggled for survival, made various adjustments, but nonetheless emerged from the Revolutionary period profoundly altered. If Austen was not just alive in her times but alive to them, as Trilling maintains, one must understand the times if one is to understand both her and her novels.

Trilling himself made two brilliant contributions to that understanding in essays on *Mansfield Park* and *Emma*, published respectively in 1954[10] and 1957[11]. One of his students, Avrom Fleishman, sees *Mansfield Park* appearing at a crucial point in the transition of English society to the modern age, when there was a fear that the French Revolution would spread to England. He argues that the themes of *Mansfield Park* grew out of Austen's responses to the French Revolution and Napoleonic Wars and their impact on English life.[12] Alistair Duckworth, believing Austen to have been deeply aware of social change, traces her response to it through an examination of the improvement theme in her novels.[13] Like Fleishman, Duckworth finds a conservatism in Austen's reaction to change that links her to Edmund Burke and the organicist political theory that was a counter to the radical ideology of the Revolution.

Marilyn Butler, in her recently published *Jane Austen and the War of Ideas*, goes further than any present study in seeing Austen's novels not as a record of provincial insularity but revealing the author's social engagement and responses to the problems of the Revolutionary age.[14] Butler makes her case by placing Austen's novels against the background of contemporary fiction, in which a war of ideas was conducted by Jacobin and anti-Jacobin writers, those who responded favourably to the ideology of the French Revolution and those who stood behind the traditional order. Both types of novel had distinctive formal characteristics, treated certain themes, and rested upon a composite of attitudes that reflected a particular social vision. Butler argues that Austen's novels are linked, at one point after another, with the anti-Jacobin novels that appeared in such large numbers, many of which she read, and whose point of view—and ideology—she shared. What Butler does not show, because it is outside the scope of her study, is how Austen arrived at the ideology, other than by reading novels. As the dust cover of her book says, 'It is often said that Jane Austen in the countryside remained isolated from the great events of her time. But she was not isolated from reading novels, and novels carried controversy.' How Austen experienced the great events of her time Butler does not attempt to explain; her interest is in the connection between Austen and other novelists. The advantage of Butler's approach is that it indicates one source of Austen's partisanship, showing how she relates to the literature of ideas; its limitation is that it does not explain how Austen connects with the actual process of historical change. If it can be shown how the political turbulence unleashed by the French Revolution entered Austen's world and affected her own life her novels can be seen in a different light, not just as a response to other fiction but as a record of her own experience.

This is precisely what I hope to do. As I will explain, Austen was connected to the great events of the day in a surprising number of ways, often through the members of her own family, whose lives were deeply affected by the political upheaval in France or who were active participants in the Revolutionary and Napoleonic Wars. For me, much of Austen's fascination is that she made a deliberate choice not to discuss directly the events that so disturbed her world, and yet incorporated many of her responses to those events into her writing. To examine her way of doing so is to enter into the very workings of history, thanks to Austen's ability to pick up the vibrations of a society that was in the throes of change and to incorporate them into her fiction. Her way of doing so was not that of an active propagandist in the war of ideas, of a Burke, Fox or Wordsworth, but a person who, as she experienced change, worked out her responses to it in her novels. Precisely because of this relationship between her experience and her novels her writing is charged with a tension that reflects and indeed is part of the history of her time. To read Austen is not only to see, as one can, how she responded to change and became politically aware, it is to enter into the life of her time in a way that one can do through no other novelist. As Fleishman has written, 'Jane Austen has become the novelist we lean on most heavily to tell us what it was like to be alive in England at the beginning of the nineteenth century.' I would add that no other writer, and indeed no other evidence, brings out as well the qualitative change that occurred in English society as it was assimilating the stresses of the Revolutionary Age.

Austen does this in part through what Trilling calls the 'hum and buzz of implication', the small actions, tone, emphasis, gesture, and words that a novelist uses with a special frequency or meaning.[15] But she also evokes that change through a careful choice of themes and a highly diverse set of *dramatis personae*, whose dialogue and actions reveal Austen's own stand on some key contemporary issues. So her novels are an invaluable way to have a sense of what it was like to go through a critical period of social change, and they tell us what one highly perceptive member of English society thought about it.

It need hardly be said that Austen's response to change reflects her own social position as a member of the English gentry. She was not an unthinking representative of her class, but viewed that class critically. According to one school of thought, Austen was a subversive, hostile to her class although not its declared enemy, while another school regards her as a pillar of the Establishment and even a reactionary. In fact, she was neither, but a person who was deeply affected by the historical impulses of her age and at the same time sought to understand change and its consequences for her class. As she lived through the Revolutionary Age she hoped, as a member of the gentry, of traditional landed society, to see the members of her class adjust to a world that was changing before her, but also she was aware of their shortcomings. Neither attacking nor defending her class, she examined its chances of survival.

I trust it is clear by now that my subject is not just Jane Austen and the French Revolution, if by the Revolution one means the period of French history between the meeting of the Estates General in 1789 and the establishment of the Consulate in 1799. Rather, my subject is the impact of the Revolution and its ideology on England and on Austen, and not just from 1789 to 1799, but to the end of her life. In some respects a more appropriate title for my study would have been 'Jane Austen and The Age of Democratic Revolution'. The advantage of this title is that it draws attention to a larger pattern of change of which the French Revolution was but a part. Some historians now regard the many conflicts that broke out in Europe and America after 1760 as preludes to the cataclysmic events of 1789. Beneath the apparent stability of the eighteenth century change was taking place, as seen in the many political collisions and the rise of a new economic order that ultimately altered every phase of life and was already making an impact at the time of Austen's birth in 1775. England played a major role in these changes, in the war with the American colonies, the bitter struggle for political reform, and the industrial breakthrough of the 1770s. James Watt took out a patent on his steam engine in 1769, in 1775 the American colonies broke into rebellion, and in 1776 Adam Smith published *The Wealth of Nations*.

So why have I chosen the title *Jane Austen and the French Revolution?* Because Austen's world was largely untouched by these earlier developments. When I say Austen's world I do not mean England as a whole but the world of Steventon, the rural insular village life of northern Hampshire. The structure of life in Steventon was traditional, and its atmosphere and feeling reflected the stability of the eighteenth century. Austen's world was not that of London or the Midlands, it was not the scene of political conflict and industrialisation. Relatively impervious to the changes of the 1770s and 1780s, Steventon was not insulated from the tremors of the French Revolution and the profound impact on English life that they caused.

My way of showing how the Revolution entered Austen's world and affected her thinking and writing inevitably reflects my training as a historian. It is not the type of approach that is characteristic of Austen studies, or indeed of literary scholarship in any of its usual forms. In each of the four chapters I have tried to fit Austen into an historical framework; in constructing these frameworks I have described sets of conditions that do not relate in every particular to Austen but do delineate patterns of change that will serve as a useful background against which she can be seen. In the historical sections I hope to convey a vivid sense of how the England in which Austen lived was changing in response to the new burdens of the Revolutionary Age. Without such a sense it is difficult, if not impossible, to grasp the type of experience that she underwent in living through such stressful times. I must say that deciding how much history to fit into the narrative was one of the most difficult of tasks. As readers bring different levels of historical understanding to such a book as this some will find my discussions more helpful than others. While those discussions could have been shorter, they could also have been longer.

Another problem was the paucity of biographical evidence pertinent to the study. If the reader's patience is sometimes tried by the piecing together of bits and pieces of biographical fact, it should be remembered that fragmentary as the evidence is there often was no other choice. Rather than abuse the author for his fragile constructions it would be kind to commend him for building so much out of so little! It would be well to remember that in none of Austen's writings did she as much as mention the French Revolution, whose impact on her thinking and writing is the book's subject. One might well feel that faced with such difficulties the book should not have been written; it is hoped that the narrative that follows will justify the enterprise.

The argument is contained in four chapters. The first, whose subject is politics, maintains that Austen became keenly aware of some of the leading social issues of the day, that her novels contain a thoughtful, searching record of that awareness, and that she took a position on these issues that was ideological. The French Revolution had an immediate impact on England and initiated a political debate that pertained not only to how the Revolution was viewed but to internal, domestic issues. While not a propagandist, Austen was a participant in that debate. In showing how she argued her case I have drawn from a number of fine studies that beautifully show how engaged Austen was by the problems of the Revolutionary Age. My indebtedness to those studies will be apparent to the reader.

While it is well known that England's war with France is a theme in *Mansfield Park* and *Persuasion* and that its presence can be felt in *Emma*, what Austen thought about the war during the long period in which it ran its course has not been thoroughly examined. Such an examination is the subject of chapter 2. I will show how profound was the impact of the war on England, the many points at which the war touched Austen's life, how she responded to it, and how her novels reflect that response. The underlying premise of the chapter is that the war was an outgrowth of the French Revolution and, as such, Austen's reaction to it relates directly to my subject.

Chapter 3, whose subject is religion, will pay particular attention to Austen's interest in Evangelicalism. The roots of Evangelicalism lay deep in eighteenth-century English life. While religious enthusiasm tended to die down in the eighteenth century, there were moments when accesses of emotional religious feeling would issue forth. The very quiet of England's religious life was a stimulus for these responses, which arose in various times and assumed different forms. While Methodism and Evangelicalism both grew up in the Church of England, the former broke away but the latter did not. Both experienced tremendous growth in the 1790s and in the early nineteenth century, and did so in direct response to the French Revolution. My discussion will be limited to Evangelicalism because of its relationship to Austen. In examining Evangelicalism and the change it wrought on Austen, I am treating a subject that at bottom is historical and one that can be understood only if it is seen as part of the Revolutionary Age. It will be seen that with the impact of Evangelicalism the contours of eighteenth-century life began to break down and new ones, those of the nineteenth century, took their place. Already in Austen's novels the Victorian world can be seen on the horizon. Evangelicalism played a key role in summoning that world into being. Without that religious movement the new pattern of life would not be fully intelligible, and without the French Revolution that movement would not have been the force that it was. Through Austen's fiction the shifting social and moral currents of the age can be seen.

Finally, the subject of the last chapter is feminism. One of the key works in the history of feminism, Mary Wollstonecraft's *Vindication of the Rights of Woman*, appeared in 1792, and quickly became part of the debate carried on in England over the French Revolution. As Wollstonecraft was close to Godwin, Priestley and Paine, and since she applied certain of their principles and those of the Revolution to the *Vindication*, this was bound to happen. Those supporting Wollstonecraft's views about the role of women were by no means all in the radical camp, at least initially. Increasingly, however, as the radical cause was discredited in England, so too was the feminist cause. Out of the debate over the position of women and a related discussion on marriage and the family came a set of attitudes that would have a deep impact on nineteenth-century English life, contributing to the primacy of the family that was such an important feature of the Victorian era. Austen lived through the period of this debate and in her fiction worked out her own responses to it. Her way of doing this was consistent with the stand she took on a wide range of other contemporary issues, and reflected a conservative social vision. In throwing her weight behind the family she valued an institution capable of maintaining order and stability and furthering social continuity. That she did so was another of her responses to the stresses and strains of the Revolutionary Age.

1 Politics

While conversing with his sister and Catherine Morland, Henry Tilney (in *Northanger Abbey*) 'suffered the subject to decline, and by an easy transition from a piece of rocky fragment and the withered oak which he had placed near its summit, to oaks in general, to forests, the inclosure of them, waste lands, crown lands and government, he shortly found himself arrived at politics; and from politics, it was an easy step to silence'. (NA,III)[1] The hero of this novel moved from politics to silence because of the female company. According to the manners of the time politics was a male preserve, not to be discussed in mixed company or by women. Not only did Henry Tilney abide by this convention, but so too, it seems, did Jane Austen. In her novels men talked about politics alone, as women, seated elsewhere, occupied themselves with subjects appropriate to their sex, such as fashions or neighbourhood gossip. Moreover, the novels did not touch upon any of the leading political questions of the day, at least directly, as contemporary readers were aware. When discussing her novels, Austen described her setting as 'pictures of domestic life in country villages',[2] (L,452) and '3 or 4 families in a Country Village'. (L,401) It would seem that Austen was the least political of novelists and, in fact, she has often been seen in this light.

J. E. Austen-Leigh wrote in 1871 that his aunt 'was always very careful not to meddle with matters she did not thoroughly understand. She never touched upon politics . . .'[3] In his opinion Austen's world was the private, domestic, provincial world of the English village, and her main concern was her family. 'Her own family were so much, and the rest of the world so little, to Jane Austen . . .'[4] William and Richard Arthur Austen-Leigh perpetuated this view in *Jane Austen, Her Life and Letters* (1913), which is subtitled 'A Family Record'. While Austen's grand-nephews felt that 'the uneventful nature of the author's life . . . has been a good deal exaggerated', they never suggested any political awareness. Her life was quiet, 'but the quiet life of a member of a large family in the England of that date was compatible with a good deal of stirring incident, happening, if not to herself, at all events to those who were nearest to her, and who commanded her deepest sympathies'.[5] Other biographers have seen Austen in much the same light as the members of the Austen family. Elizabeth Jenkins, for instance, seeing her in the midst of relatives and friends, described her world as one of 'undistracted leisure'.[6]

This view of Austen has not gone unchallenged. A number of writers have indicated that Austen was a Tory. The novelist's niece, Caroline Austen, indicated that the entire Austen family was Tory.[7] In a recent biography, Jane Aiken Hodge says the same thing.[8] Donald J. Greene has called Austen a 'Tory Democrat', [9] while R. E. Hughes considers her a 'philosophic Tory'.[10] Looking at *Mansfield Park*, Avrom Fleishman sees in the theatrical scene a criticism by the Tory gentry of 'the Whig aristocracy's flirtation with the culture of the French Revolution'.[11] This criticism, in his opinion, represents the position of the novelist.

While these writers see Austen as Tory they do not agree on the exact sense of her Toryism. Before trying to define and explain her Toryism myself it will be necessary to sketch in some political background.[12]

The Hanoverian succession was a major setback for the Tory party, whose allegiance was to the House of Stuart. In spite of this difficulty sizeable numbers of Tories continued to sit in Parliament. In 1716, 162 Tories voted against the Septennial Act, and 154 voted against its repeal in 1734. In 1760, 114 Tories sat in the first of George III's Parliaments. While it was still possible to compile a list of Tories in 1760, a decade later it was difficult to do so, and by 1780 the political term Tory no longer applied to a party, as MPs of that persuasion had largely joined the ranks of the 'Independent Country Gentlemen'. Between 1688 and 1714 there had been 'Independent Country Gentlemen' in both the Whig and Tory parties, in opposition to the Court factions in each. Gradually, after 1714, Court-minded Tories drifted over to the Whigs, while country Whigs merged with the 'Independent Country Gentlemen'. This group had little organisation, and was made up of men who voted according to their individual lights and did not share in the perquisites of office that went almost exclusively to members of the Whig party. If one wished to enjoy those perquisites one had no choice but to be a Whig. To be a Tory or 'Independent Country Gentleman' entitled one to vote as one saw fit, but not to political reward.

After 1714, there was a steady drift away from party politics until the very term Tory virtually disappeared as a way to describe a political group. There were Whigs and there was an unorganised, shifting, variable opposition. While there was no opposition party, the Whigs themselves did not constitute a party in the modern sense of the word. In addition to the 'in' faction there were various 'out' factions, also Whig, that were highly organised and fought tooth and claw to dislodge those presently exercising the levers of power. They were in the difficult position of having to attack an administration and its policies without having any ideological reasons for doing so. There were, in fact, no rival ideologies, but rather there was a division between those who aspired to the advantages of office and those who did not, and within the former there were various factions that continually hacked away at one another, for the purpose of retaining or gaining office and enjoying its benefits. The struggle took place not along party lines but within one party; in fact, the eighteenth-century political ideal was not party but the extinction of party.

While some historians have seen the emergence of a new Toryism in 1760 with the accession of George III, this view is mistaken. Lord Bute was a Whig, like George III's other favourites, even though his enemies sometimes called him Tory. In doing so, they were simply using 'Tory' as a term of opprobrium. The bitter political struggles of the 1760s, 1770s and early 1780s were not waged along party lines, and when Pitt the Younger headed his first ministry in 1783 he was but another in a long succession of Whig leaders. While Fox and others denounced Pitt as a Tory, Pitt refused to grant a monopoly on Whig principles to the opposition, and in fact he tried to 'unwhig' the 'out' Whigs by claiming to be more Whig than they. Eventually Pitt's party would become the Tory party, although it was not given that name during his lifetime. In fact, it was not until 1818, several years after the Napoleonic Wars ended, that popular writers described the government as Tory. Even then members of the government were hesitant to wear the label; it was only after 1827 that the term came into official usage.

It has been argued that once a one-party system gave way to a two-party system the term Tory was bound to creep back as the name of the second party. This is undoubtedly correct. What must be explained is the conditions that again gave rise to a two-party system. Those conditions flowed directly from the French Revolution and its impact on English political life.

English public opinion was highly favourable when Louis XVI summoned the Estates General in 1788, and continued to be so with the creation of a National Assembly and the sweeping changes that took place in the summer of 1789.[13] As those changes were accompanied by violence, some became uneasy and some hostile, but others, responding favourably to the high-minded declarations and welcoming the creation of a new society, became even more enthusiastic. Out of the disagreement came a debate over the French Revolution, with those opposing it inevitably standing behind their own social and political system and those supporting it arguing for internal, domestic change. Among the latter were some independent spirits from the upper classes, enthused intellectuals and poets, a fair number of dissenters, and a much larger representation from what might be called people 'in trade', including some businessmen and their employees and more importantly members of the artisan class. Disaffected from their own system, these radicals, 'Jacobins' as they came to be called, worked for a more democratic form of government in England. They did so through political organisations such as the aristocratic Friends of the People, the Society for Constitutional Information, and the more popular London Corresponding Society.

Some radicals, stimulated by the legislation in France, wanted to alter the entire English tax structure, and more generally to eliminate privilege. The egalitarian system that they envisioned clearly struck at the very foundations of the prevailing social and family system. Moreover, steeped as their programme was in the rational, secular ideology of the French Revolution, it is not surprising that they attacked the institution of the Church, correctly seeing it as one of the key props of the established order. Using the language of Rousseau and the Revolutionary Declaration of the Rights of Man and the Citizen, the Sheffield chapter of the London Corresponding Society demanded an equality of rights that would make 'the Slave a Man, the Man a Citizen, and the Citizen an integral part of the State, to make him a joint Sovereign, and not a Subject'.

The eruption of violence in Paris in the summer of 1792 made the English debate over the French Revolution more strident, and created a new type of political division. Initially the government had been indifferent to news from Paris, or at least disinclined to act, but the course of events eventually forced Pitt into a painful reappraisal of his position. France's declaration of war on Austria in the spring of 1792 initiated a chain of developments that brought a sudden end to the newly established Legislative Assembly and to the brief experiment in constitutional monarchy. A series of military reversals in the first months of war led to a collapse of the Roland ministry in June, and precipitated a mob attack on the Tuileries in the same month. The threatening Manifesto of the Duke of Brunswick in July further exacerbated tensions, leading to an outbreak of violence in August and September. By 21 September, monarchy was abolished and on 21 January, 1793, Louis was executed. A succession of internal convulsions quickly followed, leading to the victory of Robespierre, the domination of the Jacobin party, and the Reign of Terror, which went unchecked until July, 1794, when Robespierre himself fell.

The origins of the modern Tory party can be traced to a political crisis that broke out within the Whig party in 1792–3, in response to the upheaval in Paris. Up to this time, the English political system was that of the eighteenth century; by the time of Robespierre's fall, the old one-party system had been dealt a blow that split the Whigs into rival groups. While there had always been rival factions within the Whig party, this new division went much deeper and laid the foundations for a two-party system.

When Edmund Burke wrote the *Reflections on the French Revolution* in 1790, he appeared to other Whigs to have lost his balance in seeing such dark forces at work across the Channel. The violence that erupted in 1792 led some politicians to feel that his grave forebodings had been right and that he had seen more deeply into the Revolution than they. But not all felt that way. Even after the September Massacres in 1792 and the execution of Louis XVI in January 1793, some MPs continued to support the Revolution, whose ideals they still believed in despite the violence. Burke's former friend and sometime political ally, Charles James Fox, was the leader of this group, which became smaller and less effective as the cause they supported came increasingly to be regarded as malignant. Portland and other 'out' Whigs joined Pitt, whose party waxed stronger than ever, held together by a common fear of France and the ideology that it was spawning throughout Europe. To support Pitt was to support the established order; it meant opposing the Revolution and its beliefs; and it meant suppressing internal radicalism. The elements that were so aligned constituted the basis of the modern Tory party.

While the new Tory party rose from the conditions resulting from the French Revolution, there was a connection between the new and old Toryism. Even though 'Tory' had ceased to designate a political group during the eighteenth century, it did represent an enduring English social type. This type was committed to the Church of England, loyal to the institution of monarchy, quite possibly attached to the House of Stuart, suspicious of London and the Court, tied to local, provincial ways and customs, opposed to a standing army, and convinced that England's strength lay in her navy. If this pattern of Toryism had a nerve centre it was Oxford. This type of Tory would gravitate toward a party whose ideology was conservative once that party took shape.

Austen belonged to a family that was Tory in the eighteenth-century sense of the word. Her grandfather, father and two of her brothers were country vicars of the Anglican persuasion; her family on both sides had ties at Oxford University, an ancestor of her mother having been a Founder of St John's College, and her grandfather, uncle, father and two brothers were Oxford graduates; through her mother's family, the Leighs, there is a known history of loyalty to the Stuart dynasty; two of her brothers were officers in the Royal Navy; and, finally, she came from a part of England, rural Hampshire, that was traditionally Tory. Austen could hardly have been anything other than Tory, given the traditions of her family. Saying that the Austens were Tory, Caroline Austen was simply recording a fact. By Tory she did not mean a political Tory, but rather used the term in the earlier, eighteenth-century sense.

Yet Austen's Toryism did have a political dimension. She lived through an age of ideological conflict and social dislocation, and in responding to these developments worked out a variety of positions that connected her to writers such as Burke, Wordsworth, Coleridge and Southey. Her way of responding was unlike theirs. These contemporaries of Austen were actively political, pamphleteers in the war of ideas, occupying a prominent position on the public stage. Owing to her station in life and background, Austen related to the progression of events differently. Her writing was not political in the same way that theirs was, not being propagandistic or having the winning of minds as its objective. As D. W. Harding has said, 'Her object is not missionary; it is the more desperate one of merely finding some mode of existence for her critical attitudes.'[14] What Harding does not show is the conservatism behind those attitudes and the historical ground on which they were tested. While Austen

did not occupy the public stage and certainly was not a political
activist, her writing shows her responses to the great events of the
day, and while embedded in domestic novels they were the
responses of a person deeply engaged by the problem of how the
individual should live in society and how society should be ordered.
Like Burke, Wordsworth, Coleridge and Southey, her thinking and
writing were conditioned by the new forces unleashed by France
after 1789, and like them she was a conservative.

Austen's awareness of violence and political repression is one of
the keys to her Toryism. Living through a period of ideological
conflict and social unrest, seeing the stable world that she knew
thrown into disarray, she responded to the turbulence of her time in
a way that was consistent with her background and class position,
and also with a larger English response. Of all the countries in
Europe, the conservative reaction in England was most successful.
This did not result solely from governmental action, but spon-
taneously, the initiative coming from various quarters. While the
propertied classes led the reaction, popular demonstrations in the
early 1790s in support of King and Altar indicate a deeply
engrained loyalty to the established order across a wide spectrum of
English society.

The main source for trying to reconstruct Austen's response to the
Revolution is her fiction. The extant correspondence does not begin
until 1796, and in any event is without political observation or
discussion. The only fact about the Revolution that one can glean
from her letters is that she never discussed it. Of the considerable
body of fiction that Austen wrote during the 1790s, only two works,
'Catharine' and *Northanger Abbey*, show an awareness of the French
Revolution and its impact on English life, at least insofar as I have
been able to determine. It is entirely possible that 'Elinor and
Marianne' and 'First Impressions' also bore an impression of the
Revolutionary experience, but as these works are known only
through the later, revised versions they cannot be used in the present
discussion.

There are no direct references to the Revolution in 'Catharine'
and *Northanger Abbey*, but a careful reading of certain passages offers
clear proof that Austen was well aware of the political storm across
the Channel and the disturbance it caused in her own land. The
passages that I will discuss in 'Catharine' are intelligible only if they
are seen against the background of Austen's private life, on which
the Revolution had a considerable bearing. Austen knew about the

violence of the French Revolution through her cousin, Eliza de Feuillide. Eliza was born in India, where her mother went as a girl, penniless but with the hope of making a good marriage, as she did. Her mother took her to France in 1777, where both were received at Versailles. Still in France in 1781, Eliza married the comte de Feuillide. She became pregnant in 1785, and visited relatives in England in 1786 with her new son. Just before she went to England one of Austen's brothers, Edward, visited her in France. Another brother, Henry, stayed with her in London, where she set up a household, in 1787. In time, Steventon became almost a second home for Eliza, who was close to both of the Austen daughters, but especially Jane.

From 1788 to 1792 Eliza and her husband travelled back and forth between England and France, trying to arrange their affairs in the midst of increasingly unsettled conditions. They were often separated during this difficult period. In January 1791, Eliza, staying at Margate, wrote that 'M. de F. had given me hopes of his return to England this winter, but the turn which the affairs of France have taken will not allow him to quit the Continent at this juncture'.[15] She then explained that her husband was a strong royalist and had joined a party of *émigrés* in Turin, hoping soon 'to reinstate themselves in the country they have quitted'. Obviously apprehensive over the future, she despaired over his chances of success in a project 'which must inevitably in some degree influence my destiny'. She was hoping for her husband's arrival in England in June 1791, and sometime during the winter of 1791–2 the comte de Feuillide did come to England, it seems upon hearing of his mother-in-law's fatal illness. While he hoped to stay in London with his wife he was unable to. As Eliza explained, 'he soon received accounts from France which informed him that, having already exceeded his leave of absence, if he still continued in England he would be considered as one of the Emigrants, and consequently, his whole property forfeited to the Nation. Such advices were not to be neglected, and M. de F. was obliged to depart for Paris, but not, however, without giving me hopes of his return in some months . . .'[16] Upon returning to France to protect his property, he tried to help an aristocratic friend, the marquise de Marboeuf, who was accused of conspiring against the Republic. His strategy was to bribe a certain Morel, one of the Secretaries of the Committee of Safety, to suppress some incriminating documents, and give false testimony. Morel led the comte on and then betrayed him. Both the marquise and de Feuillide were found guilty, the latter going to the guillotine on 22 February, 1794.

It is possible that Eliza was at Steventon when she received news of her husband's death. In any event, the Austens were well-informed of the comte's difficulties in France after he returned to protect his property in 1792. Eliza visited the Austens in August or September 1792, when the French Revolution was entering its most violent stages, with the storming of the Tuileries and the September massacres. She was at Steventon on 26 September, when she wrote of the upheaval in Paris.

> I can readily believe that the share of sensibility I know you to be possessed of would not suffer you to learn the tragical events of which France has of late been the theatre, without being much affected. My private letters confirm the intelligence afforded by Public prints, and assure me that nothing we there read is exaggerated. M. de F. is at present in Paris. He had determined on coming to England, but finds it impossible to get away.[17]

Austen wrote 'Catharine' (dedicated August 1792) at the time of Eliza's visit. B. C. Southam has shown that Austen alluded to Eliza's mother through the fictional character, Mrs. Wynne.[18] That she did so is by no means unusual, as most of her youthful works are connected in some way or another to her family. Fourteen out of the sixteen pieces in the Juvenilia are dedicated to the intimate circle of family and friends to whom they were read and to whom Austen's allusive humour often referred. So fragile was that humour that the references which Austen's amused audience would quickly have picked up are for the most part lost on today's readers. But when a character such as the orphaned Mrs. Wynne was sent to India to find a rich husband the biographical reference is clear; this obviously points to Eliza de Feuillide's mother, who went to India under similar circumstances. Southam suggests that Austen alluded to her aunt, who had died eight months before 'Catharine''s dedication, as a gesture of sympathy and respect for Eliza. This would indicate that Austen was thinking about her cousin when she wrote 'Catharine', which stands to reason as Eliza arrived in Steventon either during the month of its dedication or in the following month.

Until now Austen criticism has not identified other biographical details in 'Catharine' that also related to Eliza de Feuillide. Edward

Stanley can be linked to Eliza's husband, the comte de Feuillide. As
we have seen, this French aristocrat's life became increasingly
complicated under the pressure of events in a country that was
experiencing revolution. After coming to England several times he
made a final visit during the winter of 1791–2 to see his ailing
mother-in-law, but had to return to France to protect his property.
Edward Stanley, his counterpart, was in France when he received
news of a 'melancholy event', the illness of his favourite horse.
Distressed by the news, he 'set off directly for England, and without
packing up another Coat'. (MW,222) While Edward's father,
Mr. Stanley, was delighted to see him he did not think it wise for
him to stay in England and urged him to return to France. Initially,
Edward was disinclined to follow his father's advice, partly because
he became romantically interested in the heroine, but eventually
did as his father wished. In fact, he had never been that interested in
Catharine, and having trifled with her as long as he cared he was
ready to return anyway. Point-for-point this part of the story agrees
with the movements of the comte de Feuillide, who came to
England because of an illness, returned to France to protect his
property, and was fickle and inconstant. When put on trial in 1794,
his mistress gave testimony against him. Eliza was well aware of his
romantic escapades and so too was Austen, judging from her
portrayal of Edward Stanley.

That Austen alluded to the comte's movements indicates that she
was aware of his difficulties; moreover, she was obviously sensitive to
her cousin's uncertainties and apprehensions. These allusions, like
those referring to Eliza's deceased mother, can be seen as an
indication of Austen's thoughtful concern. The allusion to Eliza's
husband and his forced separation from his wife can be viewed as
Austen's way of using comedy as a means to introduce a note of
levity into Eliza's complicated life, as a device for sympathising with
her cousin by amusing her. When the passages describing Edward
Stanley's travels are seen in this light their value is not only in their
ability to amuse but also to relieve tension.

It would be interesting to know precisely when Austen wrote
'Catharine'. Did she work on it before dedicating it (in August) or
afterwards? Also, why did she leave it unfinished? These questions
are intriguing because the answers could help explain what she
knew about the grim events that were taking place across the
Channel and how she responded to those events. In all probability
she began writing 'Catharine' soon before or at the time of Eliza's

arrival. This sequence would explain the allusions to Eliza's deceased mother and absent husband. That Austen would have decided to refer to the comte's return to France after learning about the upheaval that rocked Paris in late August and September does not seem likely, as doing so would have made light of a situation that suddenly became grave and that Eliza recognised as such. Rather, Austen probably learned about the violence across the Channel while she was writing 'Catharine', while Eliza was at Steventon, and stopped working on it under the altered circumstances. In this view, the pen of the precocious seventeen-year old writer was silenced by shock waves that moved from a politically convulsed France into the quiet recesses of rural Hampshire; as the news from Paris worsened Austen found the writing of 'Catharine' inappropriate.

Though Austen wrote *Northanger Abbey* some five years after the latest of the Juvenilia, this novel does connect with the youthful writings at several obvious points. As with the Juvenilia, Austen burlesqued fictional themes, conventions and character types through close imitation, exaggeration displaced emphasis or some other unexpected turn. She used her earlier techniques to show that artificial forms and real life can meet; burlesque became a device for reaching behind the world of illusion and showing the real world. Several passages in *Northanger Abbey* indicate that part of the reality that Austen exposed was an England that had definitely been affected by the French Revolution.

In the years after 1793, Pitt's government had to wage a two-pronged offensive against France and those in England who were inspired by the French example and wanted to create a new social and political order in their own country. This led to a widespread fear of English 'Jacobinism'. The popularity of Paine, the number and size of political clubs, the demonstrations, the monster petitions calling for parliamentary reform, and a dread of subversion led to governmental measures to silence the radical opposition. As a result, the period from 1794 to 1799 is one of the most repressive in English history. Pitt had the necessary support to carry out his measures, owing to a change of outlook among back-bench squires who feared not only the French but their 'agents' in England, and encouraged strong government action. In February 1793, John Frost, a leading figure in the Corresponding Society who had presented addresses from the Society to the French Convention, was imprisoned after he was overheard making seditious remarks in a tavern. The arrest and transportation of others followed. Some judges held that the English constitution was perfect, and that anyone proposing change was perforce an enemy of the state.

As government measures became increasingly severe, the radicals became more desperate; some made preparations for delegates to cooperate with a foreign landing and oppose English defence efforts. For this three leaders were transported, in response to which radicals challenged the authority of parliament by calling for a national convention. At the same time they called for an end of the war with France. The government then indicted thirteen leaders of the Corresponding Society for high treason, a charge that it was unable to make stick for lack of evidence. The acquittals gave fresh confidence to the opposition who, fed by popular discontent resulting from the bad harvest of 1794 and from high food prices, took even bolder steps against the government. Faced by these developments and the possibility of invasion, Pitt initiated legislation to stifle the dissidents. Having temporarily suspended Habeas Corpus in 1794, allowing political suspects to be held without trial, parliament then passed two Acts to restore order, the Seditious Meetings Act and the Treasonable Practices Act. A Newspaper Publication Act of 1799 followed earlier measures of 1792, 1795 and 1798, directed against 'criminal and seditious' writings. Other, more subtle steps to control the press were taken through new customs and procedures enabling the Attorney General to bring journalists before special rather than common juries. The combined effect of these efforts was a type of censorship that was peculiar to this period. The Acts against combinations passed in 1795 were supplemented by new ones in 1799; only now the Whigs, who had been highly vocal before, remained silent. The government, drawing support from a much broader base, was able to overcome the opposition. Finally, in 1799, the Corresponding Society and other dissident groups were suppressed as the forces of conservatism, after a long and bitter struggle, achieved a decisive victory.

In reaching behind the world of illusion and showing the real world in *Northanger Abbey*, Austen revealed the public fear and political repression that was such a prominent feature of English life when this novel was written. She did so in two passages. The setting of the first is a conversation between Catherine Morland and Eleanor and Henry Tilney. Referring to the appearance of a new novel, Catherine said that 'something very shocking indeed, will soon come out of London'. (NA,112) Assuming that Catherine meant an impending event, Eleanor inquired as to its nature. Catherine explained that 'it is to be more horrible than anything we have met with yet', and that 'It is to be uncommonly dreadful, I shall expect murder and every thing of the kind.' (NA,112) Eleanor's response was to say that 'if such a design is known beforehand, proper measures will undoubtedly be taken by government to prevent its coming into effect'. (NA,112) The amused Henry Tilney, who appreciated the misunderstanding, chose for a moment to continue it and add to his sister's fears, as well as draw Catherine into a new confusion. '"Government," said Henry, endeavouring not to smile, "neither desires nor dares to interfere in such matters. There must be murder; and government cares not how much."' (NA,112) Then he untangled the web of error that he himself had helped spin by explaining to Eleanor that there would be no riot in London.

> My dear Eleanor, the riot is only in your own brain. The confusion there is scandalous. Miss Morland has been talking of nothing more dreadful than a new publication which is shortly to come out, in three duodecimo volumes, two hundred and seventy-six pages in each, with a frontespiece to the first, or two tombstones and a lantern—do you understand?—And you, Miss Morland—my stupid sister has mistaken all your clearest expressions. You talked of expected horrors in London—and instead of instantly conceiving, as any rational creature would have done, that such words could only relate to a circulating library, she immediately pictured to herself a mob of three thousand men assembling in St. George's Fields; the Bank attacked, the Tower threatened, the streets of London flowing with blood, a detachment of the 12th Light Dragoons, (the hopes of the nation) called up from Northampton to quell the insurgents, and the gallant Capt. Frederick Tilney, in the moment of charging at the head of his troop, knocked off his horse by a brickbat from an upper window. Forgive her stupidity. The fears of the sister have been added to the weakness of the woman; but she is by no means a simpleton in general. (NA,113)

The usual interpretation of this passage is that the imagined riot was actually the Gordon Riots of 1780 and that, in exposing his sister's mistake, in explaining that no riots were expected, Henry

Tilney indicated the very different truth that precisely what Eleanor had feared would happen had already occurred.[19] Thus, Austen's irony seems to be saying that this rational young man was mistaken when he tried to show that the world was more ordinary and orderly than his sister, misled by a reference to a Gothic novel, had been led to think. The question is, how was he mistaken? Does this passage in fact refer to the Gordon Riots? Clearly, there are reasons for thinking so, but also reasons for thinking otherwise. The sequence of events described by Henry Tilney does conform in part to disturbances of 1780, which began, just as he indicated, when a mob assembled at St George's Fields. Yet, the actual mob numbered 60,000 not 3,000 as he said. Another discrepancy between the Gordon Riots and the 'riot' passage in *Northanger Abbey* is that Henry Tilney imagined a mob attacking the Bank, which did not happen in 1780.[20] A possible explanation for the inconsistencies is that Austen did not know that much about the Gordon Riots or did not bother to get the facts straight. The problem here is that Austen took pains to be factually accurate. Another problem is that if she were making the point that life in London could be violent in the way that Henry indicated, she might well have been thinking about recent disturbances with which, it turns out, she was familiar.

Eliza de Feuillide was in London when a riot broke out in June 1792, some two months before her visit to Steventon. Describing what she had witnessed in a letter to one of her cousins, Philadelphia Walter, she said:

> The noise of the populace, the drawn swords & pointed bayonets of the guards, the fragments of brick & mortar thrown on every side, one of which had nearly killed my Coachman, the firing at one end of the street which was already begun, altogether in short alarmed me so much that I really have not been well since. The confusion continued all that day & night & the following day, & for these eight & forty hours, I have seen nothing but large parties of soldiers parading up & down this street . . . my apprehensions have been that they would set fire to these houses that they were bent on demolishing . . .[21]

Given the deep impression that the riot made on Eliza she would have discussed it later that summer when she was in Steventon. There are further reasons for her to have done so. It was widely felt that a French influence was behind the riot. *The Times* reported on 6

June that 'Among the rioters we could perceive several foreigners, and it is evidont to us that many persons must have been sent to foment the disturbance . . . Frenchmen who were in the crowd bellowed *ca ira, ca ira* (go to it, go to it). This encouraged the confusion.' Given Eliza's interest in France, where she had recently lived, and where her husband at great risk was trying to sort out his affairs, she would have been struck by rumours indicating that violence was crossing the Channel, spreading from Paris to London. A few months later, upon hearing about the storming of the Tuileries in August and the September massacres, while staying with the Austens, she would have discussed the riot that she had witnessed in London earlier in the summer.

During the period of Eliza's visit to Steventon news from Paris created a wave of fear in England that reached panic proportions by the end of the year. As violent as the September Massacres in Paris were, they appeared much more so in *The Times'* greatly exaggerated report that 12,000 were butchered during one three-day spree, after an earlier massacre of 11,000 in a twenty-four hour period. The impact of this news was immense, making the last five months of 1792 a time of heresy hunts and millenarian fantasies, widespread fright and brave hope for a new future. The fact that some responded favourably to riots in Paris and the fall of the monarchy only intensified the dread of others. One result was a series of agitations throughout England and Scotland resembling Guy Fawkes demonstrations in which Tom Paine was the object of the crowd's enmity. London responded to the horrifying news from across the Channel by giving in to several days of panic beginning on 1 December, 1792, such as the City had not seen since 1642, when reports indicated that Charles I was marching on the capital. It was thought that the French were sailing up the Thames and about to raze London; that the people of the City were organising an insurrection, following the lead of their French counterparts; and that as in Paris the result would be the overthrow of Crown and Altar. The authorities were sufficiently apprehensive to make extensive preparations for the defense of the Tower, strengthen fortifications, mount cannons, erect barricades, and put a company of militia on constant alert.

The riot passage could have alluded to these as well as other disturbances. When Henry Tilney said that a mob of 3,000 men assembled at St George's Fields, Austen could have been referring to a meeting there in January 1795, in which leaders exhorted the people to oppose the repressive policies of the government. Coming at a time of extreme unrest, this demonstration aroused considerable uneasiness in official quarters and was the subject of frightened speculation in the newspapers. The part of the passage saying that the Bank was attacked and the Tower threatened could refer to the panic that gripped London at the end of 1792.[22] Fearing an uprising, the Duke of Richmond fortified the Tower and the Bank was placed under heavy guard. According to a newspaper report, 'It is generally believed that Government had discovered an infernal plot, planned by some foreigners, and certain unnatural incendiaries of native growth, to seize the Tower and the Bank, and after diverting the Stream of the New River, to set the city in Flames.'

The fact is that Austen's description does not match any event point-for-point, but the 'riot' passage does very much seem to reflect an awareness of both the Gordon Riots and those of the 1790s. The meeting at St George's Fields in 1795 brought back memories of the earlier meeting, in 1780, that led to several days of violence. And the type of rumour that circulated during the panic of 1792 also suggests a memory of the Gordon Riots, as if what happened before contributed to the shape of present fears. What the 'riot' passage refers to, then, is a type of fear that crystallised during the 1790s and resulted from the earlier experience of the Gordon Riots and the contemporary fright deriving from the French Revolution and its impact on England. If the passage is read in this way, Henry Tilney does not imagine a particular event, but alludes to a set of fears whose sources were diverse, including the Gordon Riots and the disturbances of the 1790s.

Just as the 'riot' passage in *Northanger Abbey* reveals Austen's awareness of the apprehension that gripped England during the 1790s, so does another passage suggest the repressiveness of this difficult time. We have seen that Pitt took severe measures to stifle the radical opposition, such as suspending the Act of Habeas Corpus, the passage of the Seditious Meetings Act and Treasonable Practices Act, and censorship of the press. Related to these actions was a widespread use of spies, which began in 1792. Agents, sometimes in the direct pay of the government but more often operating at their own initiative and with the hope of selling information, infiltrated illegal political organisations and helped to bring about their demise.[23] Given the nature of their activities, it was unavoidable that spies would try to sensationalise their reports, a fact of which the government was well aware. So anxious was the government for information that it accepted assistance from as many quarters as possible. One ally was the Association for Preserving Liberty and Property against Republicans and Levellers, founded in 1792, one of the conservative political groups that sprang up in an effort to defend the established order from the real or imagined forces of subversion. This group strove to suppress seditious publications and issue its own loyalist propaganda. To accomplish its objectives some 2,000 local cells were organised in towns and villages throughout England. Members eavesdropped in taverns and marketplaces for signs of Jacobin sympathies, and they scrutinised bookshops for copies of *The Rights of Man*. The central unit in London hired spies to visit bookshops and report anyone selling copies of Paine's writings. In some instances, booksellers and publishers were turned over to the government for prosecution, while in others the Association itself initiated legal proceedings.

That efforts such as these were taken by private organisations can be considered a measure of how widespread the fear of radicalism and subversion had become. In the opinion of one observer, 'A disloyal word was enough to bring down punishment upon any man's head. Laughing at the awkwardness of a volunteer corps was criminal. People were apprehended and sent on board a man of war for this breach of decorum, which was punished as a terrible crime.' A bookbinder, who was heard saying 'No George, no war', was sentenced to stand in the pillory and serve five years' hard labour. Measures of this type obviously would not have been taken in a normal or reasonable atmosphere; in fact, the decade of the 1790s was just the opposite. It was a period charged with anxiety and driven in extreme instances of over-reaction to hysteria. Out of these conditions came a national sense of uneasiness and suspicion and a tendency among the more apprehensive to see conspiracies everywhere. Writing in 1797, Thomas Bowdler said that if one of his countrymen were to take a journey across England he would see signs of material prosperity at every stage, but if he were to close his eyes and listen he would 'hear many Persons talk of nothing but Grievances and Oppressions, War and Ruin'.

The widespread use of spies during the 1790s is essential to an understanding of one of the better-known passages in *Northanger Abbey*. Her imagination having been excited by Ann Radcliffe's Gothic novel, *The Mysteries of Udolpho*, Catherine Morland came to suspect General Tilney of murdering his wife. When Henry learned of her suspicions, he not only disillusioned her but explained the fundamental improbability of her fears. The horrors that she imagined were unlikely in the present age. Remember, he enjoined her, that 'we are English, that we are Christians'; the age was too civilised for such horror, as she should have known from her education, understanding, and 'observation of what is passing around you'. Henry then asked Catherine if such atrocities could be 'perpetrated without being known, in a country like this, where social and literary intercourse is on such a footing; where every man is surrounded by a neighbourhood of voluntary spies, and where roads and newspapers lay every thing open'. (NA, 197–8)

In an analysis of this passage, D. W. Harding shows that the last sentence strikes a discordant note, and the part saying 'Where every man is surrounded by a neighbourhood of voluntary spies' is especially out of tune with the rest. He argues that the reference to spies, with 'its touch of paranoia', reveals some underlying tensions between Austen and the society in which she lived. While the novelist 'seems to be on perfectly good terms with the public she is addressing', she was, in fact, at odds with and critical towards that public. Those close to her, he contends, did probe and pry into the affairs of others, and in that sense they spied. Austen's inserting the passage about 'a neighbourhood of voluntary spies' into Henry's speech, then, was an attack on the meddling ways of her contemporaries.[24]

I should like to suggest a quite different interpretation of this passage. Austen was referring to actual spies who were serving or trying to serve Pitt and the government and whose purpose was to crush the various agents of radicalism and subversion. Such an interpretation rests upon two lines of reasoning. First, Austen wrote the novel during the very period when the activity of spies was at a peak and the atmosphere was highly charged with fear and sus- picion. Austen might not have been guilty herself of paranoia, but rather commented on that of others. Secondly, the structure of the passage supports such an interpretation. Having unburdened Catherine of her mistaken views about the death of his mother, Henry reminded her that she was living in a country and age when such things simply did not happen. This was not the southern France, Alps or Pyrenees of Mrs. Radcliffe's *Udolpho*, but a Christian land in which the rule of law was supreme and social and literary intercourse was civilised. Then, shifting gears abruptly, Henry revealed a different truth about his age when he said that 'every man is surrounded by a neighbourhood of voluntary spies'. All at once, a different view of English life has come into view. Having at first argued in a perfectly conventional, eighteenth-century way that he and Catherine lived in a nation and age when order was supreme, he revealed a much harsher reality, that of a society so fearful of disorder that spies were everywhere. This clearly was not the England whose Constitution had been venerated since 1688 as a bulwark of 'liberty', and was supposed to guarantee the rights of the individual. At this very moment, those rights were being eliminated in the struggle with the forces of subversion.

The irony is that Henry, after praising the safety and refinement in English life, exposed the underlying fears and paranoia of his society. Informed as he was, he was unable to draw the appropriate conclusions from what he knew, whereas the innocent and mistaken Catherine indirectly came closer to the truth. Admittedly, Catherine had allowed her fertile imagination, nourished by Gothic romances, to lead her into an exotic misunderstanding of General Tilney. He was not the type of villain encountered in Ann Radcliffe's novels, but as it turned out he most certainly was indecent and even brutal; his sending Catherine home on such short notice and without the appropriate escort revealed him as a villain of sorts. So the clear-headed, reasonable and politically informed Henry Tilney did not have all of the answers. Life in the English Midlands could be uncivilised, and it was by no means as calm and peaceful as he argued. Catherine, who had no awareness of or interest in politics, and considered the political pamphlets that General Tilney read 'stupid', (NA,187) was not entirely incorrect in seeing dark designs in the Midlands of England. What she had imagined about General Tilney was wrong, but the truth was bad enough, and while Gloucestershire was not the southern France of *Udolpho*, it was charged with an atmosphere of suspicion and crawling with spies. In fact, in some rather discomforting ways it was not altogether unlike France of the 1790s.

Seeing a comparison between the France of *Udolpho* and Revolutionary France might well have been part of Austen's irony. While Radcliffe's novels were set in earlier periods (1584 in the case of *Udolpho*), they were filled with contemporary topics and, more importantly, reflected the insecure, violent atmosphere of the 1790s.[25] It would have been easy enough for a reader of the time to have seen parallels between the dark dungeons, villainous designs, inquisitorial repression and generalised horror of Gothic novels and news from France of imprisonments, improvised tribunals, blood-thirsty Jacobins and mass executions.

Ultimately, whether or not one is prepared to see allusions to Revolutionary France in *Northanger Abbey* depends on how one chooses to reconstruct Austen's perception of her world. Harding's view of the 'voluntary spies' passage is that her vision went no further than her own family and neighbourhood and was fixed on private rather than public affairs. I have suggested that Austen referred to repression on one side of the Channel and violence on the other. Henry Tilney was not entirely correct in seeing a riot as a figment of his sister's imagination. Things were not exactly as they seemed, and life in England was not as rational and stable as on various occasions he indicated. Not that Austen was expressing a fear of disorder or a breakdown of stability. Above all, her writing is comic and the appropriate response is one of amusement. Yet, somewhere within the irony there is a hard, almost grim view of the world. This is what Harding correctly picked up in his reading of the 'spies' passage, in which there are traces of irritation and what he called a 'regulated hatred'. I agree with Harding when he stresses Austen's anger towards those who made up her own social world. Her private complaints were undoubtedly central in forming her view of the world and contributing to the undercurrent of tension and hostility that runs through both her correspondence and novels. But her uneasiness can also be explained by reference to public events. The 1790s was a period of unprecedented fear that sometimes bordered on paranoia, and it was a time of widespread repression. In *Northanger Abbey*, Austen commented on both fear and repression in her characteristic way, through irony. While out-wardly detached she was not entirely so. Or perhaps it should be said that the final, formal detachment, as expressed through the irony, was purchased at a definite cost. Behind the verbal artistry of the 'riot' and 'spies' passages were the troubled times of the 1790s, which Austen did experience.

Just as the French Revolution had a profound effect on English social and political life, so did it permanently alter Austen's outlook. One manifestation of the change that Austen underwent as a result of the Revolutionary experience is her Francophobia, which Ward Hellstrom has splendidly analysed.[26] Hellstrom sees Austen as a representative of the settled English Toryism that was 'threatened by French radicalism, which manifested itself in England as Jacobinism', and led to a widespread fear of internal revolution. A direct outgrowth of that fear, according to Hellstrom, was a 'hostility to Jacobinism [that] revealed itself in . . . a denigration of the national character, culture, and politics of France'. While Hellstrom makes a convincing case for Austen's Francophobia in *Emma*, the only novel that he discusses, and correctly examines it in the light of the Revolutionary experience, he does not explain its origins in her earlier writings. I believe that I have done so, insofar as the evidence permits, in my discussion of 'Catharine' and *Northanger Abbey*. In these two early works one can follow shock waves emanating from France and entering the rural quiet of Austen's world, and one can see her responding to them in passages that refer to troubled conditions in France and to the panic that gripped England.

What one finds in 'Catharine' and *Northanger Abbey* is not Francophobia, but a type of experience from which it would spring. How Austen felt about France before the Revolution is difficult to determine, but there are reasons for suspecting that as a girl she identified positively with French culture. It is not an idea that one should push too hard, but it does deserve considering. To some extent, keeping up with the latest styles and trends, for Austen and her family, related to French culture and its impact on English life. On one level, this can be explained by the hegemony of France in the world of fashion, which in the eighteenth century was widespread. More specifically, it can be explained by the impression that Eliza de Feuillide made on the Austen family, with her *savoir vivre* and sure sense of fashion. When Austen's brother, Edward, went on the Grand Tour in 1786, he followed the path of countless eighteenth-century English travellers who wanted to assimilate the cosmopolitan culture whose nerve centre was Paris. Eliza travelled to England in 1787, and again in the following year, visiting the Austens on both occasions. Through her French culture entered the quiet, rural world of Steventon, making a considerable impression on the entire Austen family and particularly on Jane, with whom Eliza was on especially close terms.

This means that Austen's Francophobia was not there from the beginning, but took shape later, and as Hellstrom explains, in response to the Revolution; while certain passages in 'Catharine' allude to events in France, this work is not Francophobic. Nor is *Northanger Abbey* so. Rather, the 'riot' and 'spy' passages comment on the repressiveness and panic that gripped England in response to the fear of domestic Jacobinism. Austen's irony is directed not at the

French or their English followers, but at the fear that swept both London and the countryside. The relevance of these passages to the present discussion is that they reveal Austen's awareness of the new burdens in English society that resulted from the Revolution. Her Francophobia was a later product of that awareness.

My discussion of Austen's Francophobia will be limited to *Mansfield Park* and *Emma*. In both of these novels some characters bear the imprint of French culture, whereas others embody and carry forward an orientation and value system that is distinctively English. Lionel Trilling has made the fascinating point that between France and England there are different conceptions of sincerity, each of which is reflected in its literature.[27] In French literature, sincerity consists in telling the truth about oneself to oneself and to others, which necessitates a confrontation with one's traits or actions that are morally or socially discreditable. One confronts what is shameful in oneself and acknowledges it. English sincerity calls for no such acknowledgement, requiring rather that one communicate about oneself to others without deceiving or misleading. The implications are important, revealing different types of moral life that convert into disparate systems of manners and that help form different national social types.

To be sincere in the French system implies an awareness of the devices that one uses to conceal what one does not wish others to see; it implies an awareness of the mask that one wears for this purpose. The sincere person takes off the mask. To be sincere in the English system is to be direct and straightforward, to be oneself in action. The sincere person does not remove a mask because living sincerely one does not practice concealment, one never wears a mask.

While the theatrical episode in *Mansfield Park* most obviously brings out the effect of mask-wearing, this is a theme that runs through much of the novel. Henry Crawford uses *Lovers' Vows* as an occasion to reveal what Trilling calls a histrionic talent and what Alistair Duckworth describes as a 'ludic' personality. Henry Crawford was never in his element more than during the theatrical, while playing a role, while wearing a mask. That Fanny was profoundly out of her element in the theatrical helps mark her as Henry's anti-type. She was sincere precisely in the English sense indicated by Trilling, 'a single-minded commitment to whatever dutiful enterprise [one] may have in hand'.

Austen also dramatised the conflict between those representing French and English cultural norms in the Sotherton episode. When

Mary Crawford made light of the elimination of family worship, calling it an 'improvement', Austen regarded Mary's *persiflage* as an aspect of her French manners. Hannah More would have done the same. More wrote in the *Strictures on the Modern System of Female Education* (1799) that the 'cold compound of irony, irreligion, selfishness, and sneer, which make up what the French . . . so well express by the term *persiflage*, has of late made incredible progress in blasting the opening buds of piety in young persons of fashion'.[28] She feared the corrosive effect of French manners on English life. In the *Moral Sketches of Prevailing Opinions and Manners, Foreign and Domestic, with Reflections on Prayer* (1819) she contrasted the mixture of French polish, urbanity, wit, and irreverence to the more sober and plain virtues of the English. What she most admired about the English character was its solidity and durability, which she compared to an oak tree. By contrast the French character was superficial and glossy, like varnish, concealing interior flaws. But French manners were infiltrating English life, even in the country, the bastion of traditional values and English morality. 'The old English gentry kept up their reverence and secured the attachments of their dependents by living among them.'[29] A modern spirit of restlessness led to travel abroad, the adoption of French manners, and an undercutting of the Protestant religion. Connected to religious decline was a weakening of the family, caused in part by females who prided themselves on wit, which the Christian should reject in horror. The best protection against foreign contamination was religion, on which the 'elevation of our national character' largely depended. 'Here then is Britain's last, best hope. . . . Why need we doubt, that the Christian religion, grafted on the substantial stock of the British character, and watered by the dews of heaven, may bring forth the noblest productions of which this lower world is capable.'[30]

In contrast to Mary Crawford's 'French' levity and irreverence was Fanny's 'English' sobriety and serious conception of religion and its impact on family life. To her it was unfortunate that the Rushworths had abandoned family worship, which she considered a custom that should not have been discontinued. 'It was a valuable part of the former times. There is something in a chapel and chaplain so much in character with a great house, with one's idea of what such a household should be! A whole family assembling regularly for the purpose of prayer, is fine!' (MP,86) While the spiritual importance of worship was not dwelled upon, the danger of irreverence was, indicating Austen's objection to the modern, fashionable tendency to be religiously indifferent, if not to ridicule religion. For Austin and many of her contemporaries religion was important as a force of social continuity and a safeguard against the secular and atheistic ideology of the French Revolution. Mary Crawford was not atheistic, but she was secular and she did ridicule religion. So the discussion is about family worship, it is about religion as a force of family and social cohesion, it is about the dangers of the modern and fashionable mockery of religion, and it establishes a dichotomy between rival outlooks and systems of value. The dialogue shows Edmund and Fanny as the upholders of tradition and custom, and Mary Crawford represents attitudes that are alien and incompatible with settled English country ways.

After leaving the chapel, Mary asked Edmund why he wanted to become a clergyman, saying that he could not distinguish himself in such a profession. Edmund acknowledged that a clergyman could not be 'high in state or fashion', and 'must not head mobs, or set the ton in dress', (MP,92) but explained that he was the guardian of 'religion and morals, and consequently of the manners which result from their influence'. Mary wondered if two sermons a week were adequate to 'govern the conduct and fashion the manners of a large congregation for the rest of the week? One scarcely sees a clergyman out of his pulpit.' (MP,92-3) This remark led to a discussion of religious life in London and the country, Edmund contending that the clergy's greatest influence was not in great cities but local parishes, and that morality depended largely on the extent of that influence. The manners that drew their substance from morality did not consist of good breeding, refinement and courtesy, but right conduct and principles. This was the calling that Edmund hoped to answer. While the obvious contrast in this passage is between morality and manners in London and the country, the English–French dichotomy in the previous dialogue is also present here. Upon reaffirming his decision to enter the clergy Edmund explained that there was not the least wit in his nature, and that 'I am a very matter of fact, plain spoken being, and may blunder on the borders of a repartee for half a hour together without striking it out.' (MP,94) In this passage Austen had in mind a distinctively English type, one who was not polished, refined, clever, urbane, and cosmopolitan, but serious, introspective, stolid, direct and forthright; the former, refined type was French or—to be more exact—bore the stamp of French culture.

Fanny was with Edmund and Mary at the time of the above conversation. At the end of it she said that she was tired and would like to sit down. ' "I shall soon be rested", said Fanny; "to sit in the shade on a fine day, and look upon verdure, is the most perfect refreshment." ' (MP,96) This passage brings to mind a similar one in *Emma*: 'It was a sweet view—sweet to the eye and the mind. English verdure, English culture, English comfort, seen under a sun bright, without being oppressive.' (E,360) The verdure that Fanny chose to observe and enjoy rather than continue the walk with Edmund and Mary can be seen to represent English culture, just as the verdure in *Emma* does. When Fanny sat down to rest, Mary said she was tired because during the tour of the great house she had had to strain her eyes and attention, listen to descriptions that she had not understood, and pretend to admire what she had not cared for. What Mary said about Fanny in fact applied to herself. Fanny both admired the great Elizabethan house and grasped the significance of its traditions, so much so that she recognised the mistake of ending family worship. Mary, lacking Fanny's appreciation of the house and grounds of Sotherton, wanted to continue the walk, as if restless and unsettled and searching after novelty. And she took Edmund with her, down a serpentine path that led into the wilderness and away from Fanny and the quiet of English verdure and culture. Not only did she not appreciate the Englishness of the Rushworth estate, but stood for a way of life that was alien to its customs and character. Also, she tried to tempt Edmund with the contrasting French values that she, as a member of fashionable London society, stood for.

Just as Mary's leading Edmund away from Fanny and down a serpentine path suggested the hazards of a certain way of life, so did the appearance and departure of Henry Crawford and Maria Bertram twenty minutes later convey a similar message, although in a different context. This time the dichotomy was between the rights of the individual and the restraints of society, between liberty and constraint. The iron gate, which was locked, can be seen as a symbol of society's iron code, and Maria's desire to climb around its edge was a sign of her rejecting that code, whose limitations she found confining.[31] That Henry was quick to agree to the plan put him in the same moral camp; he too was an advocate of individual liberty. As Marilyn Butler has pointed out, the theme of individual rights was central to English Jacobin novels of the 1790s. Reacting against this ideology, conservative, anti-Jacobin writers argued for the necessity of a social code that would limit those rights, seeing the individual in relationship to the community. Austen's position was that of a conservative who stressed the importance of continuity, tradition and the claims of society, arguing against the radical and Revolutionary ideology with its emphasis upon individual rights. So while a fashionable young man like Henry Crawford was not a Jacobin, his actions indicated a rejection of a conservative social code and ideologically put him in a rival camp.

In *Emma*, the dichotomy between English and French culture is seen in the contrast between John Knightley and Frank Churchill. As in *Mansfield Park*, one set of norms was clearly superior to the other, but each had its attractions. In both novels, the suave, elegant, refined, superficially attractive characters were most successful initially. Mary Crawford nearly conquered Edmund, and Henry won over everyone but Fanny, who was punished by Sir Thomas for rejecting his marital offer. In *Emma*, Frank Churchill was a candidate for the heroine's affection before Knightley even entered the romantic picture, but once Knightley did there was no question that he would get the upper hand. By that point, what he stood for had been shown as clearly superior to the more shallow ways of his rival. But Emma did have to choose between the two, between English 'virtue' and French 'depravity'.

Before Churchill appeared, Knightley, knowing about his reputation, saw him as an outsider, not just in the sense that he had never visited Highbury, but that he brought habits, values and manners that were foreign to local ways. Rather than doing his duty to his family by visiting them, he was in the habit of going to 'some watering-place or other', shirking his responsibilities 'whenever there is any temptation of pleasure'. (E,146) When Emma protested that Churchill's conduct should not be criticised without understanding his situation, Knightley replied that 'There is one thing . . . a man can always do . . . and that is, his duty; not by manoeuvering and finessing, but by vigour and resolution.' What followed was a long discussion of Churchill's tact, which Emma thought made him 'an amiable young man', (E,148) but which Knightley regarded as a combination of weakness and self-indulgence. 'No, Emma, your amiable young man can be amiable only in French, not in English. He may be very "aimable", have very good manners and be very agreeable; but he can have no English delicacy towards the feelings of other people: nothing really amiable about him.' (E,149) Like Henry Crawford he was outwardly attractive and well-mannered, but without resolution, integrity and moral substance. As with his counterpart in *Mansfield*

Park, his merits were 'merely personal', in the sense that he was 'good-looking, with smooth, plausible manners'. And Churchill's manners were specifically depicted as French, indicating the connection that Austen made elsewhere between refinement, social polish and French manners.

In criticising Churchill in this way, Knightley clearly regarded English manners as superior, with substance counting for more than form, directness more than adroitness, responsibility more than liberty, and strength prevailing over effeteness. Plain-spoken, forthright, not given to witticisms or interested in repartees, Knightley was in the same pattern as Edmund Bertram, and this pattern was represented as English. This was a type of person whose values and outlook were a prop to the community, furthered what was best in English tradition, and whose solidity and permanence were consistent with the rhythms of country life. Knightley was a magistrate, very active in local affairs, a working farmer, and closely connected to the members of village society, such as the worthy Robert Martin. And he was 'amiable' in the English rather than French sense, with a 'delicacy towards the feelings of other people', as seen in his reprimanding Emma over her impoliteness to Miss Bates. Knightley reminded Emma that there had been a time when this spinster had been younger and counted for more in local society, when her friendship to Emma had been freely and generously given, and when 'her notice was an honour . . .'. (E,375) This remark indicated not only a concern for and sensitivity to the feelings of others, 'delicacy', in his word, but a clear understanding of social relationships and their importance to social behaviour. For Knightley, the well-mannered person was not a display piece, refined, polished, witty and elegant, but polite on a different level, from an awareness of the feelings of others and in a way that recognised the layering and ordering of the community; the well-mannered person was sensitive to the feelings of others, but also understood how one's feelings were affected by one's social state.

Interestingly, Frank Churchill appeared polite in exactly the way that Knightley was, just as he seemed like a bulwark of the community, in whose customs and traditions he expressed a decided interest and whose retention he appeared to consider valuable. As if anxious to join his family in Highbury, he arrived a day early as his proud father had predicted. Ordinarily, Churchill explained, he would not have exerted himself so, 'but in coming *home* I felt I might do any thing'. (E,191) He said he wanted to familiarise himself with his father's home and the homes of his neighbours and was anxious to learn about the village, professing 'himself to have always felt the sort of interest in the country which none but one's *own* country gives . . .'. (E,191) At the same time, he made apparently thoughtful inquiries about his father's friends and about local societies and local practices and rituals. The next day he expressed a 'wish to be made acquainted with the whole village', and went for a walk with Emma and his parents, finding 'matter of commendation and interest much oftener than Emma could have supposed'. (E,197) He wished to see his father's house and that of his father's father, and even walked the length of the street in quest of the cottage of an old woman who had nursed him, so great was his filial devotion, his sense of family continuity, and his 'good-will towards Highbury in general'. (E,197) Carefully observing Churchill, Emma decided that a young man with such feelings was indeed 'amiable', that he was not insincere as Knightley had charged, and that 'Mr. Knightley certainly had not done him justice'. (E,197)

This positive assessment seemed to receive new confirmation as Emma, Churchill and the Westons continued their walk. Upon arriving at the Crown Inn, the other members of the party gave Churchill 'the history of the large room', explaining that it had been built many years ago as a ball-room, but in recent times had not been used for dancing. Churchill was 'immediately interested', impressed by the room's 'character as a ball-room', and sorry that 'its original purpose should have ceased'. Claiming to be anxious to maintain the ways of the past, he wondered 'Why had not Miss Woodhouse revived the former good old days of the room?' (E,198) After leaving the Crown they came to Ford's, a local shop where, Churchill's father informed him, 'every body attends every day of their lives'. Any place that important to the life of the village Churchill wanted to see, so that 'I may prove myself to belong to the place, to be a true citizen of Highbury'. Perhaps, he said, he could buy a pair of gloves, which prompted Emma to say, 'I do admire your patriotism. You will be adored in Highbury. You were very popular before you came, because you were Mr. Weston's son—but lay out half-a-guinea at Ford's and your popularity will stand upon your own virtues.' (E,200)

Churchill's professions of patriotism were completely false. When he regarded the purchase of a pair of gloves as a burst of *amor patriae* he revealed both his frivolity and falsity. Emma had been wrong about Churchill from the beginning; he had misled her every step

of the way. When he said that he had exerted himself to arrive early
so he could be with his family, he neglected the reality of his waiting
so long to pay a visit that was woefully overdue. Knightley had been
correct in saying that he 'cared for little but his own pleasure', and
had spent his time at 'the idlest haunts of the kingdom', (E,146)
rather than doing his duty to his father. His apparent interest in
everything about Highbury was insincere. When he said he wanted
to revive the earlier custom of the dance at the Crown Inn he was
really laying plans for a social occasion that served his own
scheming purposes. The truth was that he had no interest in past
ways, no commitment to tradition. Nor was he 'amiable' in the
English sense of the term, as defined by Knightley.

Examples of Churchill's falsity are legion. He had not come to
Highbury to see his family but because a young lady was there
whom he had courted under irregular circumstances, in defiance of
the social code, and in a way that compromised her and caused her
great and unnecessary anguish. Having done so, he had to throw up
one smoke screen after another, appear as he was not, and create a
network of deceptions that was necessary to the furthering of his
plans.

The party at the Coles' a few days later brought Churchill's
defects sharply into focus, as a direct comparison was made between
him and Knightley, between the 'aimable' manners of one and the
'amiable' manners of the other. Churchill had made a trip to
London under the excuse of getting a haircut, but in fact to purchase
a piano for Jane Fairfax, so that she could play on her own
instrument. Even this apparently thoughtful act was less generous
than it seemed. But before showing how this was so it will be useful
to build up to the scene at the piano, in which Churchill's true
colours became clear. Upon arriving at the Coles', he paid 'his
compliments en passant to Miss Bates and her niece', (E,220) and
then moved to the opposite side of the circle, where Emma was
sitting. He ostentatiously made her the object of his attention, using
her as a pawn in his game, a ploy in a strategy that would enable
him to get closer to Jane Fairfax. After talking to Emma awhile he
excused himself to see Jane and tell her that she had 'done her hair
in so odd a way—so very odd a way . . .'. (E,222) Before he
returned, Mrs. Weston joined Emma to tell her that Knightley had
put his carriage at the service of Miss Bates, which struck her as
'Such a very kind attention—and so thoughtful an attention!'
(E,223) Emma realised, and said, that nothing could have been

more in character. Her remarks depicted a man who was 'amiable', rather than 'aimable', and helped set the stage for the piano scene. 'I know no man more likely,' she said, 'than Mr. Knightley to do the sort of thing—to do anything really good-natured, useful, considerate, or benevolent. He is not a gallant man, but he is a very humane one . . . for an act of un-ostentatious kindness, there is nobody whom I would fix on more than on Mr. Knightley.' (E,223) Not only was Emma describing Knightley, but portraying the antithesis of Churchill, as she did again when she disagreed with Mrs. Weston, who suspected that Knightley had purchased the piano for Jane. 'Mr. Knightley does nothing mysteriously . . . if he had intended to give her one, he would have told her so.' (E,226) Knightley's kindness, then, was not gallant but useful, considerate and unostentatious, and by nature he was direct and forthright.

The scene at the piano showed Churchill to be Knightley's opposite, self-indulgent and selfish to the point of meanness. Emma was asked to play first, and was joined by Churchill in a duet. Aware of her musical limitations, she scaled the performance accordingly, only to be surprised by Churchill's breaking away from her confines, employing vocal resources that enabled him to rise above the level of her capability. This was one of his reasons for buying the piano. He was a musician of some achievement and wanted to perform, to receive the praise that he quickly got. 'He was accused of having a delightful voice, and a perfect knowledge of music; which was properly denied; and that he knew nothing of the matter, and had no voice at all, roundly asserted.' (E,227) Then it was Jane's turn to play, giving Churchill the chance to sing some more duets. Towards the end of the second piece Jane's voice 'grew thick', which prompted Knightley to say, thinking aloud, 'that will do . . . You have sung quite enough for one evening—now, be quiet.' (E,229) But it was not enough for Churchill, who said to Jane: 'I think you could manage this without effort; the first part is so very trifling. The strength of the song falls on the second.' (E,229) At this, 'Mr. Knightley grew angry.' To be 'amiable' was to be genuinely but quietly concerned for others, as from a distance; to be 'aimable ' was to give an impression of concern and to be superficial and false. To be mannered in one sense was to be direct and forthright, in the other indirect and mysterious. One pattern of conduct was English, the other French.

So Churchill made the right impression with Emma and others, until his elaborate stratagems went wrong and his true character became clear. When his juggling act broke down he wanted to get away from the complicated situation that he had created. He wanted to leave England, to go abroad. 'I feel a strong persuasion, this morning, that I shall soon be abroad. I ought to travel. I am tired of doing nothing. I want a change. I am serious, Miss Woodhouse, whatever your penetrating eyes may fancy—I am sick of England—and would leave it tomorrow, if I could.' (E,365) How beautifully Churchill revealed himself in this passage, through the grammatical 'I'—'I feel', 'I shall', 'I want', 'I am tired', 'I am sick', always the 'I'. That he should think only of himself at this moment and want to run away from his problems was completely in character, and that he should want to go abroad, to leave England, was only fitting. With his 'aimabilité', his French manners, he belonged elsewhere. John Knightley was the ideal Englishman. His integrity, sense of responsibility and tradition, his respect for the social code, his true propriety and 'amiability' made him a leading citzen of Highbury. This was where he belonged; it was not where Churchill belonged.

Austen's Francophobia was completely at one with her Toryism, just as was the case with the Francophobia of Southey, Wordsworth and Coleridge. Austen entered the Revolutionary era well disposed to French culture, and the Lake poets initially favoured the Revolutionary cause. As the poets' support gave way to opposition, their political views underwent a metamorphosis, making them ideologically conservative. They ended up embracing the doctrines of Edmund Burke, whom they scorned when the *Reflections on the French Revolution* first appeared. Austen was Tory from the beginning, although in the eighteenth-century, pre-Revolutionary sense; she became a conservative in the Burkean mould in response to the French Revolution, and at the same time that her Francophobia took shape. As with the Lake poets, her ideological conservatism was directly related to her anti-French feeling. It can be regarded as its positive counterpart, a prescription for keeping English society stable and vital, and protecting it from the subversive forces that threatened what was most valuable in English life.

Edmund Burke, the lifelong Whig, was instrumental in working out conservative doctrines that would provide the Tory party of the nineteenth century with an ideological base.[32] Always distrustful of human nature, philosophically and temperamentally opposed to change, and deeply hostile to eighteenth-century rationalism, Burke had in fact always been conservative.[33] He pulled these tendencies into a coherent doctrine in the *Reflections*, in which he stressed permanence and a 'continuity of past and present' without which there could be no 'solidarity between all parts of the political order'.[34] That order was organic and the relationship between the parts was conditioned by custom and tradition. Reacting against what he saw happening in France, Burke argued that men were bound together as members of constituent elements, and each person was a part of his subdivision. In his opinion the revolutionists across the Channel were attempting to merge everyone into an inorganic mass that, if they succeeded, would cut them off from the past and destroy the community. The concept of community was central to Burke's political thought, flowing logically from his stress on tradition and his organic view of society. For Burke, life centered on the community, and it was through it that the generations were connected to one another and the present carried forward the ways of the past. To live outside the community was to be cut off from one's ancestors; it was to be rootless and adrift in a world without structure or permanence. Taking further exception with the rationalistic doctrines of the Revolution, Burke rejected the mechanistic model of the state, stressing the role of history in shaping political institutions. In his view, change was necessary, but only within the context of present conditions. Those conditions were the result of an evolutionary process that represented the collective wisdom of the nation.

It has been argued that Burke's organic model was conditioned by his practicality, empiricism and sober Englishness, and that it was a premise for experience, not a systematic philosophy. One of Burke's main objections to the revolutionary ideology was what he regarded as its abstractness. Rooted in the tradition of English empiricism, he emphasised—perhaps it should be said had an underlying feeling for—the actual and the historical. As pragmatic and down to earth as Burke's thought was, it was not without an almost mystical sense. For him the data of historical life became a continuum, passing through time, that reflected the unconscious wisdom of the generations. While Burke borrowed heavily from Locke, he also pushed many of Locke's ideas to conservative conclusions. Locke's philosophy was based on individual right; Burke's began with religious obligation. One freed political thought from authority, the other re-inspired politics with a cosmic spirit and showed the deeper realities of social life.

Between Burke and Austen there are some obvious affinities,

common modes of perception, shared habits of mind, similar premises of thought. She too can be seen as part of the English empirical tradition, sticking very close to the facts and seeing the facts of historical experience as part of a progression that gives meaning to and provides models and guidelines for a society. Like Burke, she had a strong sense of and respect for the past, a deep feeling for custom, and saw into the intricate recesses of social life. As a novelist she had at her disposal an ideal vehicle for showing those recesses, depicting the dynamics of the collective life and representing people in relationship to others, making choices, following norms, and revealing themselves through a rich minutiae of detail that in the aggregate defined their position in society.

Of course the novel by definition is about man—and woman—in society, and by that very fact it reflects certain facets or characteristics of a historical moment. My point is that Austen's novels not only reflect the social life of her time, but with their Burkean insights yield a depth of social awareness that sets them apart from earlier fiction.

This is not to say that Austen was a student of Burke or was familiar with his writings, for which there is no evidence whatever. It is to say that she developed a social vision very like that of Burke. Like Burke and the Lake Poets and countless lesser writers her vision cannot be understood unless it is seen as a response to the French Revolution and its impact on English and all of European life, and like them it gave her rich insights into the workings of society. Her Burkean social analysis, as I shall call it, was not present in her early fiction. The themes of community and social continuity, upon which I shall concentrate, do not appear in the Juvenilia, *Lady Susan*, or *Northanger Abbey*, even though these early works contained the materials from which those themes would be constructed. They became themes only when Austen articulated them consciously and made them part of a systematic analysis. She did not do this all at once, but by stages, as she worked her way through the problems of living in an age whose settled and civilised ways were being disrupted, as it were, before her own eyes.

The estate was Austen's principal vehicle for discussing community. It did not serve as such a vehicle until *Sense and Sensibility*, even though Austen's characters obviously lived on estates in the Juvenilia and *Northanger Abbey*. The beginning of *Sense and Sensibility* indicates that the estate of the Dashwood family 'was large, and their residence was at Norland Park, in the centre of their property, where, for many generations, they had lived in so respectable a manner, as to engage the general good opinion of their surrounding acquaintance'. (SS,3) John Dashwood did not maintain this tradition, viewing the estate as an economic commodity, capable of yielding revenue, and something to be improved exactly in that sense. Eager to extract as much from it as possible, he did not have a sense of custodianship but was an enclosing landlord who extended his control over Norland Common and bought the farm of a neighbour, 'where old Gibson used to live'. In discussing the transaction he said nothing about the farmer, who undoubtedly had a long association with the Dashwood family, but did explain that 'The land was so very desirable for me in every respect, so immediately adjoining my own property, that I felt it my duty to buy it. I could not have answered it to my conscience to let it fall into any other hands. A man must pay for his convenience; and it *has* cost me a vast deal of money.' (SS,225) Having ready cash he was able to drive a hard bargain, as indicated when he explained that 'I might have sold it again the next day, for more than I gave'. (SS,225) His avarice having been established earlier, in the financial arrangements that he worked out for his mother and sisters, in this passage it acquired a new, social dimension. By aggrandising himself at the expense of the less fortunate he weakened the community, for which he obviously had no concern. His type of improvement meant the exploitation of others—of families long dependent upon the Dashwood family. Nor did John Dashwood have a sense of permanence, as evidenced by his decision to cut down some old walnut trees so he could build a new greenhouse.

Mrs. John Dashwood was as crass as her husband, equally mercenary, and like him without a sense of social responsibility. When the two of them discussed an annuity for Mrs. Dashwood she explained that her mother had been 'clogged' with payments to old, superannuated servants according to the terms of a will. That the servants had been in the service of the family made no difference. Without a sense of obligation, she regarded them as economic units and made her calculations accordingly. Such a person could only weaken the community.

One wonders about the changes that Austen made as she turned 'Elinor and Marianne' into *Sense and Sensibility*, and how those changes reflected an altered social awareness. Between the epistolary version of 1795 and the narrative version of 1797 the differences must have been largely technical. The Austen who at the age of twenty-two recast a work written at twenty did not have a significantly different social outlook. It was later, some time after *Northanger Abbey*, that a Burkean conception would take hold. Since the themes of community, social continuity and improvement are not in *Northanger Abbey* it would seem probable that she had not announced them in her earlier writings. This type of internal reasoning is consistent with the view of Austen that I have set forth, that during the 1790s she experienced the stresses and strains of this decade and in *Northanger Abbey* showed an awareness of violence and political repression, but had not yet developed a positive social philosophy. It would seem that she became a conservative in the Burkean mould some time between the writing of *Northanger Abbey* in 1797–8 and the final revision of *Sense and Sensibility* in 1809–10.

That Austen did not systematically develop the themes of community, social continuity and improvement in *Sense and Sensibility*, and treated them through negative rather than positive example, could indicate an early stage in the development of her social thought, or it could mean that she could not easily graft those themes on to an earlier work, to which they were not organic. Given the narrative framework and the characters of *Sense and Sensibility*, this novel does not contain the type of antithesis that would readily lend itself to a positive statement of the conservative position, as developed through Austen's themes. Yet John Dashwood must have been an ideal foil for pointing out the dangers of pursuing economic interest at the expense of the community. Perhaps some other character, such as Edward Ferrars or Brandon, could have offered a different set of alternatives and been vehicles for showing the advantages of social responsibility, but if this were an option Austen did not exercise it. To have treated either of these characters in this way would have required considerable adjustments, not only in the way they were depicted but in the way they fit into the narrative scheme. Such adjustments would have altered the intricate network of relationships, and introduced even greater strain into a novel that by general consent already shows the difficulties of revision. It would seem, then, that Austen fitted the theme of community into *Sense and Sensibility* as best as she could, accommodating it to the material at hand.

This is not to say that her social thought was already fully developed, and that for strictly technical reasons pertaining to the revision of an earlier work she was unable to give full scope to her ideas. In fact, her social thought was not static, but underwent considerable development between her first published novel and her last, unfinished work. Her writing and the evolution of her thought were closely bound together, the former serving as an anvil on which the latter was hammered out. It was in the act of writing that Austen's insights deepened, as she saw their varied and complex implications. Reworking 'Elinor and Marianne' into *Sense and Sensibility*, there was but limited opportunity to introduce the theme of community—and the related themes of social continuity and improvement—and little occasion for sharpening ideas through the act of writing.

Pride and Prejudice is a very different matter. Austen's social ideas are worked out in this novel with a richness and complexity that was strikingly new, setting it apart from its predecessor. A conservative argument was sustained so successfully and positively and was so organic to the story as to make one wonder if ideological underpinnings were there from the beginning. I do not believe this was the case, but that in 'First Impressions' Austen happened to have an ideal vehicle for developing a Burkean social argument. The pride and prejudice theme, undoubtedly present in 'First Impressions', lent itself to a completely different type of development than the sense and sensibility theme; this time the polarities could be tested against one another and a synthesis between them achieved in a way that was no longer merely personal, but social as well. On the personal level the errors of the hero and heroine were exposed; one was prideful, the other prejudiced. But then Darcy's pride was shown to have a positive side, and the inadequacy of Elizabeth's outlook and judgment was revealed. Once she recognised her mistaken view and saw him in a truer light the doors swung open for the inevitable romantic ending.

It was in the way that Austen showed how mistaken first impressions were that neither Darcy nor Elizabeth were exactly as they seemed; it was also how Austen invested the story with a different level of meaning, adding a new dimension.[35] As Alistair Duckworth has beautifully shown, Darcy became a Burkean figure. When he visited Netherfield with Bingley he appeared haughty and aloof, but later, at his family's estate, he was far more at ease. The change in his demeanour had a definite reason. The norms by which men had lived for generations were being undermined 'in such days as these', (PP,38) and committed to tradition and the preservation of past ways as Darcy was he made a conscious decision to set an example for others. By doing so he was trying to resist social tendencies that he considered corrosive. At his estate there was no need to make such an effort.

When Elizabeth first visited Pemberley, after having rejected Darcy's proposal, she was struck by the 'large, handsome stone building', and the magnificent setting in which it was situated, 'neither formal nor falsely adorned'. The natural beauty and moral character of the house and grounds made her feel that 'to be mistress of Pemberley might be something!' (PP,245) When she and the Gardiners knocked at the door they were received by the house-keeper, Mrs. Reynolds, who had known Dracy since he was four years old. Elizabeth was surprised at her obvious fondness for her master. Personally, Mrs. Reynolds said, Darcy was 'good-natured'. Further, he was 'the best landlord' and, like his father, 'affable to the poor'. (PP,249) As the housekeeper was describing her employer she was conducting the guests on a tour of the house, enabling Elizabeth to see Darcy in a new light, in the midst of the surround-ings in which he had grown up. Upstairs, in the picture gallery, there was a portrait of him, along with those of his ancestors. After pausing before it 'in earnest contemplation' (PP,250), Mrs. Rey-nolds explained that the picture 'had been taken in his father's life time'. As if looking down at Elizabeth, with a smile that she recognised, Darcy was part of a family tradition and he connected, through his ancestors, to the very building and grounds of Pemberley; he was part of a continuity that was architectural, familial and social. Thinking about Darcy after finishing the tour of the picture gallery, Elizabeth realised 'how many people's happi-ness were in his guardianship'. That such an 'intelligent servant' as Mrs. Reynolds regarded him as an ideal master and landlord made Elizabeth think of Darcy with 'a deeper sentiment of gratitude' (PP, 251) than ever before.

Such a landlord as this was a bulwark of a community of which he was the leading figure. Endowed with a strong sense of duty and responsibility, he cared for those in his custody. As the head of the family estate he managed the business of its operation, as indicated by his early return to Pemberley to tend to 'business with his steward'. (PP,256) His concern for Pemberley transcended his interest in its operation, as seen in his regarding himself as a trustee who was not the 'entire master', but the 'life-renter' of the estate—a nice Burkean conception, as Duckworth points out, just as he also notes that Darcy had a Burkean regard for his ancestors. The estate, then, was something to be carefully and well managed, and also to be handed down from generation to generation.

It was also something to be improved, which Elizabeth, perhaps paradoxically, could help bring about. The tradition that Darcy carried forward was coming to an end in the Bennet family. Not only did Elizabeth's father have no sons, but also his estate 'was entailed in default of heirs male, on a distant relation'. (PP,28) That he could not pass on his estate to his progeny undoubtedly contributed to his detachment and cynicism, and it helps explain his retreat from the world. Mr. Bennet is seen in the company of his wife and daughters or in the isolation of his library, not playing an active role in the management of his estate. His one achievement in life was his beloved 'Lizzy', who unlike her sisters had his clearness of mind and verbal quickness, along with her own energy and independence, the very qualities that helped her to win over Darcy. Precisely because she came from a different social stratum than Darcy and belonged to a family line that was running out, she was all the more capable of appreciating the tradition of Darcy's family and helping to maintain it. Darcy stood for permanence, while Elizabeth represented an energy that could translate into improvement. Through marriage the two were synthesised.

As represented by Darcy, the aristocracy was not a closed caste, but open to infusions of life from below. Not only did he marry down in the social sense, but also related easily and successfully to people of different classes than his own. When Elizabeth imagined herself as mistress of Pemberley during her first visit, and wondered if she hadn't made a mistake in rejecting Darcy's proposal, she thought of her aunt and uncle, the Gardiners, and 'recollecting herself' decided that she had made the right decision. 'My aunt and uncle would have been lost to me: I should not have been allowed to invite them.' (PP,246) When Darcy appeared unexpectedly he was friendly and thoughtful to Elizabeth's aunt and uncle, offering Mr. Gardiner the use of his stream any time he might choose, along with his own fishing tackle. Only knowing what Elizabeth had told them about Darcy they were surprised at such generosity, and wondered afterwards if he had been serious in the offer. In fact, he had been, partly because they were Elizabeth's aunt and uncle but also because he was polite and found them nice and agreeable people. That Mr. Gardiner was a lawyer from London certainly did not prejudice Darcy; pride he certainly did have, but not the type that made him disdainful of those beneath him socially. We read in the final paragraph of *Pride and Prejudice* that 'with the Gardiners' Darcy and Elizabeth alike 'were always on the most intimate terms'. (PP,388) As Duckworth has said, 'The three classes of [Austen's] fictional world—nobility, gentry, and trade—come together finally in the park at Pemberley.'

I have argued that in *Sense and Sensibility* and *Pride and Prejudice* Austen poured new wine into old bottles, and that in one case she found a suitable receptacle, but not in the other. At any rate, the Burkean themes that Austen added on were not necessary to the stories, but were fitted in as seemed appropriate; they could be removed from these novels and the stories would still hang together. As those themes were in Austen's mind from the beginning in *Mansfield Park*, they occupy a more central position, contributing to the novel's underlying structure. The plot is built around the community theme, of which the Bertram estate is the main symbol.[36] Of the various groups that entered this community, the Crawfords and Fanny Price were most important. The Bertram family was made up of vital and weak elements, and in that sense was divided, as by extension was the world of Mansfield Park. The subversive Crawfords would attempt to win over the representatives of order, principle and stability, and nearly succeeded in their design. Only Fanny was steadfast in opposing them, only she remained firm in the beliefs that she knew to be right. While Sir Thomas believed in duty and demonstrated his firmness and rectitude upon returning from Antigua and stopping the theatrical performance, he was prone to errors of judgment. In wanting Fanny to accept Henry's proposal he demonstrated an inability to measure character. His reason for sending Fanny back to Portsmouth was to shake some sense into her head in order that she would change her mind and marry Crawford. Rather than leading to a change of Fanny's heart, her departure resulted in a moral breakdown at Mansfield Park. Only Fanny's return, at Sir Thomas's request, led to a restoration of order. Having been an outsider at Mansfield Park at the beginning, and abused by her aunt and cousins, Fanny gradually worked her way towards its centre, as indicated externally by her moving from one of the wings into the east room. It was only upon returning to Mansfield Park from Portsmouth that she would fully and finally occupy the position towards which she had been gravitating as she grew and developed in its surroundings.

It might appear that Fanny was an unlikely heroine to provide the cohesion necessary to mend the weak parts of Mansfield Park and gather them into a strong whole. She was physically weak, even sickly, and without a vital, compelling personality. Her way was to win not by brilliant reasoning or forceful argument but by example; while the most passive of heroines, she was morally steadfast, a quality that made her the type of agent capable of stabilising Mansfield Park. She stood for stasis, the Crawfords for change. In their endless search for amusement Henry and Mary undermined the foundations of Mansfield Park and disrupted the rhythm of its rural life. As we have seen, Henry may be seen as a 'ludic' type, bent on turning life into a play. Without any fixed principles, his way was to assume various roles as prompted by his whims. Given this type of makeup, he was superficial and he represented a type of flux that could subvert the traditional pattern of Mansfield Park, for which permanence was a necessity. While his boredom led to his flirtation with Maria and contributed to his role in the theatrical episode, Mary's resulted in the revealing harp incident. Anxious to pick up the harp that she had sent from London, she found it difficult to hire a cart, as it was the middle of the harvesting season. That her plans should encounter any difficulties irritated her, especially when the only obstacle was the intransigence of the local farmers. They were preventing her from fetching her musical instrument; their harvest would keep her from a performance that would have a certain effect upon Edmund. When it was explained to her how important the carts were to the harvest and that none could be spared, Mary tried to contain her vexation: 'I shall understand all your ways in time; but coming down with the true London maxim, that everything is to be got with money, I was a little embarrassed at first by the sturdy independence of your country customs.' (MP,58) The truth was that neither Henry nor Mary Crawford was capable of understanding those customs. Made up as they were they could only regard the regularity of rural life as foreign. They did not wish to adapt to that way of life nor were they temperamentally able to do so; they could only undercut it.

In working her way to the centre of Mansfield Park and dislodging the Crawfords, Fanny preserved the Bertram estate. What she saved was not just the Bertram family but something larger and more significant. Sir Thomas and Lady Bertram and their children were but one generation, receiving an estate from their ancestors, which they in turn would hand down to their descendants. It is when the family is seen in this light, carrying forward a tradition, that the social—and ideological—dimension of

Mansfield Park comes into view. What Fanny buttressed was the community, of which the Bertram family was the head and their estate the physical centre. Anxious as the Bertrams were to accommodate their London guests, they could not assist Mary in her harp plan because they were part of rural life and understood its ways, as they had to. The well-being of the community depended on them; without their support social continuity would break down.

What separates Austen's treatment of these themes in *Mansfield Park* from their earlier treatment in *Sense and Sensibility* and *Pride and Prejudice*, in addition to their centrality, is the dynamic social ground on which they were worked out. The world of *Mansfield Park* was threatened in a way that was new, as a grim struggle was taking place beneath an apparently calm surface, making this a very different type of novel from its predecessors, one that unlike them was fully of the Revolutionary Age. Not only did Austen reveal a more complex society in *Mansfield Park*, but also something about her response to change.

The worlds of *Sense and Sensibility* and *Pride and Prejudice* were basically stable, undoubtedly reflecting Austen's social awareness in the 1790s, when she wrote the early versions of these novels. John Dashwood was a threat to the community, but just as enclosing landlords had been for centuries. There was nothing inherently or structurally wrong with the community; the problem was with the person who stood at its head. In *Pride and Prejudice* there are signs of social strain, as seen in phrases like 'such times as these'. I think that language of this type was an interpolation, used by Austen when she made the revisions of 1811–12, to dramatise and give urgency to her Burkean argument. The two estates in this novel, Longbourn and Pemberley, were not unsound. It was true that Mr. Bennet did not manage Longbourn, but one of the reasons was the absence of a male heir. The problems that were attached to this estate did not derive from internal weakness, but from the legal consequences of having only daughters. And Pemberley, as we have seen, was well and responsibly managed.

In *Pride and Prejudice* there was a synthesis of different elements through Elizabeth's and Darcy's marriage, thereby infusing new energy into the social body. This happened in a way that was normal in the old, traditional and stable society. New families had long married into old families, and Elizabeth's marriage to Darcy was consistent with that pattern. Fanny's marriage to Edmund was different. This was not just a merging of new and old, but a necessary way to preserve a community, and by extension an entire social order, that was internally weak and subject to the forces of subversion.

Improvement was a theme in *Sense and Sensibility* and *Pride and Prejudice*, and indeed in much of the literature of the seventeenth and eighteenth centuries. In *Mansfield Park* it received a new type of treatment, reflecting a Burkean conception of change. While Burke had a prejudice against change, believing that 'the cold sluggishness of our national character' and 'our sullen resistance to innovation'[37] helped to maintain the venerated ways of the past, he did recognise the necessity for change. Change should take place not violently, as in France, where the elaborate and intricate network of custom, tradition and legal arrangements had been torn asunder in the name of abstract principle, but through gradual adaptation to existing institutions, in a way that was organic to the legacy handed down by past generations. In discussing his views on this subject, Burke spoke of the state as if it were an estate.

> But one of the first and most leading principles on which the commonwealth and the laws are consecrated is, lest the temporary possessors and life-renters in it, unmindful of what they have received from their ancestors or of what is due to their posterity, should act as if they were the entire masters, that they should not think it among their rights to cut off the entail or commit waste on the inheritance by destroying at their pleasure the whole original fabric of their society, hazarding to leave to those who come after them a ruin instead of an habitation—and teaching these successors as little to respect their contrivances as they had themselves respected the institutions of their forefathers. By this unprincipled facility of changing the state as often, and as much, and in as many ways as there are floating fancies or fashions, the whole chain and continuity of the commonwealth would be broken. No one generation could link with the other. Men would become little better than the flies of a summer.[38]

When Austen used the estate as a vehicle for discussing improvement in *Mansfield Park* she made a Burkean statement about society. In the Sotherton episode the focus was on estate improvement, with one set of characters arguing for one type of change and a rival set for a different type. Those representing artificial values and symbolising flux supported architectural and landscape changes that failed to respect the work of earlier generations. Modern in outlook, they would have imposed their ideas without regard for existing structures. Anxious to be elegant and in the latest style, Rushworth would have cut down trees near the family estate. Henry Crawford agreed with the plan. The new avenue that Rushworth and Crawford favoured would have provided an alternative entrance to the house. Facing to the west rather than the east, where the present entrance was situated, it would have avoided the village, including the church, steward's house and alms-houses, all of which Maria predictably found unsightly. The improvements that fashion required would have had the inevitable effect of separating the great, stately, Elizabethan house of the Rushworth family from the various buildings that made up the nearby village, which would have weakened the organic structure of the community. Fanny disliked the idea of cutting down trees for a new avenue and wished that she could 'see the place now, in its old state'. (MP,56) Edmund would not have hired Rushworth's favourite improver, Repton, or for that matter anyone: 'Had I a place to new fashion, I should not put myself into the hands of an improver. I would rather have an inferior degree of beauty, of my own choice, and acquired progressively.' (MP,46) In saying that he preferred a beauty that was 'acquired progressively', Edmund indicated his sense of tradition.

He did so again when discussing his future parsonage house, Thornton Lacey, with Henry and Mary Crawford. Having examined the place earlier, Henry felt that it needed improvement. The farmyard should be cleared away and planted so the unsightly blacksmith's shop could not be seen, and the front of the house should be moved to improve the view. He also insisted on a new approach and a new garden. Mary agreed that the parsonage house needed improvement, which if done properly could 'raise it into a *place*'. (MP,244) Typically concerned with appearance and anxious to be in the latest style, she imagined changes that would reflect well on the occupant of an elegant establishment. 'From being the mere gentleman's residence, it becomes, by judicious improvement, the residence of a man of education, taste, modern manners, good connections.' (MP,244) Such ideas did not fit into Edmund's plan. Not only would Henry's scheme not be 'put in practice', but by satisfying himself with a far more modest proposal he hoped to satisfy 'all who care for me', (MP,242) by which he undoubtedly meant his future parishioners. Instinctively he took

into account the members of a community of which the parsonage
house was a vital part. Undoubtedly the farm that was attached to
the house was connected organically to the community, symboli-
cally representing the tradition of the village and evoking its rural
character. By wishing to remove it, the Crawfords indicated the
type of disruption that would result from their type of improvement.
When Edmund rejected this plan he revealed a very different
orientation, but without refusing all improvement. As with Sotherton, he would make changes, but they would be modest, respect the
legacy of earlier generations, and not do violence to an existing
structure.

The community was threatened in a quite different way in *Emma*
than in *Mansfield Park*.[39] To be sure, there were intruders who, like
those of the previous novel, endangered the world that they entered,
in this case the village of Highbury. But the heroine herself was also
a threat. As the only issue of a family that was 'the first in
conquence', (E,7) Emma should have been a constructive factor
in the life of the community. That she was not resulted, among other
things, from an inability to grasp the social relationships that were
the basis of the hierarchical village order. What best brought out
this failing was Emma's plan to marry Harriet Smith to Mr. Elton.
This empty-headed girl at first was favourably disposed toward the
worthy yeoman Robert Martin, who offered her his hand in
marriage. Emma would not consent to her protegée's making such a
degrading alliance, convinced that Martin was not Harriet's equal.
When she indicated to Knightley that Harriet had rejected the
proposal he became cross, instantly realising Emma's role in the
proceeding. In a moment of exasperation he told Emma the plain,
hard truth. Harriet Smith was 'the natural daughter of nobody
knows whom, with probably no settled provision at all, and
certainly no respectable relations. She is known only as parlour-
boarder at a common school. She is not a sensible girl, nor a girl of
any information.' (E,61) Under the circumstances her marrying
Robert Martin would have been to her considerable advantage.
Martin had consulted with Knightley about the proposal before he
had made it, and Knightley, realising that Harriet was basically a
girl of good disposition, had given his support. His view was that
'Her character depends upon those she is with.' (E,58) Recognising
the solid qualities of Martin, and appreciating his forthrightness, he
had no doubt that married to him Harriet would 'turn out a
valuable woman'. In Abbey-Mill farm he was well situated

materially and in a position to afford being married. By encouraging Harriet to aim higher than this 'open, straight forward, and very well judging' (E,59) farmer, Emma was threatening the girl's chances of happiness: 'If you encourage her to expect to marry greatly, and teach her to be satisfied with nothing less than a man of consequence and large fortune, she may be a parlour-boarder at Mrs. Goddard's all the rest of her life . . .' (E,64)

Besides having a clear view of the social hierarchy and understanding how its various parts could fit together without friction or dislocation, Knightley appreciated the virtues and contributions of those of more modest station than himself. As a working farmer he was well able to measure the achievement of Martin, and value his industry and the success it brought. Martin was the type of ambitious young farmer who read the Agricultural Reports, anxious to keep abreast of the latest methods of cultivation. His efforts paid off, as 'he had been bid more for his wool than any body in the Country'. (E,28) While an efficient, progressive farmer, he had a very deliberate, careful and even cautious side, as seen in his consulting Knightley, his superior in the village as well as a man he looked up to, before making the proposal.

There is, in fact, something definitely traditional and even old-fashioned about Martin, the latter attribute deriving from the class that he was described as belonging to. In calling him a yeoman Austen used a term that had definite emotional connotations, evoking memories of a type of freeholder that once played an important role in rural life but no longer did.[40] What the term did was connect Martin to an earlier tradition and summon memories of the old England in which yeomen played a central role, not only socially and economically but also militarily, helping lay the foundations of England's greatness. By scorning Martin, Emma failed to recognise a most worthy young man, one who not only was a successful and hardworking farmer but also was connected to a hallowed English tradition. Until Emma's humiliation and consequent reformation she did not support the social order as she should have.

Anne Elliot, the heroine of *Persuasion*, was deeply serious, highly perceptive, more than any other character in the novel, dutiful, socially responsible and emotionally attached to the family estate, Kellynch Hall.[41] She embodied the very characteristics necessary for the continued well-being of the community. In *Emma*, it was necessary for the heroine to mend her ways before assuming a proper place in the community; in *Persuasion* the heroine was responsible from the outset, while the community itself was in need of repair. As in the earlier novels new families were pushing upward in the social order, but they did not achieve a synthesis of new and old, nor did they reconstitute the community. Unhealthy at the beginning of the novel, the community was still so at the end. Written in the tense, post-war period, *Persuasion* reveals a bleak social vision that reflects Austen's own despair. As Litz has said, doubt and indeterminacy had been present in the earlier novels, but had been suppressed or adroitly handled. In *Persuasion* new pressures can be felt, as can an uncertain and even hostile social climate.

The Elliot estate was badly in debt, owing to the extravagance of Anne's father. As long as Walter's wife had been alive he had kept his expenses at a manageable level, but after her death he had spent on such a grandiose scale that he had to mortgage his estate. Further in debt than ever, and unable to find any new expedients, drastic measures were necessary. As he would never 'disgrace his name' by selling Kellynch, there were but two alternatives: he could greatly reduce his expenses and continue to live on his estate, or he could rent it and live elsewhere until he would be in a financial position to return. His lawyer, Mr. Shepherd, reckoned that the latter alternative would require seven years. Sir Walter, Anne and her elder sister, Elizabeth, all preferred retrenchment and staying at Kellynch, but only Anne was prepared to cut back as much as was necessary.

As attached as Sir Walter was to tradition, that attachment was superficial. This baronet loved nothing more than to read the history of his family, to see 'how it had been first settled in Cheshire; how mentioned in Dugdale—serving the office of High Sheriff, representing a borough in three successive parliaments, exertions of loyalty, and dignity of baronet, in the first year of Charles II . . . .' (P,4) While he loved to read about the achievements of his ancestors he did nothing comparable in his own right. Earlier members of the Elliot family had served in public office, on the local and national level, and then fought for the king during the Civil War, for which they were rewarded during the Restoration. Unlike them, he lived a retired and parasitical life on his beloved estate. In fact, conscious as he was of his position, he did not carry forward the tradition of his ancestors; not only did he fail to do so but through his negligence he undercut that tradition.

Sir Walter's failure of responsibility became apparent as he was leaving Kellynch, on his way to Bath. Before driving 'off in very good spirits' he 'prepared with condescending bows for all the afflicted tenantry and cottagers who might have had a hint to shew themselves'. (P,36) That he could depart in a good humour indicates the inadequacy of his attachment to his estate, as well as social neglect. There is no indication that he visited the tenantry and cottagers before leaving. Further, some who lined up to see him leave had been instructed to be there, which is not surprising given Sir Walter's ways. He was not the type of person that would endear himself to the plain, hard-working members of village society. His 'condescending bows' beautifully bring out his view of those people who were so beneath him. Anne had a completely different idea of the villagers. Before joining her sister at nearby Uppercross she did something of a 'trying nature', going 'to almost every house in the parish, as a sort of take-leave. I was told that they wished it.' (P,39) Anne found her visitations trying not just in the physical but also in the emotional sense, attached as she was to the village families.

Staying at Uppercross with her sister and brother-in-law, the Charles Musgroves, Anne again was a misfit. Mary and her husband, along with his two sisters, were flighty, irresponsible and modern. Until 'a few years back' Uppercross 'had been completely in the Old English style; containing only two houses superior in appearance to those of the yeomen and labourers', (P,36) the old mansion and the parsonage house. When Charles and Mary moved into a farmhouse they converted it into a cottage, adding a 'veranda, French windows, and other prettinesses', in other words 'improving' it according to their taste. By making those changes they added a false and artificial element to the village, affecting its character negatively. Mr. and Mrs. Musgrove, who in contrast to their children were in the 'old English style', (P,40) lived in the Great House, located a quarter of a mile away. 'Friendly and hospitable, not much educated, and not at all elegant', (P,40) they enjoyed living simply. But 'Their children had more modern minds and manners', so they brought the Great House up to date by improving it. Maria and Henrietta modernised the 'old-fashioned square parlour' by furnishing it with 'a grand piano forte and a harp, flower-stands and little tables placed in every direction'. (P,40) Through these changes, like those made by their brother, they were breaking with the past. If their ancestors, who were represented in portraits, could look down from the walls of this old room and see 'what was going on' (P,40) they would have been astonished at the 'overthrow of all order and neatness!'.

Though Uppercross was not her own village, Anne became attached to it. When it was time to leave 'she could not quit the mansion-house, or look an adieu to the cottage, with its black, dripping, and comfortless veranda, or even notice through the misty glasses the last humble tenements of the village, without a saddened heart'. (P,123) That she felt as she did about the modest houses of the villagers set her apart from the family that stood at the head of the community. Concerned only with their own amusement, the Musgroves did not play an important role in the life of the village. 'The Mr. Musgroves had their own game to guard, and to destroy; their own horses, dogs, and newspapers to engage them; and the females were fully occupied in all the other common subjects of house-keeping, neighbours, dress, dancing, and music.' (P,42–3) Engaged by these frivolous pursuits, they were unfit to occupy their social station. Just as the community of Kellynch had been weakened by neglect, that of Uppercross was harmed by the 'improvements' of the indolent, self-indulgent, irresponsible and modern Musgroves. And this did not change. No reform took place. The person who most embodied the characteristics necessary for the well-being of the community and for social continuity remained a misfit and an outsider. Her marriage to Wentworth would have had no impact on either Kellynch or Uppercross. Those communities had fallen, it appears, into permanent disrepair. Neither the hero nor heroine would be in a position to mend these weaknesses. While the new understanding between Anne and Wentworth cleared the way for their marriage it did not have any forseeable influence on the community.

In *Sanditon*, the community was threatened by new and even more disruptive forces.[42] Before, it had been possible to strengthen it through a synthesis of new and old elements, or to repair it through personal example or a reform of mistaken individual ways. Even in *Persuasion* reform was possible, although it did not take place. The characters who had the sense of responsibility to restore the community to a sound condition were not given the opportunity, so the community remained weak. In Austen's final work the community was undercut in a far more pervasive way, and no one could arrest the frightening process of change.

More than the heroines in the earlier novels, Charlotte Heywood stood apart from the activity that went on about her. She was an agent through whom the community can be seen, but she did not enter into its life. Further, her position was almost secondary; the focus was no longer on the relationship between the heroine and the community but rather on the community itself. There were, in fact, two communities, Charlotte's own village, Willingden, and the seaside resort, Sanditon. Willingden was insular, traditional, and intensely local. Seemingly at one with it was Charlotte's father, a farmer and gentleman who is first seen in a hayfield, among three or four of his men. He and his wife never left home, except for two trips to London every year to receive his dividends. This farmer did not stay home by choice but from necessity. Reasonably well off, he and his wife were unable to 'indulge' themselves with visits to Tunbridge Wells or Bath because they had fourteen children, whose 'maintenance, Education and fitting out . . . demanded a very quiet, settled, careful course of Life . . .' (MW,374) In fact, insular as the world of Willingden appeared, it was not impervious to change. While the Heywoods hardly ever left home, they were 'very far from wishing their Children to do the same, they were glad to promote *their* getting out into the World, as much as possible. *They* staid at home, that their Children *might* get out.' (MW,374) And this farmer did travel to London twice every year to collect his dividends, indicating that his economic outlook was not limited to the growing and selling of crops. Indeed, given the necessity of staying at home, it would seem that he could not have maintained his decent but modest way of life without dividends—without having been connected to the capitalistic economy.

Change took place on a completely different scale in Sanditon, where Mr. Heywood sent his daughter, anxious for her to see more of the world. As Sanditon contrasted to Willingden, so did Mr. Parker stand apart from Mr. Heywood. This entrepreneur lived inland originally, but moved to Sanditon, a burgeoning coastal resort. Eager to promote change and further growth, he worked incessantly at bringing in people from the outside world. Nothing gave him greater satisfaction than to see the visible signs of progress. Walking through the village and seeing some 'Blue shoes, and nankin Boots' in the window of a shoemaker, he could only think of the role he played in producing such positive evidence of improvement. As he climbed a hill he went past the last house of old Sanditon, coming to a row of new buildings that extended to the down above, where his own house, 'a light elegant Building', (MW, 384) was situated. A short distance away there was a 'short row of smart-looking Houses, called the Terrace, with a broad walk in front, aspiring to be The Mall of The Place. In this row were The best Milliner's shop & the Library—a little detached from it, The Hotel & Billiard Room—Here began the Descent to the Beach, & to the Bathing Machines—& This was Therefore the favourite spot for Beauty & Fashion.' (MW,384) While Mr. Parker's spirits rose as he viewed the new parts of Sanditon, his wife felt differently. She was unhappy, missing her old house, the abode of her forefathers, where she and all her brothers and sisters had been born and bred and where her own three eldest children had entered the world. For her, it was 'an honest old Place', and 'a very comfortable House'. (MW, 380) She especially missed the garden. Not Mr. Parker, who pointed out that they could still grow fruit and buy anything they wanted in their new house. In making this statement he refused to take his wife's feelings into account. What she missed was not food for their table, but a garden to which she was emotionally attached and that had aesthetic as well as functional value. It was a formal garden, unlike the 'Kitchen Garden' at Sanditon. Pragmatic and economically motivated as Mr. Parker was, he apparently had no use for the older type of garden at his new house.

Equally pragmatic and concerned with profit was Mr. Parker's friend, Lady Denham. Discussing the coming season, she was apprehensive, afraid that the lodgings might not be filled. She was relieved that Mr. Parker's sister, who had made a recent trip to London to attract paying guests to Sanditon, had lined up two large parties, one from the West Indies. But even the prospect of their coming made Lady Denham uneasy, afraid as she was that they would 'scatter their Money' so freely as to raise prices. As Mr. Parker pointed out, this evil was a blessing in disguise. Explaining the benefits of modern economics, he showed that an increasing demand for goods might indeed profit 'Our Butchers & Bakers & Traders', but they could not 'get rich without bringing Prosperity to *us*'. (MW,392–3) An infusion of wealth from rich guests would in fact make their own holdings more valuable.

Money was an obsession with the seventy-year old Lady Denham. As a woman of 'about 30' she had married an elderly and very rich man, who had left her his entire estate. She then married Sir Harry Denham, who was just as calculating as herself. She had money, he had a title; both wanted what the other possessed. Lady Denham was the winner in this unpleasant competition, outliving her husband and keeping her title without having allowed him to get his hands on her money, which he wanted for the impoverished members of his family. Lady Denham revealed her meanness by having the niece and nephew of her deceased husband live with her so that they could court her favour in the hope of inheriting her wealth. Not satisfied with their presence, she invited another relative to Sanditon from her own family, in spite of the protests of the niece and nephew. By surrounding herself with relatives who by their very circumstances were compelled to compete for her favour, Lady Denham was not only 'thoroughly mean', but 'she makes everybody mean about her'. (MW,402)

People of this type were the dominant force in Sanditon. Through their efforts the community had been transformed. Rising above the fishermen's cottages in the old village were the new, modern buildings that catered to guests during the tourist season. The life of the village was no longer the same. Before, humble families had earned a modest living fishing, following the same pattern year in and year out, generation after generation. Now, rich and vulgar tourists who poured in inevitably upset the accepted ways. Money became a corrosive force that dissolved tradition, disrupted the community and undercut social continuity.

While Austen depicted a new type of community in *Sanditon*, the seaside resort, she saw it in relationship to the traditional village which was her usual setting. The two communities, Willingden and Sanditon, were contrasted, one being local and insular, the other restless and fluid. Yet both were subject to the forces of change. That Mr. Heywood, the representative of the former, depended on his investments to maintain his way of life, and wanted his children to get 'out into the World, as much as possible', suggests that one of Austen's themes was the impact of change on the rural village. And Sanditon, a fishing village recently turned into a resort, had a rural aspect. Mr. Parker, the principal landowner, had succeeded to the family property 'which 2 or 3 Generations had been holding & accumulating before him', (MW,371) and Lady Denham occupied the 'Manor and Mansion House' and owned considerable property, of which a large part was in the parish of Sanditon. The two engineers of change were landowners who turned their backs on the occupations and traditions of rural life, and through their entrepreneurial activities were instrumental in transforming Sanditon.

To say that Austen's usual setting was the rural community is to utter a truism. Norland, Longbourn, Pemberley, Mansfield Park,

Highbury, Kellynch Hall and Uppercross are all of a type, and all gave Austen an appropriate framework to test ideas and concepts that I have described as Burkean. While Burke often referred to estates, and he clearly identified with the landowning class, his thought in one respect indicates a break from the tradition of that class. In the realm of economics Burke was an advocate of laissez-faire. The great advocate of the organic society ridiculed the opponents of enclosure, disregarding the ancient customs that were being violated, unmindful of the traditional social fabric that was being torn apart. With Coleridge and Wordsworth, and others of their generation, there was a new and highly positive feeling for rural life, and consistent with that feeling was an opposition to laissez-faire economics. Unlike Burke, their economic views agreed with their social attitudes, one of the reasons being their commitment to the ways of the past, to tradition, to custom and to the rural community which they considered a vital agent of social continuity.

It might seem paradoxical, precisely when England was industrialising and laissez-faire economics were gaining an ascendancy, that rural life was idealised as never before. In fact, it was because the tide of change moved so swiftly that such a response took place; it was because the old society was being undercut that people saw it in a new light, becoming more conscious of its virtues. This is not to say that rural life was not idealised before the industrial revolution, for it had been. But at a certain point, say after 1800, there was an increasing awareness of flux in the countryside, the result of enclosure and a flood of newcomers, nabobs, generals, admirals, contractors and the like who upset the old ways with their different habits and their cash. So when the Lake Poets embraced economic ideas that emphasised responsibility to the community, not laissez-faire individualism, they represented a position that both reflected and was a response to the changing conditions of this period.

As a class the traditional leaders of rural society did not pursue the economic policies advocated by conservative theorists who stood behind the rural community. Coleridge argued for 'the idea of a *trust* inherent in landed property', thereby putting the stress on the duties, not the rights, of property. But the landowning class, anxious to further its material interest, embraced the doctrines of Adam Smith, pursuing cash profits as they stepped away from their traditional responsibilities, abandoning the patronage system and introducing economic individualism into rural society.[43] This is not to say that they rejected protectionism altogether; in fact, they maintained controls when it was to their advantage, as with the Corn Laws, but rejected controls when it did not, as with the regulation of wages.

The period 1815 to 1820 was a time of great stress. Beside the dislocation of rural society, particularly in the southern counties and East Anglia, where riots broke out in 1816,[44] there was widespread unemployment resulting from the post-war depression. The end of the war was followed by a sense of disenchantment even though this was not the immediate result. Initially there was a mood of national rejoicing and patriotic enthusiasm, but in the difficult economic times of the post-war period the euphoria soon passed. It is important to realise that the war effort had given strength to the government and, by extension, to the established order, as a potentially divided society was held together in allegiance against a common enemy. This changed with the coming of peace. As early as 1816, the movement for parliamentary reform, long quiescent, was resumed, and during the next few years the spectre of class war hung over England.

How much of this is reflected in *Sanditon*? More than has been re-cognised. Austen's descriptions of Willingden and Sanditon show a keen awareness of change.and of the decisive role of economics in bringing it about. Capitalism reached the insular, rural world of Willingden and wealthy guests from London and the West Indies descended upon Sanditon, altering the social fabric with the corrosive effect of their money, not to mention the vulgarity of their example. Like Wordsworth and Coleridge, Austen was apprehensive about the changing conditions, as seen in her way of depicting Mr. Parker. His former house can be seen as a symbol of the old society, while his present house represents the new society. The earlier house was situated in a valley, where it enjoyed shade and was protected from the heavy winds that blew in from the coast. During the previous winter the Parkers, in Sanditon, had been thrown from their bed during a storm, while the family living in the inland house had scarcely been aware of the wind. Still, Mr. Parker felt that living in Sanditon he was better able to sustain heavy winds than he had been in the sheltered site of his old house. On the downs and above the sea, where he currently lived, the wind 'simply rages & passes on', (MW,381) encountering no resistance, but inland, in the 'Nook' where the other house was located, nothing was 'known of the state of the air, below the tops of the trees—and the inhabitants may be taken totally unawares, by one of those dreadful currents which do more mischief in a valley, when they *do* arise than an open country ever experiences in the heaviest Gale'. (MW,381) Modern and capitalistic man that he was, Mr. Parker was fully prepared to face the winds of change. In his opinion, the sheltered, traditional world of his other house was actually more vulnerable to those winds and more likely to suffer damage. To live there was to be 'totally unawares' of harsh forces that struck without warning. And Mr. Parker, Austen could well have been saying, might not have been entirely wrong; the future very possibly could be with a type of community geared to the new economic conditions, anxious to profit from them, and fully willing to part with the ways of the past.

Just as Sanditon revealed one set of problems in the fluid, post-war world of 1817, so did Willingden exemplify another. The coastal town, fully open to the forces of change, was a place of 'Activity run mad'. (MW,410) The inland village, rural in make-up, was beset by a different type of weakness. As a member of that community, Mr. Heywood revealed the inadequacy of his response to change. In his opinion the rise of new resort towns, all of them attracting people with money, were 'Bad things for a Country; — sure to raise the price of Provisions & make the Poor good for nothing . . .' (MW,368) In *Sanditon*, Austen was not commenting just on the new type of resort town, but on the social and economic tendencies that were fast altering the earlier pattern of life. And through Mr. Heywood's insularity and fear of the lower classes she showed a hardening of arteries in the old society, an inability to respond to the rapid change and particular problems of the post-war world.

Twentieth-century historians agree with this verdict. Halévy sees a growing ossification amongst the conservatives, whose exaggerated interest in honours and distinctions helped isolate them from the rest of the country—one thinks of Sir Walter Elliot in this connection—and Harold Perkin sees a massive abandonment by the landed classes of their social responsibilities. And all historians agree on the widespread fear by the upper classes of the lower classes. While historians of this period have concentrated on industrial conflict more than rural conflict, the latter was also acute, as any reader of Cobbett understands.

In a stimulating discussion of Cobbett and Austen, Raymond Williams finds Austen unaware of the economic change on the English countryside that entered so much into Cobbett's thinking and writing. He shows that Austen was keenly aware of certain economic facts, as indicated by her using incomes and the size of estates as a way to define her characters' material position. Further, he shows that the world of Austen's novels was not a settled, single society but one constantly in flux, 'an acquisitive, high bourgeois society at the point of its most evident interlocking with an agrarian capitalism that is itself mediated by inherited titles and by the making of family names'. In spite of this fluidity, he argues, Austen achieved a unity of tone, 'a settled and remarkably confident way of seeing and judging, in the chronicle of confusion and change'. Related to this confidence was Austen's concern not with the economic process, but the conversion of wealth acquired through that process into the amenities of civilised life, as in the improvement of houses, parks and artificial landscapes. Cobbett, by contrast, was deeply aware of the realities of agricultural life and the conflict between the land-owning class and the rural labouring class. Because he was aware of that conflict, Cobbett became class conscious, which Austen, whose awareness was limited to her own class, did not. In a striking image Williams sees Cobbett riding through Hampshire, not far from Chawton, where Austen was writing her novels. He is on one side of the park walls, an outsider, and she is on the other, an insider. He lashed away at the class to which Austen belonged, his rough language reflecting the angle of his social vision and her unity of tone and confidence reflecting her very different experience.

What I find striking about Austen is how much she saw from her side of the park wall. Mr. Heywood's fear of the poor, which Lady Denham shared, suggests that Austen understood the stresses of the post-war period and their translation into class hostility. Her description of Sanditon shows economic forces transforming a community, as members of the old society were instrumental in bringing about the change. She did not view change with the confidence that Williams finds in her writing. In *Sanditon*, Austen's way of treating the themes of community, social continuity and improvement indicates a definite apprehensiveness and concern over the future, as her class seemed unable to adjust to a new set of conditions.

Living through the period of the French Revolution and the Napoleonic Wars, Austen witnessed a breakdown of the stable, ordered, civilised world of the eighteenth century. A product of the old society, she saw a new society come into being. In recording her responses to that change in her novels she revealed an intense social engagement. Living in the midst of new and unsettling forces, she came to see the community as an important if not necessary agent in guaranteeing social continuity. As her world was that of the gentry, the way she viewed the process of change was inevitably shaped by the values and traditions of her class. The settings of her novels, her metaphors, symbols and themes, all reflect her social orientation. While she did not and could not transcend the limits of her class, her critique of society was not a class apology. Nor was she, as some have argued, a social subversive at war with her class, as critical of it as she was. Rather, Austen lived through a period that saw the settled way of life break down and, attached to that way of life, she examined the gentry's chances of survival. As she pondered the possibilities she became increasingly pessimistic, much as Wordsworth and Coleridge did, doubting that a traditional social order could maintain itself and its culture under the corrosive effect of a new economic system. The members of the old society, the members of her own class, seemed unable to resist the new ways, nor did they try to, at least sufficiently. Throughout her novels Austen's characters fit into certain normative patterns; those characters acted responsibly, supported the community, preserved tradition and furthered continuity, or they acted irresponsibly, weakened the social bonds, and diminished the legacy of past generations. In *Mansfield Park* and *Emma*, the constructive elements won out over the destructive; In *Persuasion* the former had no positive impact on the latter; and in *Sanditon* there were no constructive elements, only those that were corrosive.

While Austen was Tory, her Toryism was not a rationalisation of class interest. She arrived at her conservative views not abstractly but by the bits and pieces of her own experience. Having done so, she put those views to the social test. Ultimately, as seen in *Sanditon*, the members of her class came up short. Living in the post-war world of the Regency she had grave doubts about the future, resulting partly from the new material conditions of life, but also from a failure within her own class.

2 War

Austen maintained the same outward silence toward England's military struggle with France as toward the great political events of the day. Aside from a few passing references to military service, the novels contain no descriptions of a war that lasted, with one brief period of relief, from 1793 to 1815. Commenting ironically on *Pride and Prejudice*, Austen said it needed 'to be stretched out here and there' with a serious chapter or perhaps something 'unconnected with the story', such as one on 'the history of Buonaparté'. (L299–300) This was what other novelists had done, and it was precisely what she decided not to do, having chosen to limit her setting to the English country village. Austen's decision not to discuss the war was completely consistent with her view of herself as a novelist, and it was an artistic decision. And yet, it might have been more than that. Her letters are as free of military news as her novels are of passages describing the war. Given this paucity it might appear that living in the rural quiet of southern England Austen was sufficiently removed from the war that she hardly felt its impact. Another possibility is that as a creature of her sex and social station she so occupied herself with daily rituals, ceremonies and trivialities that she simply did not care about the war.

J. Steven Watson says that 'In spite of (Austen's) having two sailor brothers' she seems not to have been very aware of England's struggle with France, 'as witness the small part the wars play in her chronicles'. Asa Briggs sees Austen as a member of the 'enjoying classes', on whom the war made little impression. 'Jane Austen . . . had two brothers at sea during the wars, but she kept warfare almost entirely out of her novels.' Frederick Harrison criticised a novelist who avoided the war, 'penning satirettes about her neighbours while the Dynasts were tearing the world to pieces, and consigning millions to their graves'.[1] C. Linklater Thomas, looking at her correspondence, levelled a similar criticism: 'If it had not been that two of her brothers were officers in the navy, there would have been hardly a reference to the war in her letters. There seems a want of public spirit in this attitude, and a failure of imagination. It is as if she could clearly apprehend only what was passing immediately before her, and as if she was deeply interested in those with whom she had come into personal contact. She could not visualize a larger scene or comprehend vital issues'.[2] G. M. Trevelyan finds the answer to Austen's avoidance of the war in her class position. The landlords and clergy, he writes, were patriotic enough, but did not care particularly about ending the war, as they continued to be prosperous and were not called upon to make any real sacrifices. 'At no period had the upper class been wealthier, or happier, or more engrossed in the life of its pleasant country houses.' He uses Austen as supporting evidence for this view. 'No young lady of Miss Austen's acquaintance, waiting eagerly for the forthcoming volume of Scott or Byron, seems ever to have asked what Mr. Thorpe or Mr. Tom Bertram was doing during the Great War!'

Not every one agrees with this picture of Austen. V. S. Pritchett has been so bold as to see Austen as a war novelist, indicating that facts about the war are to be found in and indeed are basic to her novels.[3] Jane Aiken Hodge says that Austen 'knew all about the shortage of men, the high cost of living, and, most particularly, about the vital part played by the Navy' in England's struggle with France. She finds traces of the struggle in her fiction, especially *Persuasion*, in which contemporary readers would have understood how close the war was. D. H. Harding comments on the 'convincing impression' in Austen's novels of the war's impact on ordinary middle-class lives.[4] Many Austen critics have referred to Austen's sailor brothers, whose influence on *Mansfield Park* and *Persuasion* is well known. Even as they do so, however, these critics often, in fact typically, suggest that Austen kept the war at a distance. Andrew H. Wright, for example, after mentioning some of the points at which Austen's life touched on the larger events of the day, including the war, says that 'she might simply have held to the past, and rejected the present and its implications'.[5]

Before examining Austen's response to the war, it will be useful to look at the war itself. Seeing how the military struggle shaped the experience of Austen's society will help us to understand how it affected her. From Winston Churchill's point of view England's struggle with France was limited and circumscribed, in that it did not enter into people's lives in the way of the more democratic, mass wars of the twentieth century. This is undoubtedly correct. As Asa Briggs has written, 'the long wars with France were not total wars . . . From an economic as well as a military point of view, war never became "the great industry, directing, distorting, and dominating the whole of the nation's economic life."' Briggs points out that during the Second World War statisticians calculated that three civilian workers were necessary to keep one fighting man operational, while during the Napoleonic period estimates indicated a ratio not of three to one, but one to three. Comparing the Napoleonic Wars to those of the twentieth century is one way to take their measure, but it is by no means the only way; in fact, it can be positively misleading. Seen against the background of earlier eighteenth-century warfare the Napoleonic Wars emerge as something unique, as a type of experience that few were prepared for, and whose cumulative impact was enormous, helping disrupt established modes of life and conventional habits of thought. English—and for that matter all of European—society was profoundly altered by this wartime experience.[6]

It was the French Revolution that transformed the nature of war. As Corelli Barnett has written:

> The scope and intensity of war is determined by its social and economic frame. The wars of the eighteenth century had been fought by small ruling groups . . . the king, the courts, even in parliamentary England by the gentry. War had become a matter of limited liability and limited purpose. The new doctrine of liberty and equality burst this narrow frame. With the Revolution, the masses with all their passions, frustration, ignorance and idealism stepped into politics. The French armies were no longer the instrument of a limited materialistic policy, but of an ideological crusade.

As new energies were unleashed, new types of organisations and procedures took shape, such as conscription, requisition and central direction. The objectives of war changed from the capture of towns, colonies or provinces to the survival of conflicting ideologies and social systems. Commanding officers during the Revolutionary and Napoleonic era waged war in a way that departed from the theories and conventions of the eighteenth century. During the Seven Years' War Lord Harwicke quoted the duke of Alva with approval: 'It is the business of a general always to get the better of his enemy, but not always to fight, and if he can do his business without fighting, so much the better.' This point of view reflects the widely held eighteenth-century attitude that since armies and navies were expensive necessities they should be used with caution. When at war, the powers relied heavily upon defensive fortifications and siegecraft; formal fencing tended to replace fighting, as careful manoeuvring was preferred to decision by battle. As much as action was avoided on land, this was even more the case at sea. If outnumbered an admiral would keep a safe distance; if he joined the enemy in battle he would rarely use more than half of his fleet. It was not until the Battle of the Nile in 1798 that all thirteen British battleships of the line entered an engagement fully. As late as 1794 it was considered improper when French battleships departed from customary rules by firing on frigates not taking direct part in the engagement. War was fought with a new *élan*, and different tactics were introduced as the armies of France concentrated offensive might in columns that repeatedly broke through the more traditional line formations of rival armies.

France's military predominance during the Revolutionary era forced rival states to devise new strategies and alter their patterns of organisation. Also, the way people thought about war changed. Eighteenth-century historians failed to appreciate the differences in the social, economic and political structures of antagonists, or between former times and their own times, and tended to view contemporary military practices in the light of the past. Caesar and Condé were viewed as contemporaries, and the achievements of both compared to those of Frederick the Great.[7] Nor did historians pay close attention to the relationship between civilian and military institutions or lay bare the interaction between strategic plan and battle. As a result, such a history as Voltaire's *Charles XII* describes military events in great detail but without showing any understanding of the underlying social, economic and political forces that were at work and that contributed to the outcome. This historiographical mould was broken by the end of the eighteenth century in response to the new conditions of warfare. The old pattern of warfare was shattered as Napoleon employed new methods on land and Nelson at sea. No longer was war conceived or fought in the eighteenth-century way, but seen in relationship to other systems and as an instrument for advancing an ideological cause. As the lessons of victory and defeat were learned, warfare was conducted with a daring and aggressiveness that contrasted strikingly with the earlier type of caution.

In England the transformation of warfare took place gradually.

When Pitt declared war in 1793 he expected a short and limited conflict. His motive was not ideological; he was not acting against a state that threatened the established social and political system but protecting a British sphere of interest which he felt the French invasion of the Austrian Netherlands had violated. While a few men, such as Burke, saw the war as a crusade against France and wanted it to be waged accordingly, most shared Pitt's view that England should not join Austria and Prussia as a full participant; like Pitt, they expected the war to be short.

While Pitt did send troops to the defence of Holland he had no intention of enlarging the scope of operations and fighting a land war against France. Nor did he ever have any such intentions. Rather, he chose to be paymaster of Austria and Prussia, the principal enemies of France. England subsidised her allies until the end of the war, with various changes and modifications, as coalitions rose and fell. Not until years after Pitt's death did a coalition hold together and finally achieve a victory over France. By that time the scope and nature of war had changed almost beyond recognition, just as England's policies had been recast. Finally, beginning in 1808, England joined the land war against Napoleon in the Peninsular campaigns that contributed significantly to the ultimate allied victory. For the larger part of the war England's principal role was in the naval theatre, where she remained supreme. One of Napoleon's responses to that supremacy was the Continental System, whose objective was to close markets that were essential to the British economy. While Napoleon's plan ultimately broke down, it did place definite strains on England. Those strains were compounded in many ways, not the least being the repeated failures of Austria and Prussia. Time and again England subsidised her allies only to see them go down to defeat and leave the coalition. As this happened, England alone had to face an enemy that had vastly superior forces in every respect but the naval. In those moments England hung on grimly and at enormous cost, both emotional and material.

One way to measure the material cost is by examining the fiscal burdens of the war. The government tried to make ends meet at the end of the Seven Years' War by the sale of £1½ million in annuities, leading the opposition to launch an attack that forced a reduction of the land tax from 4s. to 3s. That a war debt of that amount had such political repercussions contrasts strikingly with the situation during the Revolutionary and Napoleonic era. When Pitt was faced with a deficit of £19 million in 1797 he made up £12 million through loans and voluntary gifts, himself contributing to the latter source well beyond his means as an example for others to follow. The balance of £7 million he raised from new taxation, which was direct. Existing taxes on items such as windows, houses, servants and carriages were trebled at a differential rate so that the wealthy man with four carriages paid more than four times as much as his less well-to-do compatriot paid for one. These taxes were inadequate, forcing Pitt to devise new measures, the most important being an income tax. As J. Steven Watson has said:

> There could be no greater proof of the change in political conditions since 1790 than that a nation which had resisted the excise now swallowed an income tax. It was criticized for being inquisitorial, for being radical, and for bearing too heavily on the upper class, but, nevertheless, it was accepted as the price of war. Pitt had remodelled the whole fiscal system and succeeded in making Britain's economic successes pay for her military trials.

Altogether, the cost of the wars was the staggering sum of £831 million. Such expenditures were necessary to support a military force vastly larger than ever before.

The army had been reduced from 17,000 men to 13,000 men nine months before the war began. By the end of the first year of war the government believed that an army of 56,000 would be sufficient; by 1801 Parliament asked for credits that would support a regular army of 193,000; by 1807 the number of troops exceeded 200,000 and by 1812 it went over 250,000. Besides the regular army there was a Militia, in which military training could be given to as many as 300,000 men in a given year, and whose units by the time of the Peninsular campaign provided men for the regular army. The main purpose of the Militia, however, was home defence, as was that of the fencibles. After 1801, the combined number of these home units was set down at 104,000. The enormous increase in the size of the army was achieved only in the face of intermittent opposition, which was directed particularly at the regular army. Ever since the Glorious Revolution the army had been regarded with suspicion and, as Blackstone put it, considered an 'excrescence' of the British Constitution. The twenty-fold increase of the army between 1793 and 1812 in itself was a change of enormous magnitude; what made the adjustment all the more difficult was the way the English people during the eighteenth century had been accustomed to think about the army. In 1757, in the middle of the Seven Years' War, the passage of a Militia Act led to riots because this legislation was thought to be a step towards the formation of a national army; during the Napoleonic period Acts were passed that allowed the regular army to draw recruits from the Militia, an indication of how important a fixture the army had become and how differently it had come to be regarded. Another adjustment that was made only with considerable difficulty was billeting troops in barracks. So deeply ingrained was English anti-militarism that when off duty a soldier was expected to remove his uniform and live among his fellow citizens; hence the eighteenth-century cry, 'No barracks'. The conditions and scale of warfare that began with the Revolutionary period necessitated the construction of barracks of which there were 155 by the end of the war, concentrated most heavily in southern England.

That these military changes were accepted can be considered a measure of the support given to the war effort. Just as the war became a struggle between rival systems for Pitt, so others came to see it in a similar light. Arthur Young is an interesting example of how an Englishmen could change his opinion of France and come to regard his own social and political system differently as a result.[8] Like most of his countrymen Young viewed the Revolution favourably when it broke out. He was in France at the time, attended meetings of the Estates General, and witnessed uprisings in the provinces. His response was definitely positive, and he remained friendly to the Revolution until 1792. Then his attitude underwent a sudden change with the eruption of violence in August and September of that year. When England declared war on France in 1793 he fully supported his country, although he continued to believe that the earlier wars with France had been mistaken. He felt that the present war was different from previous ones because it was fought not just against France, but the ideology that it represented. Others who still favoured the Revolutionary cause in 1792 and 1793 largely ceased to do so within a few years, after being disenchanted by France's military aggressiveness. Both of these factors—the eruption of violence in the summer of 1792, and the foreign belligerence that soon followed—helped to galvanise public opinion in England in support of Pitt and the war against France.

One result of this development was a deepening of national and patriotic feeling.[9] How far down that feeling went during the eighteenth century simply cannot be measured with any accuracy, but there can be no question that under the stresses and strains of ideological conflict and war it became far more pervasive. It has been said that nationalism feeds upon fear and hatred of a national enemy, and indeed this is almost a truism. To read English periodicals and newspapers during the period of the Napoleonic Wars is to find confirmation of this view. The *Critical Review* introduced a new heading in August, 1803, 'Loyalty and Patriotism', explaining that 'We feel ourselves particularly called upon, in the present state of the nation, to pay a pointed attention to the publications of this description.'[10] It was three months after the declaration of war, and a time when fear was running high in response to Napoleon's invasion plans. Of the seven publications that were reviewed under the new heading in the August issue three were about the invasion. The number of items reviewed in later issues is a useful index of both the national fear and the patriotic feeling that it engendered. Among those publications were pamphlets, books, poems, and sermons.

Nine years later, in 1812, the *Edinburgh Review* looked back over the war, measuring its impact on every aspect of British life and considering the heightened national consciousness resulting from this completely new type of experience. Government expenditure having reached levels never before known, taxes were imposed on a scale that was without precedent. The middle classes no longer lived in their former comfort, and families of more modest means, such as tailors or shoemakers, were able to provide for their children only with great difficulty. Someone earning his income in a 'laborious profession' had 'toiled through years of obscurity, poverty and sorrow', subject not only to bodily fatigue but fatigue of the mind, always striving to make ends meet. What made life so difficult was giving ten weeks of labour every year to the state in the form of new taxes, 'in order that the war for our happiness and security may be gloriously carried on'. The impact of wartime taxes, it was argued, was 'sufficient to awaken men to a feeling consideration of their intimate connection with the state'. The British people were affected by the war in many other ways, as they had to absorb an altogether new range of pressures. 'We used to think we could never bear a twentieth part as much as we have borne with ease; so that we may even go on and bear a little more.' Most people from twenty to forty years of age 'have passed their whole lives, politically speaking, in a state of universal war; and they only know from history, that there ever was such a thing as peace in the world'. The war that became 'the natural, certainly the ordinary and habitual, state of the country' made this a period 'quite unexampled in modern history'. The war was not only of 'long duration' but also novel in its 'extent and variety of . . . operations'. The forces let loose by the war were attended by an:

> excitement of national feeling, by hatred, rage, enthusiasm, glory, curiosity—by the alternations of hope and fear—of sympathy and selfishness—of anxiety before, and self gratulation after escapes—of despair and disasters. The burthens and actual sufferings entailed by the varied operations, have been proportionately great, and exceeding all former experience—or even imagination; and nations [have] both done and suffered what [would in former ages] have been thought impossible . . .[11]

Two years later, in 1814, with the arrival of peace, the *Edinburgh Review* looked back over the war again, emphasising its novelty and the magnitude of its impact, only now revealing a sense of relief and achievement, rather than dwelling on burdens that in 1812 were still keenly felt. All of society had been deeply stirred as never before and emerged from the toils of conflict as if regenerated:

> All the periods in which human society and human intellect have ever been known to make great and memorable advances, have followed close upon periods of general agitation and disorder. Men's minds, it would appear, must be deeply and roughly stirred, before they become prolific of great conceptions, or vigorous resolves; and a vast and alarming fermentation must pervade and agitate the whole mass of society, to inform it with that kindly warmth, by which alone the seeds of genius and improvement can be expanded.[12]

The result of this experience was a gain to society which, unified by a spirit of ambition, was improved at every level. The release of new forces had caused 'much guilt and much misery', but in time society absorbed the stresses of war. This led to 'a great permanent addition to the power and the enterprise of the community'. Thus did the nation as a whole benefit from the long and arduous struggle with France. Among the nations of Europe, none proved as resourceful as England and none covered itself with greater glory; it was as if no society had responded to the challenge with such vitality and creative energy.

> It is a proud and honourable distinction to be able to say, in the end of such a contest, that we belong to the only nation that has never been conquered;—to the nation that set the first example of successful resistance to the power that was desolating the world,—and who always stood erect, though she sometimes stood alone, before it. From England alone, that power, to which all the rest have successively bowed, has won no trophies, and extorted no submission; on the contrary, she has been constantly baffled and disgraced whenever she has grappled directly with the might and energy of England.[13]

While a sometimes misdirected government had made mistakes, the 'excellent spirit of the people' ultimately gave bearings to state policy; victory was achieved not by politicians drawing the populace into the war effort but by a spontaneous, collective effort surging forth from the people itself.

While the British people undoubtedly did throw their support behind the government in the war against France, and national and patriotic feeling did deepen as sacrifices were made in the effort to achieve victory, there were definite limits on the commitment. This world war, as it has accurately been called, did not elicit the same type of response as the Great War of 1914–18. In the first place, Francophobia was much less intense in 1793 than Germanophobia in 1914; in fact, many in Britain, at least initially, were sympathetic to France. Secondly, the outbreak of hostilities during the Revolutionary era was not preceded by the same type of patriotic fervour that was so manifest in the several decades before Sarajevo; the increase in national feeling that emerged in the eighteenth century pales before the new type of nationalism that issued from the late nineteenth century and flowed so mightily into the twentieth. England was much less prepared to enter fully and completely into the earlier than the later war effort. Contemporaries were aware of the limited commitment throughout the Revolutionary and Napoleonic Wars, aware of the reluctance of some to become emotionally involved in the struggle. This helps explains frequent appeals in books, newspapers and periodicals to people who withheld their support, living, it would seem, in their complacent, eighteenth-century way. Wilberforce wrote in 1797 that men of the world smiled or sneered at the services that some were rendering their country.[14] In 1807, the *Edinburgh Review*, discussing an anonymous publication, *The Dangers of the Country*, explained that 'the few who have allowed themselves to reflect' on the book's subject will be surprised at the alarming consequences that would result from defeat, which the book clearly spelled out. In the reviewer's opinion the book would 'startle the thoughtless, and rouse the multitude from their dream of apathy, thus to see these menaced evils embodied and spread out before them, which they have hitherto apprehended only as a remote and indistinct possibility'.[15] At the beginning of the Peninsular War a writer in *The Times* urged his countrymen to give the utmost importance to the Spanish cause, advice that he considered necessary owing to the indifference he had observed.[16] The *Edinburgh Review* wrote that 'Ordinary readers, who will cheerfully go through the details of a budget containing some half dozen of new taxes, are afraid to grapple with topics relating to distant countries, and the operations of War.' This same periodical claimed that:

the gravest concerns of this country must continue to be neglected; its whole resources—its wealth, its blood, its valour— to be squandered in the purchase of defeat and disgrace; its choicest blessings whether of solid comfort or pride and honour, wasted, only to bring its very existence into jeopardy, until the people shall be raised from the apathy in which they have been sunk.[17]

One of the groups to whom patriotic appeals were particularly made was the women of Britain. An example of this type of publication is the anonymous *Proposal to the the Ladies of Great Britain* (1794), which introduced Mrs. Brittanica, 'a lady of most estimable character and irreproachable manners', who was 'at present involved in trouble with a set of thieves, who will ruin her estate if she does not make the most active and strong defence', in other words contribute to the national effort.[18] The cool response to this work in the *Critical Review* indicates a definite area of patriotic restraint; in the opinion of the reviewer the ideas set forth in the *Proposal* were unsuitable 'to the softness, gentleness, and delicacy of the female sex'.[19] This attitude was undoubtedly widespread and unavoidable given the normal way of viewing the female role, especially in genteel society. In 1803, when Napoleon threatened

England with invasion, *Alfred's Address to the Ladies of England* urged women to exert their influence to promote country levies. The *Critical Review* responded to this appeal by saying, 'We trust England will never sink so far beneath the scale of her own native powers and *manhood*, as to render it necessary that the women should stimulate the men into the field against the common enemy.'[20] According to the *Edinburgh Review*, in 1814, private life was everything to women, and their sphere was defined by the laws of society.[21] The social code of the time consigned women to a certain place, one that was private rather than public, and in which there was little room for patriotism. Of course there were attacks on that code, and women were becoming more politically active and involved in the nation's affairs, but only in the face of stiff opposition. As the conventional role of women was being questioned by Wollstonecraft and her followers, and women authors played a more active role in the war of ideas, conservative responses became increasingly loud and frequent. Thus, women were being pulled in two directions, urged to become more interested and active in public affairs and the war effort, and told that their proper sphere was private and domestic and that they need not concern themselves with these matters. As difficult as it was for men to make a new type of patriotic commitment, it was even more difficult for women.

To see how the military crisis entered into Austen's experience, it is necessary to sort through evidence that is tantalising because of what it suggests, but too fragmentary for a fully rounded, complete picture. Still, certain biographical facts can be set forth that indicate some of the points at which the war touched Austen. Also, an in-depth reconstruction of an incident in her life will reveal how much she knew about England's struggle with France, as well as suggesting certain of her responses to it. Understanding those responses will be of the utmost importance, as they are an obvious key to her way of assimilating this part of her experience and incorporating it into the fabric of her thinking and writing.

A full discussion of the naval careers of Francis and Charles Austen will not be necessary. Both attended the Naval Academy at Portsmouth and participated in the all-important naval theatre of the war. As their biographers, E. J. and Edith Hubback, have shown, they maintained a regular correspondence with their family while serving in the English Channel, the Mediterranean, the West Indies, the East Indies and Baltic.[22] While most of this cor-

respondence has been lost, there is no question that Austen had first-
hand information of the war. Another brother, Henry, joined the
Oxford Militia in 1793, resigning his commission eight years later,
in 1801. Austen's sister, Cassandra, was engaged to a Tom Fowle,
who went to the West Indies in 1796 as a regimental chaplain, dying
there of yellow fever in the following year. A close friend, Jane
Cooper, married a naval officer who helped advance the careers of
Francis and Charles. Austen's eldest brother, James, married the
daughter of a general. And through Eliza de Feuillide Austen's
attention was fixed on the foreign power, France, with whom
England was at war.

I will now examine a passage in one of Austen's letters, dated
Friday, 30 August, 1805, and written to Cassandra. Nothing in the
passage or anywhere in the letter describes the war, and yet it does
allude to an episode in the struggle with France that made an
enormous impact on England and was the topic of many publications. Written to her sister, the letter is essentially personal and
assumes a familiarity with the people and subject under discussion.
As with so many of the letters, references are oblique and comments
elliptical, so that allusions and levels of meaning are unclear to or
lost on the twentieth-century reader. Thanks to the efforts of R. W.
Chapman, certain references in the passage have been pinned
down.

> Next week seems likely to be an unpleasant one to this family
> on the matter of game. The evil intentions of the Guards are
> certain, and the gentlemen of the neighbourhood seem unwilling
> to come forward in any decided or early support of their rights.
> Edward Bridges has been trying to arouse their spirits, but
> without success. Mr. Hammond, under the influence of daugh-
> ters and an expected ball, declares he will do nothing. (L,169)

The coded part of this letter, as Chapman has pointed out, is the
reference to 'the evil intentions of the Guards'.[23] After discussing the
letter with the military historian Sir John Fortescue, Chapman
learned that on the day of the letter troop movements took place
between Deal and Chatham in response to reports of Napoleon's
long-planned invasion of England. What appears to be a discussion
of such neighbourhood pastimes as a hunting party and a dance
turns out to have another and completely different context and level
of meaning.

To understand what Austen meant through an oblique reference to some troop movements it will be necessary to sketch in some background.[24] This background has been pieced together in an attempt to reveal the full significance of the passage that Chapman has clarified but whose implications neither he nor anyone else has explored. In showing this background I will try to explain the conditions that led up to the planned invasion of 1805 and to show, through a somewhat intricate network of circumstances, how the military operation intersected with Austen's life at a surprising number of points. By reconstructing this episode it will be possible concretely and specifically to see Austen against the background of the war between England and France.

After the death of her father in January 1805, Austen and her sister Cassandra received invitations from relatives to visit them, undoubtedly in well-meaning efforts to ease their grief and perhaps to lessen their financial strain. They went to Kent in the summer of 1805 to stay with their brother Edward, who lived on an estate in Godmersham, which was 8 miles south-west of Canterbury. It turned out that at first Jane stayed with Edward while Cassandra was with his widowed mother-in-law, Lady Bridges, at Goodnestone, which was 6 miles east of Canterbury and about 14 miles from Godmersham. The two sisters exchanged places some time between 24 August and 27 August, and Jane was at Goodnestone when she wrote the letter of 30 August. Goodnestone is 7 miles west of the coastal town, Deal, and some 40 miles east of Chatham. It is almost on a straight line between the two. On the day of the letter the First and Second Grenadier Guards marched from Deal to Chatham, while the First Coldstreams and First Scots Guards moved from Chatham to Deal. By chance, Austen happened to be in the direct path of soldiers who were changing their positions under a well-grounded fear that a French invasion of England seemed imminent.

When England declared war in May 1803, in response to France's military build-up and what she considered Napoleon's expansionist actions after the Treaty of Amiens, she did so without any Continental allies. Since Napoleon did not have to fight a land war, at least for the time, he could concentrate his forces for an invasion of England. This was to be achieved by a flotilla of small, light-draft boats that were to convey a force of 100,000 men from the French to the English coast. At first the idea was to row them across on a foggy or calm night, when English sailing ships would be caught unaware, but the plan seemed susceptible to so many difficulties and dangers that it was replaced by a different one. The new plan was to use warships to escort the flotilla to England. An invasion scheduled for November 1803 had to be delayed because the British, who were well-informed of the project, were able to blockade the warships that lay in wait in coastal ports and were essential to the operation. Napoleon then worked out a vast and complex strategy that in its essentials resembled his approach to warfare on land. The problem was to get a numerically superior fleet of warships to Boulogne, where it would make contact with the flotilla that lay in wait and then escort it to England. Since the warships necessary for the operation were at Toulon, Cartagena, Cadiz, Ferrol, Rochefort and Brest, with the Brest fleet being the largest and most important, it was necessary to devise some way to outmanoeuvre the English ships that bottled up the French ones. Various tactics were worked out, all of which provided for a series of feints that would deceive the British and allow a large force to concentrate itself off French waters and then sail up the Channel to Boulogne, where it would free the flotilla for the invasion. After many delays the feints were made as two fleets, one from Rochefort in January 1805, and another from Toulon three months later, set sail for the West Indies. This led to a series of chases reaching from the Mediterranean to the Indies and back to the Spanish coast, where an indecisive battle was fought on 22 July at Finisterre. Even though the French had not outwitted the British, Napoleon, misinformed about the enemy's dispositions, and thinking that he was in a stronger position than in fact he was, gave orders to send a fleet north to bring the project to a final conclusion. By 22 August it became clear that Napoleon's admirals could not carry out his instructions, and one of them, Decrès, advised him that it was 'the decree of destiny, which reserves the fleet for other purposes'.

Napoleon realised that he had to abandon the invasion plan which, owing to new conditions, could not await further delay. In an effort to forge another coalition against France, and thereby distract Napoleon from his single-minded pursuit of England, Pitt had begun diplomatic discussions with Russia in June 1804, which resulted in a formal alliance ten months later. But Russia was too distant to present a direct threat to France, making it necessary to bring Austria into the alliance. This proved difficult, until Napoleon provoked Austria when he crowned himself King of Italy in May 1805, a measure that drew Austria into the Anglo-Russian alliance in August. When Napoleon realised on 22 August that the

English had frustrated his invasion plans he moved swiftly to strike against this new enemy. He withdrew troops from Boulogne between 24 August and 28, thus initiating a campaign that resulted in a string of dazzling victories that put him in Vienna on 13 November. But as Napoleon first sent his troops to the east he remained at Boulogne, where he had been situated for several weeks, ostensibly making final plans for the invasion of England. In an attempt to conceal the movements of his soldiers toward the Rhine, he encamped a large body of troops upon the heights of Boulogne, above the gun-vessels in the basin below. He appeared to be bringing the plan to invade England to a final resolution during the last week of August and the first two or three days of September, and it was in response to this situation that coastal defences were tightened up in Kent, which lay directly across the Channel from Boulogne and was almost certain to be the invasion point.

So Austen was at Goodnestone Farm, 7 miles from the coast and almost exactly where the invasion would probably have taken place, when she wrote the 30 August letter to Cassandra. Did she know about the invasion plan? As she and Cassandra had stayed with Edward in Kent before, she was no stranger to this area. Everywhere in England counties had organised defences at the outbreak of war in 1803. Kent, which was particularly vulnerable, was the first county to install beacon stations that, in the event of invasion, would have alerted both troops and populace. The closest concentration of these stations reached inland from Deal and included beacons at at Sholden, Canterbury and Barham. The Sholden station lay 6 miles east of Goodnestone, the Barham station was 4 miles to the south, and the Deal garrison was 7 miles away. To live in that part of Kent was to be aware of the beacons and the garrison, and the reasons for their being there.

In fact, the Bridges and their neighbours had to be more than just aware of the invasion plans. People living within 15 miles of the coast were given evacuation instructions in the event of an invasion. Local farmers made plans to assist the Volunteers and evacuate women and children, while parish priests were instructed to guide them to safety by local paths to keep the main roads open for supplies. To be at a Kent farm 7 miles from Deal in August 1805 was to be in a neighbourhood that for two years had lived under the threat of invasion. Austen could not have been uninformed of this menace.

The truth is that she knew a great deal about Napoleon's plan.

Soon after England declared war on France in 1803 her brother, Francis, a Captain in the navy, was stationed at Ramsgate on the northern coast of Kent. His assignment was to organise corps of fishermen in various districts along the coast. These corps were under the command of a naval officer who exercised his men and had the beaches watched whenever the weather was suitable for a landing. While he undertook this task, Francis drew up a report on coastal defences, indicating where he thought the invasion would take place. He decided on Pegwell Bay, 'where the enemy would have no heights to gain', and where the tides 'would be equally favourable for the debarkation of troops on this shore'.[25] Pegwell Bay was 7 miles north-east of Goodnestone. In May 1804, Francis was assigned to the *Leopard*, the flagship of Rear-Admiral Louis, who held a command in the squadron that was blockading Napoleon's flotilla in Boulogne. During the eight months that he was on board the *Leopard*, Francis, in his characteristic way, made a careful study of the flotilla and the coastal geography in and around Boulogne. Unfortunately, none of his letters to his family have survived from this period, but there can be no doubt that he wrote some. During the years 1803–4, only one of Austen's letters is extant, but from the following year, 1805, there are eight extant letters, three of which were written to Francis, three of which indicate that she had written additional letters, and one of which mentions a letter from him. Austen wrote to her brother regularly, and he sent letters to his family that she read describing his maritime service. Further, it is known that she visited Francis while he was at Ramsgate and she was staying with her brother Edward. Through that visit she would have found out about his efforts to organise coastal defences against the French invasion.

The question now is what type of letter might Francis have written Austen while he was aboard the *Leopard*, blockading the Boulogne flotilla? Judging from a later letter from Austen to her brother, he was a thorough and even long-winded correspondent.

> I am very much obliged to you [she wrote in 1813] for filling me so long a sheet of paper, you are a good one to traffic with in that way, you pay most liberally;—My Letter was a scratch of a note compared with yours—& then you write so even, so clear both in style & penmanship, so much to the point & give so much real intelligence that it is enough to kill one. (L,336)

A letter written from Francis to his fiancée on 15 October, 1805, is not only long, detailed and informative, but reveals a naval officer of large ambition and deep feeling. He wrote it over a three-week period, while he was aboard the *Canopus*, which was under Nelson's command at the time of the Battle of Trafalgar. Before the battle he was anxious to play an active role, and when it turned out that he missed the opportunity he said that he could not 'help feeling how very unfortunate we have been to be away at such a moment, and by a fatal combination of unfortunate though unavoidable events, to lose all share in the glory of a day which surpasses all which ever went before'. To read Francis' letters is to read the correspondence of an English naval officer who clearly had a strong, personal dislike of Napoleon and who felt that he was participating in events of great significance.

Exactly how much Austen knew about Napoleon's activity in Boulogne in the last week of August it is impossible to ascertain. There is reason to believe that she thought that the invasion plans might be in their final stage. In a letter written to Cassandra on 27 August she commented on the Duke of Gloucester's death, which had been reported in the newspaper on the previous day.[26] It is virtually certain that Austen learned about this event from a London newspaper, as none of her letters contain any references to the one local paper, the Canterbury *Gazette*. Which paper she read cannot be determined, although the three most obvious choices would be *The Times*, *Sun*, and *Chronicle*. I have not been able to obtain copies of the *Chronicle* from the year 1805, but the copies of *The Times* and *Sun*, which I have seen give substantially the same news of French activities in the Channel from Tuesday, 27 August to Friday, 30 August. As it would be superfluous to describe the reports from both papers, I will limit my discussion to *The Times*. The following item appeared on the same day as the report of the Duke of Gloucester's death, and directly below it: 'Among a variety of reports circulated on Saturday, it was rumoured that an embargo had been laid in all the French ports in the Channel, and that the Brest fleet had actually put to sea.' The significance of this news could not have been lost on Austen. Through Francis she must have known how critical to the invasion the Brest fleet was. Long under blockade by Cornwallis, any attempt by that fleet to break out could only mean that the invasion plans were moving ahead. Had the Brest fleet actually put to sea, as rumours indicated, the results would have been alarming. The rumours were in fact incorrect, as indicated by more precise information in subsequent editions of *The Times*. The lead article on the 28th explained that the fleet had appeared outside the harbor, but that no engagement had taken place. The fleet was still under blockade. *The Times* reported a 'partial action' between Cornwallis and the French fleet on the 29th, and on the 30th it said that the action had been much sharper than first reported. Another article in this issue, titled 'The Invasion', said that 'The fact is undisguised that the very first favourable opportunity will be seized.' It cannot be proven that Austen read all of these issues of *The Times*, although it is known that she was a regular newspaper reader and, given the type of news that appeared during this four-day period, there can be little doubt that she followed the accounts. She knew that the French fleet was directly across the Channel and that invasion reports had a particular significance for the local inhabitants and authorities. She would have understood the meaning of the troop movements from Deal to Chatham and from Chatham to Deal on the 30th.

This being the case, how can the reference to those movements in Austen's letter to Cassandra be interpreted? What can be determined about her response to this incident? Austen does not attempt to explain the manoeuvres, nor does she speculate over what to expect from the military operation. The focus is not on the soldiers, neither the nearby English ones nor the French forces across the channel, but on the Bridges and their neighbours, and in particular on a partridge hunt scheduled for the following Monday and an upcoming ball. By referring to the 'evil intentions of the Guards' Austen has seen the movements through the eyes of some neighbours and recorded their responses. The full sting of her irony would not have been lost on Cassandra, who of course knew the neighbours well and would undoubtedly have appreciated what her sister was saying about them. Soldiers were marching across their farms because France appeared to be close to executing a long-planned invasion, and all these people could do was grumble about the effect on a hunting party and complain about the possibility of poaching. What rendered them all the more absurd was their unwillingness to stand up for their 'rights', in other words to try to prevent what they feared. While 'Edward Bridges has been trying to arouse their spirits . . . Mr. Hammond, under the influence of daughters and an expected ball, declares he will do nothing.' How incongruous and ludicrous is this Mr. Hammond, who has yielded to the influence of his daughters over the matter of a ball, when he is seen against the larger backdrop of events. England was tightening up her coastal defences against a possible invasion and country gentlemen of this type responded in such fashion. Completely impervious to political and military issues, they could only think about their diversions and amusements which, thanks to their spineless ways, they were unwilling to safeguard.

By now it is clear that Austen knew about England's struggle with France. Exactly how much she knew need not concern us; what must be considered is her way of responding to that part of her experience. Raised into genteel society, Austen assimilated many of its values, quite possibly including those that considered an active interest in the war improper for females. As Austen's relationship to genteel society will be discussed in a later chapter, it will suffice here to indicate that in avoiding direct discussion of the war in both her letters and novels she was only doing what was regarded as proper for someone of her sex and class. Another explanation for her keeping the war at a distance, even though it had a large impact on her life, is that of Andrew Wright: She 'might . . . have held to the past [and] rejected the present and its implications'. Austen's world, that of the country village, patronage system, close-knit family and Sunday sermon was stable and ordered, as if its beats, measures and cadences followed a strict rhythm. The authors that she read as a girl moved within a set of assumptions that agreed with this regularity, which their writings both reflected and seemed to confirm. The victory of the gentry and parliament in 1688, the scientific achievements of Newton, the writings of Locke and Shaftesbury, the decline of religious enthusiasm, the correctness and propriety of classicism, and the clarity of Augustan writing and thinking all contributed, in their various ways, to the collective security that was such a vital aspect of eighteenth-century English life. Raised into this world, Austen shared its principal character-istics; its contours were also hers. As Arnold Kettle has said, 'Jane Austen belongs to the eighteenth century in that her world is still the world established by the English revolution of the seventeenth century', and that world was one of stability and security. The 'classical' or 'Johnsonian' dimension of her thought and method of perception can be related to this orientation. As a member of the old society and a product of eighteenth-century culture it is no wonder that she did not come to terms with the present easily, the present being, among other things, the age of Revolutionary and Nap-oleonic Wars.

When Austen ridiculed the likes of Mr. Bridges and Mr. Hammond because they thought about a partridge hunt or an upcoming ball when faced with events of much larger significance, she kept those events at a distance. She did so, characteristically, through irony. One view of Austen's irony is that it was a defence, a way to detach herself from conditions that if faced directly could be discomforting. It has been said that 'To events, literary and actual, she allowed herself no public response except the socially conventional or the ironic; for neither of these endangered her reserve, both put off self-commitment and feeling . . .'[27] Her irony, in this view, was a strategem to avoid commitment and to stifle feeling; it was a mechanism to protect her from emotional involvement and a way to prevent her from passing moral judgment. This interpretation of Austen's irony has not been unchallenged. A rival view is that her irony was not a way to 'put off' feeling but a device for controlling emotional responses for the very reason that they ran so deep.[28] Applying these interpretations to the passage under discussion the results are obviously different. In the former Austen would be seen as indifferent to the military threat, even though she understood it. In the latter she understood the threat and reacted through irony, but irony that was rooted in an excess of feeling.

While there are but few references to military events in the letters, those that do appear sometimes support the former of the above views, the one that sees Austen as detached, indifferent, and incapable of open responses. On occasion, however, the letters reveal Austen responding to events in a way that indicates a genuine concern and consequently supports the second interpretation. It is this type of response that is the key to Austen's eventual way of relating to the stresses and strains of war.

In support of the view that she was detached, not only did Austen not discuss news of the war directly and freely, but also made a clear distinction between public and private affairs. In doing so she commented only on the private side of an event, blocking out or denigrating the public side. When a Major Byng was killed at the Battle of Salzburg, Austen asked Cassandra, in a letter of 14 January, 1801, if she had 'seen that Major Byng, a nephew of Lord Torrington is dead?' (L,111) It seems that she mentioned this fallen officer only because he was the relative of someone else; moreover, she did not say that he was killed in battle, but rather that he 'is dead'. Discussing an officer's death in this way, she lifted the event out of its military context and thereby deprived it of its public significance. The one reference in her letters to Francis' hero, Nelson, is to Southey's *Life of Nelson*. "I am tired of Lives of Nelson, being that I never read any. I will read this however, if Frank is mentioned in it,' (L,345–6) In this terse, brittle and ironic comment Austen limited Nelson's importance to his relationship with her brother.

On 24 January, 1809, she ended a letter to Cassandra with the remark, 'This is grievous news from Spain—It is well that Dr. Moore was spared the knowledge of such a son's death.' (L,258) The person whose death she referred to was Sir John Moore, whose death had been reported in *The Times* on the previous day in an article describing a campaign in the Peninsular War. In that article one of *The Times*' correspondents wrote, 'We are not in the least dismayed by the rapid advance of NAPOLEON, the force of his armies, or the utmost extent of his efforts. We have made up our minds to resist to the last moment. Our courage increases daily, and our hatred of the tyrant becomes more and more inveterate.' At this point in the article the press was stopped and the following announcement made: 'We stop the press to announce . . . that the French attacked General Moore in great force during his embarkation: they were repulsed on all sides with great loss, and the embarkation continued: the 4th, 42nd, and 50th regiments suffered most: General Moore was shot in the breast, and died at twelve o'clock of the ensuing night.'

Austen would have had reason for knowing who this general was, in fact for knowing a good deal about him; moreover it can be demonstrated beyond any question that she followed the course of the Peninsular War, in which Moore played a major role. She wrote Cassandra on 10 January, 1809, thirteen days before news of Moore's death reached England, that 'The *St. Albans* perhaps may soon be off to help bring home what may remain by this time of our poor army, whose state seems dreadfully critical.' (L,246) This was indeed the case. Moore, attempting to help a battered Spanish army and faced with French superiority, daringly advanced towards the enemy, which temporarily paralysed Napoleon's victorious force and saved the situation in Spain. Napoleon himself then turned against the British, leading to Moore's retreat to Corunna, where the battle took place in which he lost his life. Austen must have had a clear understanding of the strategic and logistical aspects of this campaign when she speculated that Moore's retreat would require an evacuation and that British losses would be heavy, as this is precisely what happened.

While Francis Austen, as captain of the *St. Albans*, did not sail to Spain to transport Moore's Army back to England as his sister thought he might, he was at Spithead when it returned and took charge of the disembarkation. It was undoubtedly through him that Austen understood the main outlines of the Spanish campaign and was able to predict the evacuation that did take place. At the beginning of the Peninsular War, in July 1808, Francis took Brigadier General Anstruther and his staff to Portugal, accompanied by twenty-three transports. In the following month, while aboard the *St. Albans*, he saw the Battle of Vimiera and sent boats ashore to collect the wounded. While he returned to England in September, one can assume that he would have followed developments in a campaign with which he had already become involved. He might have been particularly interested in Moore's role in the movements leading to the Battle of Corunna, and not merely because Moore was commander of the British army.

Francis might also have followed Moore's movements because his career and that of the British general seem to have intersected before. Both played a role in defending England against a possible French invasion in 1803, Francis by organising fencibles from Ramsgate, and Moore as commander of the force assembled at Shorncliffe to meet the projected enemy force. The Shorncliffe camp was directly above Sandgate, some 15 miles below Ramsgate, and part of the very coast whose defence Francis was helping to prepare. Later, in 1808, when Francis' movements again intersected with Moore's, he must have followed those of the British general with greatest interest. The evidence is his sister's letter of 10 January, in which she speculated that Francis might have to sail to Spain to pick up the 'poor army' that was taking such a beating. Austen was at Southampton when she wrote this letter, where her brother was stationed and from whom she undoubtedly received the information about Moore's army. She was also in Southampton when she wrote the letter of 24 January in which she commented on Moore's death. That she commented on Moore's father, a well-known physician and writer, is evidence that Austen not only knew about Moore as a military figure but something about his background.

The phrase in Austen's letter, 'such a son's death', is puzzling: Does it have favourable or unfavourable connotations? Before considering its meaning it will be useful to follow later reports of Moore's death and see how Austen responded to them. On 26 January *The Times* said that Moore was 'a perfect military character' and that this 'gallant officer had devoted the whole of his life to the service of his country'. On the following day *The Times* carried a description of the fallen general's death, written by an eyewitness. 'The first question he asked was—"Are the French beaten?"'—which inquiry he repeated to all those he knew, as they entered the room. On being answered by all that the French were beaten, he exclaimed—"I hope the people of England will be satisfied. I hope my country will do me justice. You will see my friends as soon as you possibly can—tell them every thing—say to my mother"—here his voice *failed him*—"HOPE—HOPE—I have much to say, but cannot get it out."' The description then says that he had his will read, that he feared he would be a long time in dying because he felt so well, that he asked again if the French were beaten, and upon hearing that they had been said, 'it was a great satisfaction to him, in his last dying moments, to *know he had beat the French*'. After thanking his doctors for their attention, 'He pressed my hand close to his body, and in a few minutes died without a struggle.' Austen must have read this account, as she referred to Moore's mother in her letter of 30 January, 1809: 'I am sorry to find that Sir J. Moore has a mother living, but tho' a very Heroick son, he might not be a very necessary one to her happiness . . . I wish Sir John had united something of the Christian with the Hero in his death.—Thank Heaven! we have had no one to care for particularly among the Troops.' (L,261–2)

It would appear that in both letters, those of 24 January and 30 January, Austen was ill-disposed towards Moore. The direct criticism of the second letter would seem to explain the ambiguous phrase, 'such a son's death', in the former, indicating that it too was critical. In each instance Austen's ill-feeling related to the impact of a soldier's death on a parent, in one case when she thought it fortunate that the father was no longer alive and in the other when she referred to a mother who was. Austen's response to this wartime fatality was private; she focused not on the significance of a battle, but on a general's death and what it meant to his family. Not only did she view Moore's death from such a perspective, but regarded it with a certain displeasure. The usual explanation for that displeasure was Moore's not praying on his death bed or making some appropriate religious utterance. In fact, the reason for Austen's negative reaction went much deeper, and relates to her larger way of responding to the war. In this instance the key to that response is the suffering and heavy loss of life that Austen accurately associated with the battle. In the first letter she wrote 'this is greivous news from Spain' before saying that it was well that Dr. Moore was spared the knowledge of his son's death. After thinking, and writing, about a battle that she knew was bloody, after an initial but brief public response, Austen changed her perspective, looking at the event privately, scaling down its significance, and characteristically resorting to irony. This is also what she did in the second letter. After saying that she wished Moore's death had been more Christian she said: 'Thank Heaven! we have had no one to care for particularly among the Troops', indicating that she and Cassandra were fortunate not to have any neighbours or relatives among the British army. Unable or unwilling to express concern over all the wounded and dead, she limited her response to those close to or known by her sister and herself, and her way of doing so was by expressing relief. This was her way of blocking out a larger response that if left unchecked could cause discomfort and hurt. A public and patriotic response she avoided, just as she again did several years later, in another letter.

Buried in a letter to Cassandra written on 31 May, 1811, in which Austen discussed some sick mulberry trees, a visit by some friends, visiting and having tea with some others, and 'the Gaieties of Tuesday', are the following two sentences: 'How horrible it is to have so many people killed!—And what a blessing that one cares for none of them!' (L, 286) She was referring to the Battle of Albuera, news of which began to appear in *The Times* on 22 May, and which continued to be newsworthy until 29 May. The article in the issue of the 22nd called the battle a 'glorious occurrence' but hinted at heavy English losses in the 71st regiment. Subsequent issues gave full details of the battle. On the 29th *The Times* gave a description of the battle taken from a French newspaper, claiming that the English had suffered very considerable loss both in 'prisoners killed and wounded'. Austen's reaction to this news was to shudder at the thought of so much death, and then, in an abrupt shift, to say 'what a blessing that one cares for none of them'. What makes this sentence so interesting and revealing is the connection between its two parts. Having admitted at first that it was horrible to have so many killed, Austen stepped back from a position that acknowledged her feelings and, in what seems to have been a reflex action, took back what she had just allowed. The detachment of the second part of the sentence is conditioned by the involvement of the first part. It is as if the thought of so much death was more than she could bear, more than her emotional apparatus could sustain. It is this very pulling back in the face of such news that reveals how deeply Austen's feelings about the war went and how the suffering and loss of life did make her an involved spectator of the great events of her day. Her involvement was not gained easily, and would seem almost to have been involuntary; it was something that she resisted, from which she tried to detach herself, and to which she reacted with irony. It was an irony that flowed from genuine feeling.

Just as Austen's society was drawn into the war at considerable emotional cost, so too was she. Her initial response, as seen in her letters, was to keep the war at a distance; she wrote freely and often about her brothers' professional advancement, but in those letters one would scarcely know that England was at war and what role these two sailors played in the struggle. As a creature of her times, and class, and sex, she avoided discussing a part of her brothers' life that was best kept in a separate and closed compartment. But she did know about their wartime experiences, and thus about the war, just as she knew about it through other sources. In fact, the war impinged on her life and created definite tensions, which are the key to her irony, to her feigning relief over news that was painful. That type of response is what one particularly finds when England's wartime hopes were at the lowest ebb, between 1809 and 1811, when newspaper and magazine articles commonly conveyed a sense of despair, when British forces in the Peninsula were sustaining heavy losses against seemingly insuperable odds. It is as if Austen's ironies became more callous and unfeeling as England's hopes became dimmer, and as the toll in suffering increased. In fact, it was precisely because she felt that suffering so keenly that her ironies became more brutal.

In 1812, and even more in 1813, the war in the Peninsula began to take a different turn, as Napoleon was no longer able to maintain the old supremacy. With the disastrous Russian campaign France was permanently weakened, and the various allied armies began to close in on an enemy that was everywhere in retreat. A sense of relief and pride in British successes was reflected in the journalism of the time, and it was reflected in Austen's letters. When Austen read about Wellington's stunning victory at Vittoria, she wrote in a letter of 6 November, 1813, 'What weather! & What news!—We have

enough to do to admire them both.—I hope you derive your full
share of enjoyment from each.' (L,372) As the fortunes of war
changed, Austen was able to take pride in the achievements of the
now successful British army. She did so in a way that connects to the
upsurge of patriotic feeling that had long been gathering momentum, and reached a climax during the final stages of the war.

In her letters Austen's patriotism is most evident in her remarks
on Sir Charles William Pasley's *Essay on the Military Policy and
Institutions of the British Empire*. When Pasley wrote this work in 1810,
England's military successes had almost entirely been achieved at
sea. Unwilling to assume that she could maintain her naval
supremacy, he asked what would happen if she lost it. His objective
was to demonstrate that even if this were to occur, England could
maintain her independence, that she could do so without 'a single
ship on the ocean', and that she could realise this goal by using the
nation's resources to build an all-powerful army.[29] As the *Quarterly
Review* noted, Pasley did not stop to consider whether or not a
standing army was constitutional, disregarding Bolingbroke's dic-
tum that the British should only occasionally be soldiers, and in
those rare cases only to a limited extent.[30] Given England's wartime
experience, it is no wonder that Pasley parted company from
Bolingbroke and rejected the eighteenth-century view of land war
and standing armies. That he went so far as to say that England
could if necessary defend herself completely with an army made him
an outspoken and daring proponent of a radical position, whose
implications he fully understood. Considering such factors as
population, industry, science and the availability of capital, Pasley
felt that England was capable of building an army that could
achieve successes comparable to those of the British navy, and
would make the 'tyrant of Europe' tremble on his throne. To do this
it would be necessary to construct a new set of military institutions
and utilise all of the nation's resources, not the least being the spirit
and patriotism of a unique people. The *Essay* was a blueprint for
total victory over France, military, political and economic. Pasley
praised the English constitution 'that alone has preserved our
independence', urged his fellow countrymen to make every
necessary sacrifice to protect that constitution from the French
threat, and said that in order to do so England had to 'become a
military nation'. The victory that he foresaw would be a 'blessing to
mankind'.[31]

Upon first reading Pasley's *Essay* Austen 'protested' against it, but ended up admiring an author who 'does write with extraordinary force & spirit'. (L,292) Later in the same letter, written on 24 January, 1813, she compared her Chawton book society to that of Steventon and Manydown. The other group read travel books and the like, while she and the members of her group read Captain Pasley, evidence of its 'superiority'. A few weeks later, on 9 February, 1813, Austen again ridiculed the travel books that women read. 'Ladies who read those enormous great stupid thick quarto volumes which one always sees in the Breakfast parlour . . . must be acquainted with everything in the world.' (L,304) She found this type of female fare superficial, and it irritated her that ladies would read about Iceland or the history of Spain and not learn about or concern themselves with the war in Spain. They read Bigland's *History of Spain* (1810) and Mackenzie's *Travels in Iceland* (1811), but not a book that addressed itself to the foremost military problems of the day. But, Austen concluded, it was just as well that these ladies did not read Captain Pasley, as 'Capt. Pasley's book is too good for their Society'. (L,304) Far from being a genteel female who was indifferent to the war, Austen poured ridicule on those who remained so. It was not easy for her to become involved in England's war effort, but she did precisely that. The full extent of that involvement is apparent in her letters in 1813, by which time she was able to read and admire such a work as Pasley's *Essay*. That she objected to it initially is not surprising. This was one of the most outspokenly and stridently patriotic and militaristic books to appear during the period of the Napoleonic Wars, one that called not only for the total defeat of France but an expansionist foreign policy. The fact is that she shook off her initial objections and did regard this book favourably, evidence of her involvement in the war and her being caught up in the patriotism that was an outgrowth of the wartime experience.

Austen seems deliberately to have avoided the war in the early novels. In *Northanger Abbey* life at Bath and the Tilney estate went on in the customary, eighteenth-century way, even though England was at war and the hero's father was a general and his brother a captain. There is no indication that either General or Captain Tilney fought in any of the campaigns against France, or that they or anyone else were aware of the war. In *Sense and Sensibility*, Colonel Brandon served in the East Indies, but not in connection with England's expansion in that part of the world, which was very active

and took place because a revival of French power was feared.
Brandon is seen not as an officer who fought in India in the last years
of the eighteenth century or the early years of the nineteenth, that is
to say in a contemporary context, but as an eighteenth-century
soldier who found life in India harsh, not for military reasons but
because of the hot climate and mosquitoes. When others speculated
about his stay there they discussed 'nabobs, gold mohrs [mohurs],
and palanquins', (SS,51) which suggested the wealth and amenities
available to the English; they did not refer to Brandon's military
role. There are no direct references to the war in *Pride and Prejudice*,
but there is an important area of allusion and innuendo that does
relate to England's wartime experience. We have seen that during
the eighteenth century there was a definite animus against standing
army, and that 'No barracks' was a common cry. The soldiers who
became part of a vastly larger wartime army after 1793, and were
billeted most heavily in Southern England, made their presence felt
in *Pride and Prejudice*. Austen did not raise the old cry of 'No barracks'
or declaim against the large army on English soil, but the soldiers
stationed at Meryton did turn the eyes of susceptible young ladies in
the Netherfield drawing room. Catherine and Lydia collected
gossip about the nearby Militia, learning that several officers had
dined with their uncle, and that Colonel Forster might be married.
Having a romance with an officer was what they hoped for, as
became clear when Lydia devised the scheme to vacation at
Brighton so she could follow Wickham's regiment, which was being
transferred to a camp close to that resort town. Elizabeth's response,
when she heard of the scheme, is interesting: 'Good Heaven!
Brighton, and a whole campful of soldiers, to us, who have been
overset already by one poor regiment of militia . . .' (PP,220). Her
fears were well grounded; the menace that she associated with the
army camp was only too real as events soon proved. The trip to
Brighton created a sense of impending disaster, which clearly
connected to the army camp. And it would seem that Elizabeth's
fears were partly based on past experience, as she had already seen
Meryton 'overset' by soldiers and had learned of their ways in
chance meetings and monthly balls. So Austen did not protest
against the billeting of soldiers among the civilian population, but
she did show what could happen as a result. The innuendo builds
slowly, until by the time Elizabeth's sisters and mother go to
Brighton there is little question that something will go wrong,
something connected with the army camp.

With *Mansfield Park* the war made an impact that sets this novel apart from the earlier ones. One example of that impact is the Antigua episode. Judging from internal evidence, Sir Thomas would have left for his West Indies estate in 1805 and returned home in 1807. For both political and military reasons these were difficult years for Antigua.[32] When France abolished slavery in her colonies, rebellions broke out that affected the British as well as French Indies. Napoleon re-introduced slavery, but his doing so by no means ended the ferment. Also, the war affected the economy of Antigua, along with the other sugar-producing islands, through a contraction of markets resulting from the Napoleonic blockade. Begun in 1803, the blockade coincided with a time of increased sugar production, which caused prices to decline sharply. From 1805 to 1807 the price of sugar dropped from 55 shillings a quintal to 32 shillings. So severe were the economic repercussions in Antigua that the local government declared bankruptcy in 1805; by 1807 numerous plantations failed. So Sir Thomas went to Antigua to solve problems that related directly to England's struggle with France.

Also related to the war was the question of abolition, a cause with which Sir Thomas became involved during this stay on his plantation. Austen's concern with slavery is similar to that of her brother, Francis. After sailing to the Cape of Good Hope in 1807, Francis accompanied a convoy to St Helena in the following year. Writing from and about that island, he said that slavery was tolerated, but was not maintained with the same 'harshness and despotism which has been so justly attributed to the land-holders or their managers in the West India Islands . . .'[33] An owner on St Helena could not 'inflict chastisement' at his own discretion, which Austen's brother considered a sound policy as far as it went, but however modified, slavery was still slavery, and in his opinion it was much to be regretted in any countries dependent on England or colonised by her subjects. And he did have occasion to see slavery in the West Indies at first hand in the course of two voyages, first in 1805 when he actually landed on Antigua, and again in 1806. Austen's other sailor brother, Charles, served in North American station for several years prior to 1811, searching American ships that might have had goods originally taken from the West Indies. He, too, was in a position to discuss those islands with the members of his family. So the Antigua episode in *Mansfield Park* can be seen against the background of the war in two respects. The conditions on the island that necessitated Sir Thomas' visit were largely determined by the war. Also, this episode can be seen in the light of Austen's two sailor brothers' wartime experiences, in which they became familiar with the West Indies and, in the case of Francis, became concerned with the slavery question. Austen's views on slavery seem exactly to have coincided with those of that brother. So while the war is never mentioned in the Antigua episode, that part of the novel clearly bears the imprint of England's—and Austen's—wartime experience.

Austen was certainly familiar with wartime suffering, most evidently through the death of her sister's fiance. The resulting sorrow must not have been unlike that of Fanny Price and Jane Fairfax, the former because her father, a lieutenant in the marines, was disabled while on active service, the latter because her father, also a lieutenant, was killed in action abroad. The injury of Lieutenant Price reduced the family to such hardship that Fanny's mother swallowed her pride and wrote to her sister inquiring in the fullness of despondence if she might take one of her children. This background of gloom is the condition leading to Fanny's departure for Mansfield Park, and it helps explain the pale, timid, shy and sad girl who appeared at her aunt's estate. The wartime death of Lieutenant Fairfax left behind a 'melancholy rememberance', a widow who soon sank under consumption and grief, and a daughter who was left to the care of her grandmother and aunt. While a wartime friend of Lieutenant Fairfax, a Colonel Campbell, provided for Jane's education and even provided her with a home while growing up, she had no prospects beyond entering domestic service, the 'white slave trade', in some respectable establishment.

The war entered into *Mansfield Park* discreetly through the Antigua episode, the injury of Fanny's father, and a conflict between the representatives of settled English ways and subversive French ways. It entered into this novel more directly through William Price, an officer in the Royal Navy who was clearly patterned after Austen's own brothers. When William returned to England on furlough he brought stories of the war to the insular world of *Mansfield Park*. In working out this part of the novel Austen did not focus attention on the war, but on the responses of various characters to William's stories. How people responded to William helped define them in various ways. Those who were indifferent to William's narrations were deficient in one way, and those critical of the navy revealed a different type of shortcoming.

William 'had been in the Mediterranean—in the West Indies—
in the Mediterranean again—had often taken on shore by the
favour of his Captain, and in the course of seven years had known
every variety of danger, which sea and war together could offer'.
(MP,236) Such a sailor 'had a right to be listened to', (MP,236) but
only some people did so. As he described his adventures, including
an 'account of a ship wreck or an engagement, every body else was
attentive', but not Mrs. Norris, who could only 'fidget about the
room, and disturb every body in her quest of two needlefulls of
thread or a second hand shirt button'. (MP,236) The well-meaning
but indolent Lady Bertram 'could not hear of such horrors
unmoved, or without sometimes lifting her eyes from her work to
say, "Dear me! how disagreeable.—I wonder any body can go to
sea."' (MP,236) A symbol of passivity and insularity, Lady
Bertram was unable to comprehend the stories that her nephew had
described or appreciate his sacrifices. Her response was to say 'how
disagreeable'. One can almost see her beginning to sew faster and
then lift her eyes from her work, looking next to her to make certain
that her pug was there. Henry Crawford, who was also present and
also heard William describe his life at sea, greatly admired such
energy and heroism. Indeed, 'the glory of heroism, of usefulness, of
exertion, of endurance, made his own habits of selfish indulgence
appear in shameful contrast; and he wished he had been a William
Price, distinguishing himself and working his way to fortune and
consequence with so much self-respect and happy ardour, instead of
what he was!' (MP,236) But Henry Crawford could only be what he
was, a selfish and self-indulgent young man much given to fantasies.
In his characteristic way he imagined himself as a William Price,
achieving fame as a sailor, but he soon fell from this dream. 'The
wish was rather eager than lasting. He was roused from the reverie
of retrospection and regret produced by it, by some
inquiry from Edmund as to his plans for the next day's hunting.'
(MP,236-7)

As a favourable character, it was only natural that Edmund
would view William positively. Not only did he do so, but also said
in an earlier conversation that the navy was 'a noble profession'.
(MP,60) He said this in response to some double entendre
comments on naval officers made by Mary Crawford. Edmund had
explained to Mary that Fanny had a brother at sea, and then
remembering that the Crawfords had several relatives in the navy
he inquired about them. She replied by saying, 'we know very little

of the inferior ranks. Post captains may be very good sort of men, but they do not belong to *us*.' (MP,60) She then indicated that she knew a great deal about Admirals, the type of officer she was acquainted with. She was aware of their bickerings and jealousies, and had seen how unfairly they felt the navy treated them. Yes, she said, she saw many of them at her uncle's house. 'Of *Rears*, and *Vices*, I saw enough.' (MP,60) Having said that the admirals she knew vented their feelings of abuse through complaining and quarrelling, she suggested dissipation and moral irregularity. Playing on the words 'Vice' and 'Rear' she said, 'Now, do not be suspecting me of a pun, I entreat.' (MP,60)[34] It was this comment, which appeared to discredit the naval profession, that prompted Edmund to defend that profession. He certainly did so from conviction, but also from a concern for Fanny, who could only have been hurt by Mary's taunting words. Even after Edmund became grave and serious Mary continued in her light and deriding way, having the final word when she said: 'Yes, the profession is well enough under two circumstances; if it make the fortune, and there be discretion in spending it. But, in short, it is not a favourite profession of mine. It has never been an amiable form to *me*.' (MP,60)

Austen's most direct statement about the war is in *Persuasion*. Begun in the summer or autumn of 1815, this is the only finished novel that was written at the end of hostilities. It is also the only one that is fixed in time. Frederick Wentworth had proposed to Anne Elliot in 1806, before beginning his rapid ascent as a naval officer. Eight years had passed, and when the story commenced it was the summer of 1814. Both Wentworth and Admiral Croft appeared because England, after twenty years and more of conflict, had finally defeated France. Details of this type were new, and they were applied with a density that sets *Persuasion* apart from the other novels. The military exploits of William Price were certainly described in *Mansfield Park*, but this sailor was seldom heard in conversation, and when he was he appeared in the role of Fanny's brother as much as that of a naval officer. In *Persuasion* there were several officers—Admiral Croft, Wentworth, Captain Harville and Captain Benwick—all sailors to the ends of their fingers. Austen described the ships they sailed, the actions they were in, how their careers progressed, the type of enemy vessels they captured and how they profited from doing so, how they lost fellow officers at sea, how they suffered injury, and how their very complexions and appearance reflected long and hard years of maritime service. These men made their presence felt, and through the plainness and straight-forwardness of their manner, and the self-confidence that they projected, they inspired admiration. This admiration was inseparable from the qualities that resulted from their experiences at sea and from their achievements as sailors.

These naval officers differed sharply from the Elliots and Musgroves, whose quiet and backward world they entered. Thumbing through his Baronetage and pausing, as he always did, to 'read his own history', (P,3) Sir Walter Elliot was an emblem of aristocratic pride and a distillation of class attitudes that had outlived their use and become anachronistic. Unable even to manage his estate properly, he had to rent it and temporarily enter into a period of economic retrenchment. At every point in his negotiations with Admiral Croft his main concern was his own dignity and importance; never did he show any respect for an officer who helped lead his country to victory. From Sir Walter's point of view it was to the Admiral's credit that he had the necessary money to rent Kellynch Hall, and it was fortunate that he had no children, but little else could be said in his support. In fact, Sir Walter had a clear dislike for a man who could only be viewed as an upstart, and who belonged to a profession that he considered undignified. Certainly, no sailor or soldier would have access to his pleasure grounds, which were strictly reserved for the socially fit. While Sir Walter conceded that the military profession was not completely without utility, he had two grounds for objecting to it. 'First, as being the means of bringing persons of obscure birth into undue distinction, and raising men to honours which their fathers and grandfathers never dreamt of; and secondly, as it cuts up a man's youth and vigour most horribly; a sailor grows old sooner than any other man; I have ever observed it all my life.' (P,19) These comments clearly reveal the smugness and snobbery and the concern with appearances of this vainglorious baronet, who was so utterly out of touch with his time, and on whom England's long struggle with France had no apparent effect.

Of the four officers in *Persuasion*, Wentworth was of course by far the most important, and he most thoroughly embodied the ideals of his profession. At the time of his proposal to Anne eight years earlier he was penniless, but certain in his own mind that he would rise high as a naval officer: 'He was confident that he would soon be rich;— full of life and ardour, he knew that he should soon have a ship, and soon be on a station that would lead to every thing he wanted. He had always been lucky; he knew he should be so still.' (P,27) When his first opportunity to command a ship presented itself he was quick to seize it, in spite of the ship's defects, which rendered it hardly 'fit for service'. (P,65) Eager to make his mark, he considered the command of even such a ship the chance he was waiting for. 'I was as well satisfied with my appointment as you can desire. It was a great object with me, at that time, to be as sea,—a very great object. I wanted to be doing something.' Perfectly willing to run the risk, he set sail and waited for the engagement that would decide his future. He knew that he and his ancient ship would go down together, or that he would succeed and reap the benefits. After 'taking privateers enough to be entertaining' (P,66) he had the good luck to fall upon a frigate, which he captured and took into port. This action won him a large prize, secured him a better ship, and led to future campaigns in the Mediterranean, where he was a participant at the Battle of Trafalgar, and in the East Indies. His subsequent exploits had been attended by danger, as the time when he made port only twenty-four hours before a four-day gale that in no time would have put his ship on the bottom of the ocean. Had he not made port, 'I should only have been a gallant Captain Wentworth, in a small paragraph at one corner of the newspapers.'

As in *Mansfield Park*, characters defined themselves by their responses to a naval officer. Wentworth first appeared at Upper-cross, where Anne was staying with the Musgroves. While Charles Musgrove and his sisters were favourably disposed to Wentworth, the Elliots, with the obvious exception of Anne, were not. Anne's sister, Mary, had the soul of a true Elliot. When her husband thought that 'Captain Wentworth was as likely a man to distinguish himself as any officer in the navy', and that he 'would be a capital match for either of his sisters', (P,75) she found reasons to oppose such a match. She reasoned that this naval officer might become a baronet, which would make his wife Lady Wentworth, and give her precedence over herself. This 'would be but a new creation . . . and I never think much of your new creations'. Acutely aware of her own pedigree, Mary looked down on anyone that she considered beneath her, and bitterly resented the upward movement of intruders from below.

At the beginning of the novel Sir Walter's agent, Mr. Shepherd, was trying to represent the Crofts as acceptable tenants for Kellynch Hall. After describing the Admiral he mentioned Mrs. Croft, who 'was not quite unconnected in this country', and was 'sister to the gentleman who lived a few years back, at Monkford'. (P,22–3) Sir Walter, who prided himself on knowing all of the local notables, could not remember any gentleman living there in recent times. When it was pointed out that Mr. Shepherd was referring to a Mr. Wentworth, Sir Walter explained that his agent had been mistaken. 'You misled me by the term *gentleman*. I thought you were speaking of some man of property: Mr. Wentworth was nobody, I remember; quite unconnected, nothing to do with the Strafford family. One wonders how the names of many of our nobility become so common.' (P,23) Edward Wentworth was the brother of Frederick Wentworth, with whom Sir Walter had had a brief and unpleasant acquaintance eight years earlier, in 1806. Just embarking on his naval career at the time, Wentworth lived briefly with his brother at Monkford. This was when he first fell in love with Anne and proposed to her. Sir Walter never withheld his consent, but he gave the marriage offer 'all the negative of great astonishment, great coldness, great silence, and a professed resolution of doing nothing for his daughter. He thought it a very degrading alliance.' (P,26)

Sir Walter was somewhat better disposed toward Wentworth in 1814 than he had been in 1806. At the time of Sir Walter's departure for Bath, Wentworth had not yet appeared, and he did not see him until later, towards the end of the novel, when, accompanied by his daughter Elizabeth, he entered a room and saw the now wealthy and well-known officer. In what must have been an instant calculation, he decided to acknowledge him. Elizabeth 'even addressed him once, and looked at him more than once'. (P,226) These signs were not without a reason. The Musgroves had just arrived in Bath, and Sir Walter and Elizabeth had decided on a party to celebrate the occasion. This was when they had planned to give invitations, and Elizabeth decided to extend one to Wentworth. She put all the invitation cards on a table, indicating with a smile and 'one card more decidedly for Captain Wentworth' (P,226) that he was to be among the select few. According to her way of reckoning, an officer of his reputation was not without value. The truth was that Elizabeth had been long enough in Bath to understand the importance of a man of such an air and appearance as his. 'The past was nothing. The present was that Captain Wentworth would move about well in her drawing room. The card was given, and Sir Walter and Elizabeth arose and disappeared.' (P,226) When Wentworth took all of this in he was somewhat puzzled by it, so he picked up the invitation in 'a manner of doubtful

meaning, of surprise rather than gratification, of polite acknowledg-
ment rather than acceptance'. Anne observed the scene with the
fullest care, and knowing Wentworth as she did understood his
reaction. She 'saw disdain in his eye, and could not venture to
believe that he had determined to accept such an offering, as
atonement for all the insolence of the past'. (P,226–7) How
perceptive she was, and how opaque her sister Mary was. Looking
at Wentworth as he fingered the invitation card, Mary whispered
'very audibly' that Elizabeth had included everybody, meaning
even Wentworth. 'I do not wonder Captain Wentworth is delighted! You see he cannot put the card out of his hand.' This new
display of Elliot arrogance sent a flush across Wentworth's face, and
his mouth formed itself 'into a momentary expression of contempt'.

When Elizabeth gave Wentworth the invitation card she did so,
at least outwardly, because of his attractiveness, not because of his
military reputation. It certainly was not her intention to honour a
war hero, but nevertheless she was doing precisely that, in spite of
herself. What she understood was the social value of a man of 'such
an air and appearance as his'. (P,226) This was a recognition of
Wentworth's good looks, but it was more than that. Wentworth was
physically much the same person in 1814 as in 1806, when Elizabeth
had had nothing to do with him. Without realising it, she now
responded to something else in Wentworth beside his fine features.
He was a force, a man fully confident of himself and quietly but
deeply aware of his achievements, making his presence felt
wherever he went. This fact, when translated into terms that
Elizabeth could understand, meant that he had a distinctive 'air
and appearance'. Sir Walter's response to Wentworth was basically
the same. Eight years earlier, before Wentworth made his mark, Sir
Walter had opposed his marrying Anne. Now, with a £25,000
fortune and a position 'as high in his profession as merit and activity
could place him', Wentworth 'was no longer nobody'. This being
the case, Sir Walter lifted his objections, having decided that it was
far from a 'bad match'. (P,248)

The young sailor whom Anne had fallen in love with in 1806 had
already possessed the self-confidence and sense of mission that
would make him a brave and distinguished sailor. Now, in 1814,
having played an important role in the war against France, he
returned home, a hero. Austen did not let the reader know that
Anne saw Wentworth in this light until the final sentences of the
novel, when she thought of herself as the wife of a sailor. 'His

profession was all that could ever make her friends wish [her] tenderness less; the dread of a future war all that could dim her sunshine. She gloried in being a sailor's wife, but she must pay the tax of quick alarm for belonging to the profession which is, if possible, more distinguished in its domestic virtues than in its national importance.' (P,252)

In trying to measure the war's impact on Austen it is useful to divide the novels into two groups, those first written in the 1790s, and those written between 1811 and 1816. In the first group, *Sense and Sensibility* and *Pride and Prejudice* were completely rewritten between 1808–12, and *Northanger Abbey* might have been revised about 1809 and again in late 1816. Whatever Austen's views of the war might have been when she reworked these novels, those views did not find a place in her writing. Rather, she kept the war out of the revised versions just as she had the original ones written in the 1790s. Of course, since 'Elinor and Marianne,' 'First Impressions' and 'Susan' are not extant it is impossible to say definitely that Austen did not discuss the war, but this does seem a safe generalisation. In letters written between 1796 and 1799, Austen often referred to her sailor brothers, but without commenting on their wartime experiences. Typically, the focus was on their careers, and showed a sister's happiness over their advancement. Nothing in Austen's early correspondence indicates an awareness of the war, even though the war did touch her life at many points, such as the wartime death of Cassandra's fiancé, the enlistment of her brother, Henry, in the Militia, and the role of Francis and Charles in the naval theatre of the war. That Austen appeared to remain unaffected by the war in spite of its obvious effect on her life has led to criticism. While some writers have seen Austen as the representative of a class that continued its customary way of life through the war years, other writers have censured her for standing aloof from a crisis that threatened her nation's survival. And there was an aloofness, in fact there seems to have been a deliberate detachment.

Given the expected role of a young lady in genteel society this is not surprising. Members of Austen's sex and class were not supposed to concern themselves with public affairs, whether political or military. While Austen internalised these values, the war did enter her genteel world, and it did affect her, creating tensions that can be felt in both her correspondence and her fiction. In fact, her very detachment contributed to, or perhaps it should be said intensified, those tensions. Austen began by accepting a code that defined a pattern of conduct that increasingly she found difficult to observe. Exactly when the walls of social convention began to break down cannot be determined. Neither her correspondence of the 1790s nor the first three novels significantly reveal her feelings or attitude toward the war, other than her decision not to write about it. There was one exception, the presence of soldiers in *Pride and Prejudice*, which undoubtedly can be viewed as a reflection of Austen's own response to the extensive billeting of troops in southern England during the 1790s. This billeting was a radical departure from the established practice of housing soldiers within the civilian population, with which they were supposed to blend, so strong was anti-militaristic feeling in eighteenth-century England. While Austen did not comment adversely on soldiers who now appeared in civilian gathering in uniform, or on the newly established army camps, a sense of menace was attached to both. The one clear response to the war in the early fiction was consistent with Austen's aloofness and detachment, indicating what must have been a deeply engrained tendency to resist changes that disrupted her genteel world.

When Austen revised the early novels she felt the war's presence in ways that she had not when she wrote the original versions. My reconstruction of her response to two wartime incidents, the 1805 invasion plan and Sir John Moore's death in 1809, reveals the density of the war's impact, and the distance from it that she maintained. She did not maintain that distance permanently. Like much of her society, Austen was made conscious of and was drawn into England's struggle with France. The collective wartime experience was different in kind from that of England's eighteenth-century wars, when the nation's survival had not been an issue, when the objective had been Hanoverian intervention in continental affairs, the conquest or retention of overseas territories, and when ideological conflict had not been a significant factor. After 1793, the role of the military changed beyond recognition, the cost of the war was altogether new, and wartime hopes and fears were felt with an immediacy that altered established modes of thought and broke down old patterns of life. Austen's experience was part of this larger, social experience, but her type of response was her own. It consisted of three phases. First, she ignored the war, following a code that said she should. Both her correspondence and fiction indicate such a tendency. Next, she feigned indifference but was no longer so, the evidence being remarks in her letters that made her appear callous to the men who suffered as they fought against France. Basically, this phase coincided with the revising of the early novels. While the war had made a definite impact on Austen by this time, she kept it out of her fiction, meaning that in this respect the first three novels, as revised between 1808 and 1812, reflect an earlier set of feelings and attitudes, an earlier state of consciousness, that of the 1790s.

But even as Austen kept the war out of her revised versions, it was beginning to find its way into her fiction. She did not work just on one novel at any given time, but on several simultaneously. During the years 1811 to 1812, she completed her rewriting of *Pride and Prejudice* and began *Mansfield Park*. It was in the latter novel that the war finally made a definite impact, affecting its structure and organisation. This novel can be regarded as the beginning of the final phase, in which Austen became openly involved in the war effort. The evidence is both in her fiction and her correspondence.

It showed up in comments on Pasley's *Essay* and a favourable comment on a victory in the Peninsular war; it showed up in *Mansfield Park* through a sailor, William Price, whose wartime stories elicited responses that indicated an important way of measuring people, such as Mrs. Norris and Henry Crawford. While responses to William and the naval profession are the most obvious evidence that Austen worked the war into this novel, she did so in other ways that, though less apparent, are no less important. Both the Antigua and theatrical episodes relate to the war, albeit indirectly. In working those episodes into the novel Austen drew from a wide range of her experience, the war being one part, and in connecting those episodes to later ones the war entered directly into the fabric of the story.

The theme of patriotism found its fullest expression in *Persuasion*, when England's wartime heroes returned home after the final victory over France. Through the members of the Elliot and Musgrave families Austen satirised the members of her own class who still lived in their insular world, concerned with the same trivial concerns as before the war, seemingly unaffected by the struggle for national survival and unmindful of those who were responsible for victory. The exception was Anne Elliot. She was dedicated to tradition, socially responsible, and as Wentworth's wife gloried in his military achievements. The pride that Anne took in Wentworth's wartime role reflects Austen's own feelings and state of mind when, with the war just over, she wrote about it with a directness and immediacy that might well have been possible only with the final achieving of victory. The Austen who wrote *Persuasion* was a very different person and writer from the author of the first three novels who, still in her early twenties, lived in the quiet, conventional world of the old society. The war helped disrupt that society, and both Austen's fiction and correspondence reveal traces of this change. Just as English society emerged from the long years of war with a new sense of national awareness, and with a realisation of the cost of victory, so too did Austen. *Persuasion* could only have been written by someone whose life was deeply affected by the Revolutionary and Napoleonic Wars.

3 Religion

Jane Austen's father, the Reverend George Austen, was Rector of Steventon in the county of Hampshire. Austen grew up in the village Rectory, which no longer stands but then was situated a short distance from St Nicholas's Church, where Sunday after Sunday her father delivered sermons. When George Austen retired in 1801, his son James succeeded him as Rector. In 1816, after many years of wavering, another of Reverend Austen's sons, Henry, entered the clergy. In addition to the father and two brothers, other members of Austen's family belonged to the Church. Her mother's father, the Reverend Thomas Leigh, was Rector of Adlestrop, in Berkshire, and her grandfather, also Thomas Leigh, was Rector of Harpsden, in Oxfordshire. A cousin of George Austen was a clergyman, as was the son of another cousin. One of Austen's maternal aunts married the Reverend Samuel Cooke, Rector of Cotsford in Oxfordshire, both of whose sons took religious orders, and another aunt married the Reverend Edward Cooper, Rector of Hamstall, in Staffordshire. His son was Rector of Hamstall–Ridware, also in Staffordshire. Two of Austen's brothers, James and Francis, married sisters, Martha and Mary Lloyd, whose father was the Reverend Nowis (or Noyes) Lloyd of Enbourne, in Berkshire. Reverend Lloyd's third daughter married the Reverend Fulwar Craven Fowle, whose family consisted largely of clergymen. A brother, Reverend Thomas Fowle, was engaged to Cassandra. To this list of ecclesiastical relatives others could be added, and many of the Austens' friends were also clerical. Besides being the daughter of a country parson in Southern England, Austen was connected in countless ways, through friends and relatives, to the conventions, customs, ways, traditions and outlook of the clerical profession. While her world was that of the English village, her view on to that world was through the Rectory window.

This fact is reflected in the novels. The heroes of *Northanger Abbey*, *Sense and Sensibility* and *Mansfield Park* are clergymen, and other clerical figures appear frequently. They include the Reverend

Richard Morland in *Northanger Abbey*, Mr. Collins in *Pride and Prejudice*, the Reverend Howard in *The Watsons*, Mr. Elton in *Emma*, and Charles Hayter and Dr. Shirley in *Persuasion*.

Despite the presence of so many clergymen, religion has not been considered a central or even very important theme in Austen's fiction. The historian, Frederick Artz, has written that 'Jane Austen's novels depict a variety of clergymen, some amiable, some ridiculous, but few who seem to have anything to do with religion. The novelist never even notes this deficiency.'[1] Lawrence Lerner has argued that Austen was a 'Truthteller', and disbeliever who put clergymen in her novels but not God.[2] Those clergymen have been seen as conventional fictional types or as social types that differed little if at all from the other male characters, possessing the same strengths and weaknesses as their lay counterparts. Alistair Duckworth feels that Austen's morality was rooted in the Christian tradition, but that her main concern was social and ethical.[3] Even the Christian underpinning of her moral values has been questioned. Gilbert Ryle argues that her value system came from the classical and secular ethics of Aristotle and Shaftesbury, not from a dualistic Christian morality.[4] While Ryle is willing to concede that Austen was the pious and dutiful daughter of a clergyman, he contends that she kept her piety and for that matter religion altogether in a separate compartment of her life, not allowing it to pass into her fiction. Thus, while her heroes sometimes entered church they are never seen on their knees in prayer, and her heroines solved their moral problems without recourse to religious doctrines or seeking the counsel of a clergyman. Privately religious, in this view, she drew a curtain between her Sunday thoughts and her creative imagination.

Did Austen draw this curtain, did she deliberately keep, or attempt to keep, religion out of her novels? And if so, why? These are difficult questions. Any attempt to answer them must consider her actual religious views, the ones that in the above metaphor lay behind a drawn curtain. Certainly the members of her family saw her as a pious and faithful Christian. Two days after Austen's death Cassandra described her last moments: 'When I asked her if there was any thing she wanted, her answer was she wanted nothing but death & some of her words were 'God grant me patience, Pray for me, oh Pray for me.' (L,514) Deeply grieved over the loss of her sister, Cassandra looked forward to the day when she would join her in the hereafter. Five months later Austen's brother Henry wrote,

'Neither her love of God, nor of her fellow creatures flagged for a moment. She made a point of receiving the sacrament before excessive bodily weakness might have rendered her perception unequal to her wishes.' (NA,4) In his opinion the Cathedral of Winchester, were she had been buried, 'does not contain the ashes of a brighter genius or a sincerer Christian'. (NA,5) As if these remarks were not enough he concluded the brief biographical notice of his deceased sister by saying, 'One trait only remains to be touched on. It makes all others unimportant. She was thoroughly religious and devout; fearful of giving offence to God, and incapable of feeling it towards any fellow creature. On serious subjects she was well-instructed, both by reading and meditation, and her opinions accorded strictly with those of the Established Church.' (NA,8) James Edward Austen-Leigh, writing many years after his aunt's death, believed that 'piety . . . ruled her in life, and supported her in death', but he was hesitant to discuss her religious beliefs. 'I do not venture to speak of her religious principles: that is a subject on which she herself was more inclined to *think* and *act* than to *talk*, and I shall imitate her reserve; satisfied to have shown how much of Christian love and humility abounded in her heart, without presuming to lay bare the roots where those trees grew.'[5] Austen's niece, Caroline Austen, drawing from the testimony of a Mrs. Barrett, said that 'the true spring of religion . . . was always present, though (it) never obtruded'. This Mrs. Barrett had told her that 'Miss Austen . . . had on all subjects of enduring religious feeling the deepest and strongest convictions, but a contact with loud and noisy exponents of the then popular religious phase made her reticent almost to a fault.'[6] The two persons who were probably closest to Austen described her as a devout, sincere, and completely orthodox Christian of the Anglican faith, well instructed in the articles of her religion and at pains to observe the Church's last rites as her end neared. While agreeing that Austen was deeply religious, James Edward Austen-Leigh and Caroline Austen, drawing in the former instance from youthful memory and in the latter from direct witness, arrived at the same conclusion: that their illustrious aunt had lived the life of a good Christian. Both added that religion was a subject that she did not discuss.

Austen's letters present a somewhat different and clearly more complex picture. Certainly, there are no indications of disbelief. The letters show a normal, conventional religious life of the type that might be expected of the daughter of a country parson. We know from the correspondence that Austen attended evening as well as morning service, that she read sermons, that she was well informed about, and concerned over, various contemporary developments in the Church, that she wrote prayers, and that in moments of reflection she pondered the mysteries of life and death. Those moments would appear to reveal a religious sense, if such a generalisation is permissible. Religious in a different way were some remarks from the last months of her life. Thankful over a remission of her illness, she said that 'the Providence of God has restored me— & may I be more fit to appear before Him when I *am* summoned, than I sh^d have been now!' (L,495) As the illness resumed its final course she discussed her 'beloved family' and anguished over some unfortunate domestic difficulties, the details of which have been deleted from the letter. The sentences that follow the missing passage read as follows: 'But I am getting too near complaint. It has been the appointment of God, however secondary causes may have operated . . .' (L,498) Undoubtedly aware that she was mortally ill, she saw that illness as divinely ordered. These are indeed the utterances of a sincere, devout Christian.

But the letters sometimes reveal a different picture. In 1799, Austen's mother received a letter from her sister's son, Edward Cooper, a clergyman in Staffordshire. Austen said that it did not announce 'The birth of a child', as expected, 'but of a living'. Her cousin having received a curacy, Austen chose the occasion to play with the word 'living'. This was no more than a light verbal touch of the type that one might expect from Austen under the circumstances. The next sentences are less innocent: 'We collect from his letter that he means to reside there, in which he shows his wisdom. Staffordshire is a good way off; so we shall see nothing more of them till, some fifteen years hence, the Miss Coopers are presented to us, fine, jolly, handsome, ignorant girls. The Living is valued at £140 a year, but perhaps it may be improvable.' (L,55) In this passage the irony is turned first on the decision of this clerical relative to reside in his parish, which was a good thing not because it was wise and responsible, but because she would not have to see him in the future. In another remark she said that perhaps the living was 'improvable', meaning that possibly her cousin could increase the tithe, as she implied he would have to in order to turn out the affected and mis-educated daughters that she was counting upon. Adding fresh barbs to her irony, Austen next said, 'Our first cousins seem all dropping off very fast. One is incorporated into the family, another dies, and a third goes into Staffordshire. We can learn nothing of the disposal of the other living.' (L,55) Obviously, there is nothing irreligious in these passages. The irony is directed at a cousin and his family; that he happened to be a clergyman might well have been coincidental. Still, Austen mocked this country parson for becoming a resident cleric, she showed that 'improving' a living can be a selfish business, and she expressed wry amusement over life, death, marriage and the clerical profession by playing on the word 'living'.

Two years later, in 1801, as Austen's father was making plans for his retirement, he offered his curacy of Deane to a certain Peter Debary. The offer was declined on the grounds that Deane was too far from London. This decision prompted the following comment: 'I feel rather indignant that any possible objection should be raised against so valuable a piece of preferment, so delightful a situation!' (L,105) But since the offer had been turned down, it had been necessary to offer the curacy to someone else. That person, a James Digweed, would probably not take it either, 'Unless he is in love with Miss Lyford', and indeed, very much so, as the 'salary' was but £50. In this letter Austen ridiculed a clerical office because of the modest living attached to it, she poured mock scorn on a person who declined it, and indicated that another would do the same unless falling in love had impaired his judgment. And calling the clerical stipend, the living, a 'salary' implied that the curacy was more of an economic office than a pastoral post.

In 1809, Austen wrote to her sister about a Dr. Mant, a clergyman who had broken his marital vows. She did not want to 'undeceive' the unfortunate wife, wished her 'happy at all events', and knew 'how highly she prizes happiness of any kind. She is moreover so full of kindness for us both, and sends you in particular so many good wishes about your finger, that I am willing to overlook a venial fault; and as Dr. M. is a clergyman their attachment, however immoral, has a decorous air,' (L,258) To say that she did not want to tell the wife about her husband's affair because this unfortunate woman wanted above all to be happy, and because she had been so solicitous towards Cassandra's injured finger, was to mock her; to say that these were sufficient reasons to 'overlook' adultery was to make light of the marital relationship; and to say that in any event the affair had a 'decorous air' because Dr. Mant was a clergyman was to be cynical towards his profession.

None of these passages express sceptical or any other irreligious tendencies. They do indicate that Austen was fully able to be ironic toward clergymen, sometimes brutally so, and in much the same way as toward anyone else. There was nothing unusual in this, and it is what a reader of the novels, familiar with Mr. Collins, Mr. Lucas and Charles Hayter, might expect. But it does not agree with the descriptions of Austen by the members of her family. In his *Notice* of his sister, Henry Austen connected her piety to what he described as a sweet and loving disposition. 'She was thoroughly religious and devout; fearful of giving offence to God, and incapable of feeling it towards any fellow creature.' (NA,8) He made this connection after having touched on some delicate and difficult points. 'Though the frailties, foibles, and follies of others could not escape her immediate detection, yet even on their vices did she never trust herself to comment with unkindness.' Willing to admit that his sister recognised faults in others, he added that her response was one of tolerance. Continuing along the same lines he said, 'Faultless herself, as nearly as human nature can be, she always sought, in the faults of others, something to excuse, to forgive, or forget.' Then, having established her charity toward others, regardless of their errors, he turned, in the final paragraph, to the one trait that remained to be touched on, the one that made all others unimportant. In describing that trait, Austen's piety, he connected it to the tolerant and charitable spirit he had already mentioned.

James Edward Austen-Leigh projected the same image of Austen when he commented on her 'sweet temper and loving heart' and called her 'the delight of all her nephews and nieces', just as Caroline Austen remembered her 'great sweetness of manner'. These remarks reflect actual childhood memories. Also, they conform with the family view of Austen, the very view that appeared in Henry Austen's *Notice* a few months after her death. It is a view that is both right and wrong; it describes one Austen, but not the other. For the letters reveal a deeply divided person, one given by turns to kindness and charity and eruptions of ill feeling and verbal malice. Somewhere in the deepest recesses of that division lay problems that were religious, as Henry Austen either intuited or understood when he tried to see his sister's piety and charity as complementary, as connecting parts of a unified whole. In his mind, the two had to be linked; to be devout without being kind and compassionate was inconsistent and probably a logical if not moral impossibility. So he made the connection, describing the sister who was devout and kind at the exclusion of the one who was hostile and ironic.

Describing a ball that she had attended in 1800, Austen said that there were only a 'very few Beauties'. One acquaintance had not looked well, leaving the field to a married woman, Mrs. Blount. 'She appeared exactly as she did in September, with the same broad face, diamond bandeau, white shoes, pink husband, and fat neck.' (L,91) Among the other guests was a 'vulgar, broad-featured girl', another girl who was 'a queer animal with a white neck', a married woman who had 'got rid of some part of her child, & danced away with great activity looking by no means very large', a girl with 'a good deal of nose', two sisters who were dressed 'all in black' and had 'bad breath', a husband who was 'ugly enough; uglier even than his cousin', and a general and his wife who had, respectively, 'the Gout', and 'the jaundice'. (L,91–2) The following year she described a 'stupid party' that she had attended the previous evening. She respected Mrs. Chamberlayne for 'doing her hair well', but she 'could not feel a more tender sentiment'. Miss Langley was 'like any other short girl with a broad nose & wide mouth, fashionable dress, and exposed bosom'. Admiral Stanhope was 'a gentlemanlike Man, but then his legs are too short, & his tail too long'. In a masterpiece of understatement she summed up her feelings about these people by saying 'I cannot anyhow continue to find people agreeable.' (L,128–9)

She did not limit her disagreeable feelings to chance acquaintances at evening parties. Few were exempt from her mockery. We have seen how she ridiculed a clerical relative in Staffordshire. Even the members of her immediate family were not immune. When a local farmer died she fancied that her brother Edward intended to get part of his farm 'if he can cheat Sir Brook enough in the agreement'. (L,12) Commenting, undoubtedly with unerring accuracy, on her mother's self-styled grandness, she said, 'My mother made her *entrée* into the dressing-room through crowds of admiring spectators yesterday afternoon . . . She has had a tolerable night, and bids fair for a continuance in the same brilliant course of action today.' (L,34) Nor did Austen always respond sympathetically to the illness or injuries of others. While her inability to have 'much compassion' for her mother's complaints can be explained by their frequency, it is less easy to explain away her description of a riding accident in which a Mr. Heathcote's horse 'trod upon his leg, or rather ancle I beleive, & it is not certain whether the small bone is not broke'. Austen called this mishap, which was undoubtedly the occasion of considerable pain, 'a genteel little accident'. (L,85) Towards death she sometimes responded unfeelingly, if not harshly. When she met a certain Dr. Hall he turned out to be in 'very deep mourning', so much so that 'either his mother, his wife, or himself must be dead'. (L,60) When a Mrs. Rider died she commented that 'the Neighbourhood have quite recovered', and indeed she thought that 'they are rather rejoiced at it now'. (L,114)

The sympathetic, charitable Austen was uneasy about these barbed comments and flashes of hostility. The letters sometimes contain expressions of displeasure over remarks that have just been made. After bidding 'adieu' to Cassandra and all her 'agreeable inmates' at Steventon, and making an undecipherable but clearly ironic comment about her sister-in-law, who had just given birth to a son, she said 'How ill I have written. I begin to hate myself.' (L,18) In another letter, she made a witticism about an acquaintance and then decided that the remark was 'stupid' and that 'nobody can smile at it'. Innocent as the witticism was, it made Austen 'sick of myself, & my bad pens'. (L,197) On another occasion she said 'I am still a Cat if I see a Mouse.' (L,330) To have made this comment was to indicate a clear understanding of a very real tendency, one that she was often unable to control and that made her unhappy with herself. More than unhappy: guilty. And when she expressed dismay with herself over her cutting ironies she was repentant. This is not to say that her self criticism was entirely a religious response, but to some extent it could not have been otherwise. Austen was the daughter of a country parson, she did write her own prayers, she did attend church regularly, she did read sermons, and she was an orthodox and sincere Christian. Given these facts, it is not unreasonable to see a sense of religious contrition in her expressions of self dismay.

The two Austens were not fixed identities. Rather, each changed over the years. As a generalisation, it can be said that the compassionate and religious side became more prominent and that the hostile and cutting side diminished. The shift was gradual. In such a process there are no markers that indicate clear and definite signs of change, but beyond a certain point the letters have a different tone and reveal a kinder, more humane view. The earlier tension diminished, or if still present it shaped thoughts and attitudes in a new way. And the really brutal ironies by and large disappeared. Those ironies were most frequent from 1798 to 1801.

From 1801 to 1805, there was only one letter, but by 1805 Austen seems to have been aware of a change that had passed through her and altered her way of viewing things. Writing to Cassandra in that year, she said, recalling a riding exhibition that had taken place in 1798, 'What a different set we are now moving in! But seven years I suppose are enough to change every pore of one's skin, & every feeling of one's mind.' (L,148) Later in the same letter there is a passage, written the next day, describing the mortal illness of a friend, Mrs. Lloyd. First Austen said, 'Poor woman! May her end be peaceful & easy, as the Exit we have witnessed! And I dare say it will. If there is no revival, suffering must be all over; even the consciousness of Existence I suppose was gone when you wrote.' (L,149) Reflecting on this woman's withdrawal from the world, Austen became uneasy with herself. 'The nonsense I have been writing in this and in my last letter, seems out of place at such a time; but I will not mind it, it will do you no harm, & nobody else will be attacked by it.' (L,150) She was not disturbed over biting or malicious comments, for there had been none, but rather over ordinary descriptions of daily happenings; she was not repentant over cutting ironies, but rather the 'nonsense' she had written while a friend, unknown to her at the time, was passing through the final stages of life. Her final comment was a self irony: she would not mind the trivia she had written, as it would do Cassandra no harm nor would others be 'attacked by it'. Two years later, in 1807, Austen commented on a 'nice, natural, openhearted, affectionate girl' that she had just met. Her response was to say that this girl was 'so unlike anything that I was myself at her age, that I am all astonishment & shame'. (L,179) In saying this she was implying that she had not been like the girl, not 'nice, natural, openhearted, affectionate'.

Perhaps the most interesting and revealing retrospective view of herself is to be found in a letter of 1813, when Austen said, 'I am still a Cat if I see a Mouse.' She said this after some hard but not ironic and certainly not malicious comments concerning her mother's latest illness and the unkindness and pettiness of some friends. Even these restrained remarks made Austen uncomfortable and conscious of her feline tendencies. But by saying that she was still a cat when she saw a mouse she was recognising an internal change that had taken place. What the word still implies is that while a tendency that she disliked did persist, it had diminished, and her letters from this period of her life are ample testimony of that fact. The Austen who, at the end of her life, at the age of 41, was careful to receive the sacraments before joining her Maker, who in her final moments 'wanted nothing but death', was different in both the personal and religious sense from the Austen of age 25. In the interim, and especially it seems between 1801 and 1805, there had been a marked change of outlook, one that made Austen more reflective and self aware, uneasy over certain of her own tendencies, guilty over earlier manifestations of those tendencies, and in response to her guilt feelings religious in a way that she had not been before. Or, to put it differently, the compassionate and religious Austen achieved definite gains over the cutting and hostile Austen.

The change that passed through Austen was by definition personal, but it was not completely isolated from outside influences. Most importantly, her struggle, and it was precisely that, was within herself and it was of a type that people have experienced through the ages. Still, for the sake of the fullest possible understanding it is necessary to see it within the historical framework of Austen's lifetime. This was a time not only of political upheaval and military conflict but also religious ferment. In fact, the latter type of change was connected to the former, making it part of a larger historical process. While the 'collective security' of eighteenth-century England, to use the phrase of J. Steven Watson, was subjected to new pressures after 1760, those pressures did not overturn the settled system of life. But the French Revolution violently disrupted the established regime, sending out shock waves that had a highly disturbing effect not only upon English political and military but also religious structures.

Within two years of the fall of the Bastille the National Assembly launched a massive and devastating attack on the Church, confiscating its land and making it a department of state. Some revolutionaries did not hesitate to announce their hostility to Christianity, as English observers soon became aware. Commenting on Dupont's speech in the National Convention, given on 16 December, 1792, Hannah More said that initially the cause of the Revolution appeared to be that of mankind, but since then dark and evil forces had come to the surface. 'What English heart,' she said, 'did not exult at the demolition of the Bastille? . . . Little was it then imagined that anarchy and atheism, the monsters who were about to succeed them, would soon slay their ten thousands.'[7] This is a revealing and important comment; for Hannah More there was a definite connection between 'anarchism and atheism', the twin 'monsters' that had released savagery on such a scale. As she denounced what was happening in France some of her compatriots were responding otherwise, welcoming attacks on the Church. The combined effect of a successful Jacobin Revolution in France and the appearance of 'Jacobinism' in England led to intense fear, at least in certain quarters.

My discussion of English religious responses to the Revolution will centre on Evangelicalism because of its relevance to Austen. She wrote in 1809 that 'I do not like the Evangelicals', (L,256) but seems to have changed her mind by 1814, saying 'I am by no means convinced that we ought not all to be Evangelicals.' (L,410) In 1816 she apparently returned to her earlier disapproval, writing 'We do not much like Mr. Cooper's new Sermons;—they are fuller of Regeneration & Conversion than ever—with the addition of his zeal in the cause of the Bible Society.' (L,467) That Austen should have found the solemnity, piety and enthusiasm of Evangelicalism distasteful is not surprising, but the fact remains that she was attracted to it. Since this attraction will play a key role in my examination of religion and its impact on Austen's thinking and writing, it will be useful at this point to discuss Evangelicalism.

While Evangelicalism is a broad term and can be used in many ways and to describe many things, the following discussion will limit itself to a movement within the Church of England that began in the 1780s and became vastly more powerful in the 1790s and early nineteenth century.[8] As its decisive growth period coincided with the period of the Revolution, it can be viewed as one of several religious responses to an age of political and ideological upheaval. Its leaders stood behind the established social order and consciously strove to use religion as an instrument of stability. William Wilberforce wrote that 'the state of religion in a country at any given period . . . immediately becomes a question of great political importance.' Addressing himself to middle and upper-class readers, he said that Christianity 'renders the inequalities of the social state less galling to the lower orders, whom also she instructs, in their turn, to be diligent, humble, patient: reminding then that their more lowly path has been allotted to them by the hand of God; That it is their part faithfully to discharge its duties, and contentedly to bear its inconveniences . . .' Is it any wonder that Edmund Burke was attracted to Wilberforce and his views? That Burke was reading his *Practical View of Christianity* while on his death bed is a perfect indication of the confluence of conservative political and religious movements in a common social cause. Members of the established order turned to Evangelicalism to maintain the world that they knew and wanted to preserve.

The religious enthusiasm unleashed by Evangelicalism had an enormous impact on nineteenth-century English life. Convinced that the choice was between 'Reform or Ruin', the Evangelicals launched a massive and highly successful campaign to promote their views. Countless organisations spearheaded one innovation after another, working for reforms that were at once social and moral. Benevolent societies founded hospitals, organised opposition to the slave trade, tried to improve the lot of deprived children, strove for prison reform, and endeavoured to assist the aged and destitute. Humanitarian in inspiration as these causes were, they also furthered social cohesion by helping a beleaguered and troubled society to have faith in itself.

The reform movement helped turn English society away from the urbanity, cosmopolitanism, scepticism, deism and polite sociability of the eighteenth century and towards the earnestness, sobriety, moral strictness, self-discipline and domesticity of the nineteenth century. Evangelicals had excoriated the profligate before 1789, but achieved only minor successes. After 1789 they issued a new type of warning: not only did the dissolute work toward their own spiritual ruin, but contributed to the ruin of society. Alarmed over the popularity of Paine and a considerable enthusiasm in England for the French Revolution, the reformers maintained that moral improvement was necessary for the survival of the established social order. The middle and upper classes, it was argued, should not be idle and dissipated, but set a proper example for the lower classes. A reformation of manners and a renewed commitment to the Christian religion were seen as necessary antidotes to the spreading contagion of Jacobinism and infidelity. Believing in a hierarchical society, the reformers felt instinctively that if the existing order were to be preserved it would have to rest on new moral foundations, that for the privileged classes to maintain their advantages they would have to command respect.

Like Edmund Burke, the Evangelicals were persuaded that sound manners were essential for social health. Burke had argued that 'the most licentious, prostitute, and abandoned . . . and at the same time the most coarse, crude, savage, and ferocious' manners had weakened French society, making it ripe for Revolution. Fearing that loose manners had weakened England, John Bowdler asked, 'do not Luxury, Corruption, Adultery, Gaming, Pride, Vanity,

Idleness, Extravagance, and Dissipation prevail too generally?'
Believing that they did, he argued that it was necessary for the
English people to 'BE GOOD!' Wilberforce warned that the upper
orders were accustomed to riches, comfort and refinement, and
neglected the strict precepts and self-denial of Christianity.
Thomas Gisborne wrote, 'Let the man then who loves his country
endeavour to render *himself and his family* a pattern of Christian
virtue, of useful but unassuming knowledge.' Arthur Young argued
that the lower classes would not be virtuous while the upper classes
indulged in 'Sunday parties, excursions, and amusements, and
vanities'. The *Annual Register* wrote that the 'French Revolution
illustrated the connection between good morals, and the order and
peace of society more than all the eloquence of the pulpit and the
disquisitions of moral philosophers had done for many centuries'.

The world, argued the reformers, was not to be enjoyed as it had
been; places of amusement, such as Ranelagh and Vauxhall, led
people astray and should be avoided. Anxious to improve society at
all levels, their strategy was to begin with the upper classes and, by
winning them over, to reach the middle and lower orders; by
starting at the top of the social pyramid they hoped to work down to
the base. Their programme included criticisms of masquerades,
Sunday concerts, gambling, drinking, Sunday newspapers, Sunday
travel and prostitution. The more austere broadened their attack by
opposing the theatre, opera and magazines. Objecting to 'heathen'
influences and verbal irregularities in such authors as Shakespeare
and Pope, they expurgated their works to make them acceptable.
Their appeals were made in grave and earnest language that
reflected their seriousness and piety; so frequent and successful were
the appeals that the very language in which they were expressed
contributed to a more sober and solemn atmosphere.

Thomas Gisborne urged females particularly to mend their ways,
to avoid 'vanity, affectation and frivolousness', to be less occupied
with amusements and more concerned with virtue, to enter into
'serious reflection' rather than dwell on 'exterior ornaments'.
Parents should instill in their daughters a sense of duty, obedience
and sobriety to arm them against the world's snares and defend
them against the temptations they were bound to encounter at
dances and the theatre.[9] Hannah More called on the women of
England in 'this moment of alarm and peril' to 'raise the depressed tone of public morals and to awaken the drousy spirit of
religious principle.'[10] Continuing, More wrote: 'At this period

when our country can only hope to stand by opposing a bold and noble *unanimity* to the most tremendous confederacies against religion, and order, and governments, which the world ever saw, what an accession would it bring to the public strength, could we prevail on beauty, and rank, and talents, and virtue, confederating their several powers, to exert themselves with a patriotism at once firm and feminine, for the general good!'

The Evangelicals felt that for the Church to be fully effective it would have to eliminate certain abuses, such as pluralism. No longer, they argued, should elegant, fox-hunting clergymen support their worldly habits at the expense of congregations they seldom or never visited. In part, pluralism had been necessary because of the small livings, sometimes but a few pounds, that were attached to curacies. Under the patronage system many of the Church's offices were controlled by persons, sometimes secular, who were religiously indifferent. Patronage, of course, was a vital feature of eighteenth-century society and one of the principal means by which privileged individuals and groups exercised power. To dispense favours was to build loyal followings that were both visible signs of dignity and instruments of control. That the Church had been brought into and indeed was a central part of this system led to abuses, in the opinion of Evangelicals. It led to clergymen at all levels who were in varying degrees unfit to exercise their pastoral responsibilities. The Evangelicals urged members of the clergy to reside in their parishes, they worked for the appointment of their own adherents, and they urged those already entrusted with offices to reform.

The rapid growth of Bible Societies is one index of how successful the Evangelical movement was. In 1810, 64,468 Bibles and Testaments were printed and distributed; by 1815 the number increased to 249,932. Writing in 1815, and undoubtedly reflecting the sense of national achievement that was in the air, a friend of Hannah More looked back over the previous twenty years, contemplating the improvement in English life that she felt had taken place. Before the Evangelicals began their work the state of morals and religious opinions had been deplorable among all ranks. 'The poor were in profligate ignorance—the rich in presumptuous apostasy.' She remembered a dinner party years earlier when she had burst into tears over someone's scoffing at religion without having been reprimanded. And this had been at 'what was called a most respectable circle'. As a result of Evangelical reform 'such conduct now would not be tolerated for a moment in any company'.

While the infidel had been subdued at home and the enemy defeated abroad, reformers thought it necessary to continue the cause of religious improvement. Two years after the end of the war a society was founded for the construction of churches. In the following year Parliament appropriated £1,000,000 for this purpose, later adding additional funds. From 1818 to 1824 alone, 212 new churches were built as a result of combined public and private initiatives, and church construction would continue on a large scale throughout the nineteenth century. If the nineteenth century was not a great spiritual age in the sense that the Reformation had been, it most certainly was an age of piety, thanks in no small part to Evangelicalism.

Lucy Aikin, herself an Evangelical, understood the impact of her party when she said, 'at length [it] became great enough to give the tone to society at large'. Originating as a small group within the Church of England, it developed into a powerful force as it denounced ecclesiastical abuses. The times were propitious for their purposes, giving them a moral advantage over the more relaxed partisans of the High Church. Placed on the defensive, the High Church party had to organise itself not only against the attacks of Evangelicals, but also Methodists and Nonconformists. In fighting their adversaries these churchmen adopted some of their tactics, particularly those of the Evangelicals. They revived older religious societies and modelled new ones after those of their opponents. As rival programmes for popular education had been extremely successful, the Church established its own national system of elementary education. It also produced a sizeable amount of religious literature in the form of tracts and books. By taking over many of the practices of the Evangelicals, the High Church party ended up resembling them in ways that had not been intended. The wave of piety and seriousness that flowed outward from the Evangelicals and passed through much of English life had a definite and lasting effect upon the High Church.

This is not to say that churchmen of a traditional persuasion came entirely to resemble Low Church zealots. On the contrary, many fought them blow for blow, attacking the Sunday School movement as subversive and accusing the Evangelicals of stirring the politically dangerous waters of Puritanism. Further, some considered their pious and earnest rivals sanctimonious and insufferable, anxious in their enthusiasm not so much to prevent various innocent practices that provided some small pleasure as to blot out pleasure itself.

Writing in the *Edinburgh Review* in 1808, Sydney Smith said:

> It is not the abuse of pleasure which they attack, but the in-
> terspersion of pleasure, however much it is guarded by good sense
> or moderation:—and it is not only wicked to hear the licentious
> plays of Congreve, but wicked to hear *Henry V* or *The School for
> Scandal*; it is not only wicked to run about to all the parties in
> London and Edinburgh, but dancing is not fit for a person
> preparing himself for eternity.[11]

Smith had good reasons for mounting a High Church counter-
offensive against the Evangelicals. When he wrote polemical
articles in the *Edinburgh Review* in 1808–9, Evangelicals seemed to be
making inroads everywhere. Perceval, the prime minister, was
highly sympathetic to their cause. Not only had Wilberforce
become one of the most powerful men in the Church, but he also
exercised enormous political influence. The fact was that
Evangelicals were to be found in key positions everywhere,
as the High Church periodical the *Anti-Jacobin* recognised in
1816:

> With puritans in the senate, and in the army; with the spread of
> schism over the land; and with encouragement to its diffusion in
> quarters whence effectual remedies might have been expected;
> the man who does not discover, in the signs of the times, sufficient
> ground for apprehension, must be either stoically indifferent, or
> willfully blind. Let churchmen stand firm at their post—let them
> rally round the altar—let them 'cry aloud and spare not,' or we
> may be destined to witness a second *usurpation* without the chance
> of a second restoration.

While the High Church writer who issued this warning was correct
in seeing a puritanical strain in Evangelicalism and in recognising
its recent success, he was mistaken in regarding it as politically
subversive. The truth was just the opposite. Evangelicals were the
least radical of people; they worked not to overthrow the established
order, but to give it their unyielding support. But their way of doing
so happened to remind nervous and apprehensive High Churchmen
of an earlier time in English history, when religious zealots
contributed to social and political upheaval. Such a misunderstanding, such exaggerated and groundless fears, indicates the confusion

of this trying and difficult time. But this is what happens in the midst of conditions as volatile and unstable as those created by the French Revolution.

In examining religion in Austen's fiction it will be necessary to begin with her early works, written before she came under the influence of Evangelicalism. In discussing the early fiction I will not limit myself to the first three novels, but also include the Juvenilia and *Lady Susan*. Austen's treatment of the clergy and religion in the Juvenilia is satirical and ironic, an example being some short works that she wrote for her neice, Jane Anna Elizabeth Austen, in 1793. In a dedication she said, in mock serious style, that her advice offered 'very important Instructions, with regard to your Conduct in life'. (MW,71) While three of the four items in the 'collection' played lightly on themes of sentimental literature, the first piece, 'A Fragment written to inculcate the practise of Virtue', has a different frame of reference. It relates not to fiction, but to another genre, the sermon.

> We all know that many are unfortunate in their progress through the world, but we do not know all that are so. To seek them out to study their wants, & to leave them unsupplied is the duty, and ought to be the Business of Man. But few have time, fewer still have inclination, and no one has either the one or the other for such employments. Who amidst those that perspire away their Evenings in crowded assemblies can have leisure to bestow a thought on such as sweat under the fatigue of their daily labour. (MW,71)

In 'The Generous Curate', which is part of the same collection, Austen dismissed an idealised, fictional view of a good country clergyman by parodying a passage in a novel through close imitation. In the 'Fragment' she seems to have dismissed a sermon by the same imitative device. While it could be argued that this genre of homiletic writing was a normal and even natural field of satire for the youthful Austen, she herself would appear not to have thought so later, when she erased the entire piece. Interestingly, she wrote in the dedication that she hoped that she would not 'regret the Days and Nights that have been spent in composing these Treatises for your Benefit'. It seems that there was an unintended irony, that she did regret writing one of the pieces, the 'Fragment', at least to the extent that she erased it at some later time. She might then have thought that in writing this short work she had tread on dangerous ground.

The 'Fragment' demonstrates how thoroughly satirical Austen's way of viewing the world had become at the age of eighteen. Already in the Juvenilia certain of the mature habits of mind and mental processes had begun to take shape. A study of the literary activity of Austen's elder brothers, James and Henry, helps explain how this happened, how her satirical view developed as it did. Austen said that her family were 'great novel readers'. The literary culture that was part of the Austen family life is reflected in a weekly periodical entitled *The Loiterer*, which James Austen began in January, 1789, and to which Henry later made contributions.[12] The appearance of this work coincided with Austen's early writing, with which it has various similarities and affinities. Not only did the two university students treat many of the same themes as their precocious sister, but did so in much the same way. They too satirised the themes and style of the sentimental novel, poking fun at the stock material of fiction with which the entire Austen family was familiar. That Austen was influenced by her brothers would appear to be a virtual certainty and that she satirised eighteenth-century fiction was only to do as they were doing.

In the 'Fragment' it can be seen how a satirical view became detached from a fictional framework as the focus shifted from the novel to the sermon. This was not a large departure, and can be seen as a redirecting of satire from one genre of literature to another. What Austen demonstrated through the 'Fragment' was an ability to view a sermon simply as literature, to poke fun at its style in the same way that she would a novel. Of course she did not limit her satirical view to literature, of whatever type, but rather directed it to life itself. Just as she poked fun at novels, and on this one occasion at a sermon, so too did she mock the people that she encountered in her own world, as the letters provide ample proof. Her satirical bent of mind, then, whose origins can be traced at least in part to the literary tastes and interests of her own family, became a way of looking at the world. This helped form the first of the two Jane Austens, the one who stood back from the stage of life, wryly amused over the vagaries of its actors.

Without this detachment Austen the novelist would be inconceivable. To the end of her life she correctly saw herself as a comic writer. Were it not for the keen eye for human folly and social error that in a sense was her birthright, her comic art could not have been realised. This is not to suggest that the comic dimension of her fiction was inconsistent with the religious tradition that was equally her birthright. Not only was it consistent with that tradition, but was deeply rooted in it.[13] For a hard core of religion and morality was essential to Austen's comic art, in which the exposure of error required norms. Interestingly, James Austen made this very point in the last number of *The Loiterer*, as he explained the purposes of his periodical. Its aim had never been to promote virtue and learning directly, but always '*Through* the exposure of folly and error, and the recommendation of those inferior Virtues, which, though not of the greatest value, are of more frequent currency in Society.' In the first number of *The Loiterer* Austen's brother placed his periodical in a literary tradition, describing it as a descendant of the London 'essay serials' made famous by Addison and Steele and continued by Johnson. Austen was in the same moral and religious tradition as these essayists, much as the novelists Defoe, Fielding, Richardson and Goldsmith also were. Just as all of these novelists assumed a religious structure with positive norms, so did Austen, and just as they showed departures from those norms so did she. Austen's fiction resembled that of the eighteenth century in the additional sense that while it assumed religious norms it avoided religion as a conscious theme.

While religious norms are implicit in *Lady Susan*, the upholding of those norms would appear to have been remote from Austen's purpose. Opinions are divided as to the sources of *Lady Susan*. One view is that Austen drew this realistic work from life. Another and more widely accepted opinion is that its origins are literary. While J. A. Levine and B. C. Southam argue their cases differently they both arrive at the latter conclusion.[14] Levine places the heroine of this work in a literary tradition, that of the Merry Widow, that extends as far back as Roman Comedy and was well represented in seventeenth and eighteenth-century theatre as well as eighteenth-century fiction, and connects her to two literary predecessors, the hypocritical, lascivious widow of Restoration comedy and the villainesses of such novels as Sophia Lee's *Life of a Lover* and Frances Sheridan's *Memoirs of Miss Sidney Bidulph*.

While there is a definite similarity between these Merry Widow types and Austen's heroine, there is also a striking difference. Unlike the English literary antecedents discussed by Levine, Lady Susan possessed an iron will, which she used for the sake of revenge. While seduction was her goal, she was indifferent to love. She did find

Reginald de Courcy sufficiently attractive to be amusing and to make her design interesting, but her real goal was domination. 'I have made him sensible of my power, & can now enjoy the pleasure of triumphing over a Mind prepared to dislike me, & prejudiced against all my past actions.' (MW,257) By 'subduing' a young man who was 'pre-determined to dislike' her, Lady Susan would achieve two objectives: she would make this young man, whose entire family despised her, acknowledge her superiority, and she would 'humble' the rest of 'these self-important De Courcies'. Her strategy was to disconcert him by a 'calm reserve' which would weaken his defences and thereby facilitate a successful completion of the operation. As she began her campaign she took pride in its progress. 'My conduct has been equally guarded from the first, & I never behaved less like a Coquette in the whole course of my Life, tho' perhaps my desire of dominion was never more decided.' (MW,258) What made that desire so intense was her wish to inflict 'every sort of revenge' that was within her power.

The love–vengeance theme, the carefully laid strategies, the dissimulation, the absolute control of every facial gesture, the perfection of manners for evil purposes and the sexual domination of man by woman do indeed suggest that *Lady Susan's* origins are literary, but not just those indicated by Levine or Southam. A work that appeared in the late eighteenth century contained all of these themes and characteristics and bears such a striking resemblance to *Lady Susan* that it can be considered almost certainly to have been Austen's model. That work was Choderlos de Laclos' novel, *Les Liaisons Dangereuses*.[15] This is not to say that Levine and Southam were wrong in emphasising the influence of English theatre and fiction on *Lady Susan*. That influence might well have been present as Levine demonstrates it had been in the Juvenilia and Southam shows it would be in the novels. But in *Lady Susan* Austen seems also to have drawn from a very different type of work, a libertine and in many quarters scandalous French novel; that novel contained the highly distinctive features of *Lady Susan*, which are not to be found in English literary sources.

How might Austen have known about Laclos' novel, whose heroine is so similar to Lady Susan? The answer is undoubtedly through Eliza de Feuillide. Eliza had married the Comte de Feuillide in 1781, one year before the appearance of *Les Liaisons Dangereuses*, which was a succès de scandale. Between 1782 and 1788, fourteen French editions appeared, as well as various others, including an English translation in 1784. One suspects that it is precisely the type of novel that Eliza would have been attracted to, and one can well imagine her taking a copy to Steventon, either a French edition or the English translation, knowing that the Austens were 'great novel readers' and that her cousin Jane was an aspiring authoress.

Lady Susan maintains a seriousness of tone and non-ironic temper so consistently that this work stands apart from the earlier Juvenilia as well as the later novels. Austen never attempted anything else quite like it. *Lady Susan* does have certain similarities with the rest of her writing, in which she exposed the gap between illusion and reality, and in doing so revealed hypocrisy, error and self-deception. Assuming implicit positive norms, the reader is amused by departures from those norms. In *Lady Susan*, those same norms are present, but the heroine's transgressions occur within a framework that is not comic. The literary model that Austen followed undoubtedly goes far towards explaining this feature, but why she chose that model is another question. Austen could have patterned Lady Susan Vernon after Laclos' heroine not just as a literary exercise, but because depicting such a character gave new scope to her satirical bent of mind and her tendency to question and even ridicule social forms. Through the heroine both the manners and morals of society are viewed with contempt and brought under systematic and brutal attack. This is not to say that Austen felt such contempt herself, or imagined the destruction of conventional morality, but in writing *Lady Susan* she not only depicted the most wicked of all her characters but also made scandal and the moral subversion of society central to what she was doing. To be sure, it can be argued that evil received its just punishment at the end. As in Austen's later novels traditional moral norms remained intact, but this does not alter the fact that in *Lady Susan* evil was the dominant force, which makes one wonder about Austen's interest in the heroine. Just as Laclos' readers differed over his intentions, so too can Austen's perspective be questioned. Certainly the view of the world that one sees through the eyes of Lady Susan Vernon is not what one might expect from the pen of an eighteen-year-old daughter of an English country Rector. One might suspect of this singular work that Austen was exploring a subject that was interesting precisely because it was wicked.

In discussing the first three novels I will limit myself to one topic, Austen's way of depicting clergymen. Both the hero and the

heroine's father were clergymen in *Northanger Abbey*, and yet if that
fact were not spelled out the reader would hardly guess it, as nothing
in their manner seemed clerical. Good and decent they certainly
were, but not pious. When Austen first presented Mr. Morland she
sketched him in with light and comic touches. He 'was a clergyman,
without being neglected, or poor, and a very respectable man,
though his name was Richard—and he had never been handsome.
He had a considerable independence, besides two good livings—
and he was not in the least addicted to locking up his daughters.'
(NA,13) When Henry Tilney made his first appearance at a dance
he was described as 'a very gentlemanlike young man' who 'talked
with fluency and spirit' and whose manner had an interesting
'archness and pleasantry'. Amusing himself with the self-
consciousness of the heroine, he asked exactly the questions that
were expected when a young man met a young lady at Bath, and
then demonstrated his understanding of the ways of the opposite sex
by imagining the entry that she would make that night in her
journal. His tone throughout the ensuing discussion was wry and
ironic. Only after bringing out his amusement over the social
niceties at Bath did Austen indicate that this sophisticated young
man was 'a clergyman, and of a very respectable family in
Gloucestershire'.

The 'simpering air' that he sometimes maintained when he first
met Catherine did not bespeak affectation. Rather, as a person of
sense he ridiculed the forms and refinements of genteel Bath. That
he was a person of sense had nothing to do with the fact that he was a
clergyman. This civilised cleric, who was 'about four or five and
twenty', enjoyed a sizeable income from the family living, which his
father had given him. There is no indication that he resided in his
parish, Woodston, although he did go there twice, as a result of some
'engagements or on business'. So Henry Tilney was a rational,
clearheaded young man, sometimes given to wryness, he had done
the rounds at Bath often enough to be thoroughly familiar with
them, and met the expenses of these visitations with the handsome
income derived from his living. Just as General Tilney provided for
his son through the gift of a curacy, so did Mr. Morland plan to do
the same for Catherine's brother, James. When James announced
his plan to marry Isabella Thorpe, Mr. Morland decided to give
him one of his two livings, 'of about four hundred pounds yearly
value'. (NA,135) This was precisely what Austen's own father did
for his son when he retired in 1801, soon after the completion of

Northanger Abbey. In this respect Austen's treatment of the clergy was at one with the ways and practices of her own family. The clerical father and the hero of this novel were good and decent men whose characters were defined in social terms rather than by their profession. One was a pluralist, the other a non-resident clergyman.

Edward Ferrars, the hero of *Sense and Sensibility*, was also a clergyman, although he did not become one until the latter part of the story. While he had always 'preferred the Church' as a profession, his family recommended the army or navy as more appropriate, and were willing to concede that law was 'genteel enough'. He was either uninterested in or considered himself unfit for any of the fields that his family favoured; they refused to approve his choice, so he decided to do nothing, to live a life of idleness. When Edward did enter the Church, it was after being disowned by his mother and through the good offices of Colonel Brandon, who offered him a curacy. Brandon had understood that Edward intended to take orders, but that was not why he made the offer. Rather, he acted from generosity toward a person that he felt had been treated unfairly by his family. When Edward heard of the proposal he was noncommittal, neither accepting nor declining it. His initial concern was not with the curacy nor with the possibility of entering the clerical profession, but rather with the role that Elinor had played on his behalf. It was not clear at the time, but later became apparent, that Edward was actually depressed over the offer, assuming that with it he would have to go ahead with his plan to marry Lucy Steele. When Lucy married his brother instead the way was clear for him to marry Elinor, the prospect of which made him think again of the curacy that he had already accepted. The fact was that he had 'never yet been to the place' and had taken virtually no interest in it. What he did know he learned through Elinor. This pertained to such matters as the 'house, garden, and glebe, extent of the parish, condition of the land, and rate of the tythes', and related only outwardly to his spiritual duties.

Initially Edward did not think about the curacy or what it would mean to become a clergyman, but about the impact of the change on his own life. And even after his attention turned to his living the focus continued primarily to be private and domestic, rather than clerical and pastoral. That he felt astonishment over never having taken an interest in or having visited his living suggests embarrassment over his neglect, but such feelings were not spelled out. He still did not think openly about the responsibilities that he was about to undertake or the condition of his parishioners; never did he reveal demonstrably clerical attitudes. During the first month of the marriage he and Elinor improved the parsonage house and gardens, choosing wallpaper and planning new shrubberies. Even after moving into the house and assuming his new station, Edward appeared as a private person, not a clergyman: 'if Edward might be judged from the ready discharge of his duties in every particular, from an increasing attachment to his wife and his home, and from the regular cheerfulness of his spirits, he might be supposed no less contented with his lot, no less free from every wish of an exchange'. (SS,377)

Mr. Collins, the clergyman in *Pride and Prejudice*, was shown as a person of his profession as neither Henry Tilney nor Edward Ferrars had been. As Rector of Hunsford he lived in the parsonage house, delivered sermons every Sunday, and expressed opinions that were consistent with his clerical office. When visiting the Bennets he was asked to 'read aloud to the ladies' after tea, and a book was duly handed him for that purpose. When it happened to be a novel, 'he started back' and 'protested that he never read novels'. Finally, 'Other books were produced' and he chose one of sermons, from which he began his recitation, in a tone of 'monotonous solemnity'. Bored by it, Lydia interrupted him by relating some local gossip, which provoked this man of the cloth, 'much offended', to put down his book and say, 'I have often observed how little young ladies are interested by books of a serious stamp, though written solely for their benefit. It amazes me, I confess,—for certainly, there can be nothing so advantageous to them as instruction. But I will no longer importune my young cousin.' (PP.69)

Mr. Collins' solemn and scrupulous ways led Elizabeth to assume that he would refuse to dance and therefore decline Mr. Bingley's invitation to the Netherfield Ball. Even as he was assured that the host was 'a young man of character' and that the guests were 'respectable people', he felt that attending could have no 'evil tendency', and under the circumstances he was 'far from dreading a rebuke' from either his archbishop or patron, Lady Catherine de Bourgh. What he revealed in making a demonstration of his scruples in the same moment that he accepted the invitation was a mixture of sanctimoniousness and deference to his social betters. He would show those same tendencies again a short time later when he explained that the 'very noble lady whom I have the honour of calling my patroness' had told him he had to marry. In Mr. Collins,

Austen depicted a clergyman whose 'good opinion of himself, of his authority as a clergyman, and his rights as a rector, made him altogether a mixture of pride and obsequiousness, self-importance and humility'. (PP.70) A comic figure, his cowing to his patroness in one moment and assuming pious airs in the next made him an object of ridicule. Here was a clergyman to be laughed at.

Religion occupies a much larger position in *Mansfield Park* than in any of the earlier novels. The hero, Edmund Betram, wanted to become a clergyman, he did so, and he openly and frequently discussed the clerical profession, as did his father and Mary Crawford. Among the religious topics in this novel are ordination, sermons, residency and private chapels, as well as other subjects with a religious connection, such as private theatricals and the abolition of the slave trade. Yet, Austen's reasons for working these topics into *Mansfield Park* are not entirely clear. One view, and probably the dominant one, is that frequent as the religious theme was it was subordinate to other interests, such as the moral criticism of the gentry. Avrom Fleishman has given weight to this argument, having carefully considered the critical question of Evangelicalism. That Austen appeared to comment favourably on this group in 1814, but unfavourably in 1809 and again in 1816 leads Fleishman to conclude that she was not consistently Evangelical, but was receptive to the movement's moral programme even while she found its tone distasteful. He furnishes further evidence of her ambivalence towards Evangelicalism in the fact that her father was a pluralist but her more serious and fastidious brother refused a second living because he opposed simony. In this view she might have been attracted to Evangelicalism in one moment, just as her brother was, while in another she could have felt differently, perhaps reflecting the more relaxed ways of her father.

According to Fleishman, even when Austen discussed topics in *Mansfield Park* that were important to the Evangelicals she did not adopt their point of view. Thus, her treatment of ordination did not echo the Evangelical sentiment of the day, but stressed the abuses and religious shortcomings of the gentry. Drawing from the research of Clarence L. Branton, Fleishman shows that Edmund appears to have been a pluralist and not to have been ordained canonically.[16] Even as Austen settled Edmund and Fanny in Mansfield parsonage, in an apparent alliance of the gentry with the Established Church, she revealed the precariousness of the alliance. Thus, the novel does not end with a vindication of the Church, but a criticism of the gentry; her goal was the self-evaluation of the gentry, not its conversion. Nor was Austen, in Fleishman's opinion, stirred by religious faith when she wrote *Mansfield Park*. She most certainly was concerned, like the Evangelicals, with the scepticism that had attacked the gentry, and she felt that Christian belief was a powerful corrective to this insidious tendency, but she kept her focus on the social and political side of the problem. Again, her concern was not with religion, but with the impact of religion on the gentry.

As clearheaded as the above interpretation is, it can be questioned at several points. Austen was not completely opposed to Evangelicalism in 1809. As early as 1805 she wrote to Cassandra that 'I am glad you recommended "Gisborne", for having begun, I am pleased with it, and I had quite determined not to read it.' (L,169) These remarks are interesting for several reasons. First, they indicate that Cassandra encouraged Austen to read an Evangelical publication, probably Gisborne's *An Enquiry into the Duties of the Female Sex* (1797). As Cassandra also recommended Hannah More's *Cœlebs* in 1809, it would seem safe to infer that she favoured the Evangelicals and encouraged her sister to do the same. On both occasions Austen did not expect to like the books that Cassandra urged her to read: 'I had quite determined not to read [Gisborne]. You have by no means raised my curiosity after Caleb;—My disinclination for it before was affected, but now it was real . . . of course I shall be delighted, when I read it, like other people, but till I do I dislike it.' (L,256) It turned out that she did like Gisborne, but not More's *Cœlebs*. This makes one wonder about Austen's saying 'I do not like the Evangelicals' in the middle of her remarks about More's recently published novel. Austen's opinion of Hannah More appears to have caused her to censure Evangelicalism with a severity that did not accurately reflect her views. That she liked Gisborne earlier would seem to indicate that to some extent she had already become favourably disposed to the Evangelical programme. And when she wrote in 1816 that 'We do not much like Mr. Cooper's new Sermons;—they are fuller of Regeneration and Conversion than ever—with the addition of his zeal in the cause of the Bible Society' she was referring to a cousin that she had always disliked, and describing a side of Evangelicalism that had long made her uneasy. She was not making a negative pronouncement on that religious movement.

Nor does Fleishman's argument hold up that Austen's Evangelical tendencies were 'strangely inconsistent' because some of the clergymen in her family embraced the Evangelical cause while others did not. To say that her father, as a pluralist, violated her brother's strict standards is meaningless. When the Reverend George Austen took possession of his two livings in 1761 and 1773, those standards had not been established, nor had they fully taken hold when he retired in 1801. In fact, George Austen, while a pluralist, cared for both his curacies, which were little more than a mile apart and together had a population of some three hundred families. By the standards of his time this was by no means abusive. While the matter of her father's pluralism is beside the point, the 'conscientious refusal' of a living worth £100 by her brother James in 1808 is more relevant. What this decision indicates is precisely the type of response toward which the Evangelicals were working. His scrupulosity reflected his awareness of a problem that was of central importance to the Evangelical party. Henry Austen also appears to have come under the same influence when he became a clergyman, in 1816, of a decidedly Evangelical bent. It is not convincing, then, to argue from the clerical practices of Austen's family that the evidence for her so-called Evangelicalism is 'strangely inconsistent'. The one safe conclusion is that both Austen and her two clerical brothers came under Evangelical influence. Cassandra also did so, as did Francis Austen, who was known as '*The* officer who knelt in church' and was the protégé of Admiral Gambier, a leading Evangelical.

Fleishman might well be correct in arguing that Edmund's ordination was not canonical and that he was a pluralist, and from those facts generalising that Austen was laying bare the inadequacies of the gentry. But it does not necessarily follow from this line of reasoning that her main concern was social rather than religious. Of course, Fleishman does advance other reasons to support his view. The two country houses in the novel were not conspicuously religious, he maintains, nor were the hero and heroine. Edmund was 'strikingly devoid of religious doctrine or sentiment', and Fanny's values were only 'tangentially religious', just as, he concludes, were those of Austen. Fleishman seems to have arrived at this view of Austen through his reading of *Mansfield Park*, and more particularly through an analysis of Fanny Price. Thus, he contends that Fanny favoured private chapels because they supported the country house ideal; that her doing so revealed a concern for secular more than religious ideals; and that just as Fanny favoured religious practices because they were socially useful, so too did Austen.

We have some problems here. Fleishman has argued that Fanny Price's values were not basically religious, that Austen's were not either, and that while there was religious affirmation in *Mansfield Park* it was put, as in the Evangelical criticism of the time, 'to the service of maintaining the strength of the gentry, bolstering its self-assurance and correcting its lapses, in the face of the threats of a revolutionary age'. The first two parts of this formulation might well be correct, just as they might not be. We shall have to examine both propositions, but only after considering the implications of the final contention. While it is accurate to see Evangelicals urging the gentry to reform or face ruin, it is misleading to say that because religious affirmation was 'put to the service of maintaining the strength' of this class that social considerations came first and that religion was a mere device for buttressing the gentry. It is of course true that Evangelicalism is unintelligible unless it is seen against the background of the French Revolution, and as a response to radical social and political forces that swept over England, just as it is right to see an upper-class orientation within the movement. Religious and social factors were inextricably intertwined. But this is frequently true of religious movements.[17] The extent to which other movements, or Evangelicalism in particular, are rationalisations for social, political or economic objectives is not our present concern. Once they become religious movements they are religious movements. And Evangelicalism was indeed a religious movement, however important the social factor might have been. This raises an interesting question: If religious and social considerations were bound together so closely in Evangelicalism, might not the same have been true with Austen, who, ambivalent though her feelings might have been, was attracted to Evangelicalism?

In trying to answer this question, perhaps the best place to begin is by identifying elements in the novel that can be connected to the Evangelical programme. The value in doing so will be to determine as precisely as possible how importantly Austen, in writing *Mansfield Park*, quarried her building materials from this contemporary religious movement. Two of those materials were pluralism and non-residence, which the Evangelicals regarded as abuses and sought to eliminate. In 1796, 1803 and 1813, Parliament passed bills that attempted to reduce multiple incumbencies and encourage clergymen to reside in their parsonages. In fact, the measures had little effect, as the High Church party found ways to avoid their stipulations. Correctly perceiving the initiative of Low Church reformers in the bills, the High and Dry party worked to keep power as much as possible in the hands of the episcopate and to allow vicars to make private arrangements with their curates that would enable them to continue in their customary way. Ineffective as the various bills were, they do reflect a concern over pluralism and non-residency that took hold in the late 1790s and gained added momentum in the years after 1800.

Austen's novels reflect a growing awareness of the problem. That Henry Tilney did not live in his parsonage, Woodston, and was not criticised for being a non-resident clergyman, would appear to indicate that Austen regarded the practice as normal or at least acceptable when she wrote *Northanger Abbey*. Nor does she seem to have been critical of Mr. Morland's pluralism. Between 1798 and 1811, the respective years in which she began *Northanger Abbey* and *Mansfield Park*, she became aware of the questions that Evangelicals were raising about these practices. Thus, in *Mansfield Park*, when Henry Crawford indicated his wish to rent the parsonage house at Thornton Lacey, which was soon to become Edmund's curacy, Sir Thomas explained that it would be impossible, as his son would assuredly reside there himself. Turning to Edmund for a clarification, he was prompt in receiving it. 'Certainly, sir, I have no idea but of residence.' While Sir Thomas would regret his son's living there, even though it was but 8 miles away, he would be mortified if he were to do less. He did not hesitate to spell out his reasons:

a parish has wants and claims which can be known only by a clergyman constantly resident, and which no proxy can be capable of satisfying to the same extent. Edmund might, in the common phrase, do the duty of Thornton, that is, he might read prayers and preach, without giving up Mansfield Park; he might ride over, every Sunday, to a house nominally inhabited, and go through divine service; he might be the clergyman of Thornton Lacey every seventh day, for three or four hours, if that would content him. But it will not. He knows that human nature needs more lessons than a weekly sermon can convey, and that if he does not live among his parishioners and prove himself by constant attention their well-wisher and friend, he does very little either for their good or his own (MP,247–8)

Did Edmund later become a non-resident clergyman and pluralist, as Fleishman maintains? At the very end of the novel, after marrying Fanny and moving into Thornton Lacey, Dr. Grant died, thereby making Mansfield parsonage available. Under these circumstances 'they removed to Mansfield, and the parsonage there'. (MP,473) From this Fleishman concludes, in the absence of information to the contrary, that Edmund retained his living at Thornton Lacey while accepting the additional one at Mansfield. Perhaps and perhaps not. It should be remembered that Sir Thomas had originally intended Mansfield for Edmund, but the extravagance of the elder son, Tom, had forced him to sell it to Dr. Grant. As he also held a second and less valuable family living, Thornton Lacey, he was able to keep it for Edmund until he was old enough to take orders. The inference is that since Sir Thomas was unable to give Edmund one living, he would give him the other, as indicated by his later comments about residency. From these facts it should follow that when Edmund moved into his new living he gave up his former one. If so, why did Austen neglect to say so? The answer might be that the focus was not on Edmund, but on Fanny. As soon as the marriage took place, and Sir Thomas settled her at Thornton Lacey, his object 'almost every day was to see her there, or to get her away from it'. There is no indication, incidentally, that Edmund's residence 8 miles away, which began before the marriage, had been so painful for Sir Thomas. In any event, Fanny's return to Mansfield brought her back to the centre of a world toward which she had long been gravitating and which she had helped rescue from disorder. For her to have remained at Thornton Lacey would have been inconsistent with the ever more central role that she played in the life of the Bertram family and at Mansfield Park. So, when Fanny and Edmund moved to their new parsonage house only her feelings were recorded, not his. Might it not be assumed that, left in the background, Edmund would have done his duty and put Thornton Lacey in trustworthy hands, or that Sir Thomas, feeling as he did about residency, would have done so?

Of all the Evangelicals' successes, none had greater contemporary impact than the abolition of the slave trade. While the Evangelicals played a leading role in the campaign, they did not act alone, drawing necessary support from Methodists, dissenters, and even radicals. The opposition was formidable, led by reactionary Tories who considered the movement for abolition an attack on property and therefore a threat to their own vested interests.

Wilberforce, the driving force behind the cause, was faced by another group of enemies who, paradoxically, tended to favour abolition but questioned his motives. This group, made up of liberals and radicals, saw a vicious contradiction between the Evangelicals' support for liberty in Africa and their opposition to working-class reform in England. As Hazlitt said, 'What have the SAINTS to do with freedom or reform?' For him, and others, abolition was a pious fraud and deceit, a device that posed as humanitarian reform but in fact diverted attention from the distress of the labouring classes in England. Neither of the opposition groups understood Wilberforce. Clearly, he was no enemy of property; yet he did work tirelessly for a cause that conservatives bitterly opposed as radical and Jacobinical, owing to its attack on certain existing arrangements and to its inherent reformism. Nor were liberals and radicals any more accurate in viewing abolition as a scheme for holding the lower orders in England in their present state of subjection.

Wilberforce was very much in earnest. When Parliament passed the Act of 1807, a group of elated Evangelicals met at his house in Old Palace Yard. According to one account, 'When the first rush of congratulations was over, Mr. Wilberforce turned to Henry Thornton and said exultingly, "What shall we abolish next?" The answer fell with characteristic seriousness from the lips of his grave friend: "The lottery, I think." ' Clearly, Wilberforce saw abolition as part of a larger cause, not as an end in itself. Important as humanitarian considerations were in that cause, and anxious as the Evangelicals might have been to preserve the established social and political order, their main goal was religious reform. What the abolition movement did was to pull them together, give them a sense of cohesion, and galvanise them into a committed and highly effective party. While it did have a highly practical value, it would be misleading to think that for a man of Wilberforce's stamp pragmatic considerations came first. Political person that he was, and inured to the ways of the world, he believed that God had entrusted him with the task of reform, and in his mind religious considerations were central to his goals. He himself said in 1813 that abolition was not his proudest achievement, but rather legislation that introduced missionaries into India and the Far East. Referring to some recent measures, he said 'This East India object is assuredly the greatest that ever interested the heart, or engaged the efforts of man. How wonderful that a private man should have such an influence on the temporal and eternal happiness of millions; literally, millions on millions yet unborn.' Along with abolition the project of missions to the Heathen not only gave the Evangelicals a sense of dedication and purpose, but also had the same effect on countless numbers of English men and women who needed the moral conviction that these measures offered. These were years of enormous emotional strain, caused by year after year of military reversals, taxation of unprecedented severity, serious economic dislocation resulting from a loss of markets, and rioting that was a response to widespread unemployment. Religious reform helped English society to believe in itself; it did this through measures whose immediate objectives were sometimes humanitarian and social, but whose core was religious. In carrying the reform movement forward Wilberforce made himself one of the most influential men of his time, 'The most loved and respected man in England', 'the conscience of his country', 'the foremost moral subject of the crown', and 'the most powerful man in England who owed nothing to birth or office'.

While Austen touched only passingly on the slavery question in *Mansfield Park*, her way of doing so suggests that she considered it an important issue. When Sir Thomas visited his Antigua estate he was in financial difficulties. His eldest son had spent beyond the family's means, and unless the West Indies plantation could yield greater profits the economic future of the Bertrams would be uncertain. Plantations were failing, owing to the effects of the Napoleonic blockade and falling sugar prices. Adding to the economic difficulties was the problem of abolition, a hotly debated issue precisely at this time. As the passage of an act ending the slave trade would permanently have limited the availability of slave labour plantation owners began to improve the condition of slaves, introducing humanitarian measures for pragmatic reasons. Like other owners, Sir Thomas had to protect the lives of his slaves, which he could have done through the establishment of better working conditions, better nutrition and more decent housing. He probably went to Antigua for economic reasons, to repair 'some recent losses on his West India estate', (MP,24) but upon arriving and becoming acquainted with conditions on the island and on his estate, he became interested in the slavery question on grounds that were not strictly economic. One can well imagine him going through stages leading from the strictly pragmatic to a mixture of practical and humanitarian and then centring on the ethical. Certainly the slavery question was very much on his mind when he returned to Mansfield Park.

Anxious as he was to discuss it, the members of his family were indifferent. When Sir Thomas raised the subject there was a 'dead silence', as his own children sat by 'without speaking a word, or seeming at all interested in the subject'. (MP,198) Only Fanny wanted to hear Sir Thomas discuss his views on slavery, but keenly aware of her position in the family she did not want to appear in a more favourable light than her cousins 'by shewing a curiosity and pleasure in his information which he must wish his own daughters to feel'. (MP,198) Restrain herself as she did, Fanny talked more than usual and made direct inquiries about the slave trade, which led Sir Thomas to see her differently. Not only had Fanny changed physically during the period of Sir Thomas's absence, but also matured, unlike his own daughters, into a person of sound judgment and moral substance. Edmund was quick to explain to his father that only Fanny had steadfastly refused to enter into the theatrical plans; she alone, he said, did as Sir Thomas would have wished. The slavery and theatrical episodes fitted together, then, in redefining Fanny's position in the opinion of her uncle, who began to view her with greater respect. Of course, this was but a stage in a progression of incidents that would eventually place Fanny at the moral centre of the Bertram·family and Mansfield Park. Passing as the references were to the slavery question, they played an important role in establishing attitudes and relationships that were central to the plot and basic to the structure of the novel.

When Sir Thomas returned from Antigua his household was barely recognisable, thanks to the preparations for the private theatrical. Like the abolition theme, the theatrical episode relates to Evangelicalism. In a study of that episode William Reitzel sees Austen working under the influence of Evangelicalism, which in his opinion came through as an anti-theatrical prejudice.[18] It is true that the Evangelicals did attack the theatre as immoral, but since Austen attended plays not infrequently and both before and after writing *Mansfield Park*, this view does not hold up. If Evangelicalism made itself felt in this episode it must have been in some other way. Denis Donoghue sees an Evangelical influence in the stern ethic and seriousness that permeates this part of the novel. Plausible as this view might be, it is but a tempting suggestion unless what Austen was doing through the episode can be connected more directly to Evangelicalism.

As David Lodge has shown, a question of judgment was central to the private theatrical.[19] There is no doubt that the undertaking was wrong. The arguments for and against it gave the various disputants an opportunity to exercise their powers of judgment and to apply both social and moral values. The former, expressed through decorum, propriety and fitness, were valid only if they rested upon principle. To cultivate one without invoking the other was to run a definite risk; without a proper exercise of judgment, the necessary balance between social and moral factors would break down. Unless objections to the theatrical were based on principle they lacked efficacy, which leads Lodge to conclude that in theological terms the theatrical was a 'proximate occasion for sin'.

All of this sounds very Evangelical. Wilberforce or Hannah More would also have said that social values were hollow unless based upon principle. But Evangelicalism can be seen even more importantly in the stress that Austen gave to choice, which is by no means isolated to the theatrical episode but runs throughout and indeed is crucial to the entire novel. One function of *Lovers' Vows* was to establish a moral division, with one side representing right and the other wrong. The partition that ran through the episode extended, in various ways, to the end of *Mansfield Park*, giving the characters various opportunities to line up on one side or the other. Eventually, in the last chapter, there was a final settling of moral accounts, as those who had gone astray went to their just punishment and those who were deserving received their fair rewards.

This interpretation does not agree with the view of Gilbert Ryle, who sees the moral world of Jane Austen as 'Aristotelian' or 'Shaftesburyian', by which he means monistic rather than dualistic, as in the Puritan moral tradition. Austen's characters, Ryle argues, are neither black nor white, but compounds of good and bad tendencies. None of the exceptions that he notes come from *Mansfield Park*, whose monism, then, would appear to be uncompromised. And yet the moral world of this novel was not monistic. Even though none of the characters are black in the way that Wickham was in *Pride and Prejudice*, there is an underlying dualism in *Mansfield Park*.[20] Paradoxically, the very mixture of positive and negative qualities in such a character as Henry Crawford dramatised the conflict between right and wrong and in that sense reinforced the dualism.

The attractive qualities in both Henry and Mary Crawford have not gone unnoticed, and in fact have been a source of misunderstanding. That some readers should prefer the Crawfords to Edmund and Fanny in a way indicates how successful Austen was. As amusing, clever and charming as Henry and Mary were, they lacked principle; moreover, they stood for the values and ideas that Austen represented as wrong. What adds immensely to the novel's depth and complexity is the surface attractiveness of characters who, so to speak, occupied negative moral ground, and the surface plainness of those who occupied positive ground. The choices that Henry and Mary offered did have appeal, just as those held out by Edmund and Fanny were not without a certain forbidingness. In the context of the theatrical episode the former translated into play, fancy, amusement, make-believe, romance, flirtation and intrigue, and the latter into self-denial, restraint, limit, seriousness, sobriety, permanence and respect for authority. By making such choices available, and focusing attention so sharply upon the faculty of judgment, Austen did something new. There was nothing quite like this episode in the earlier novels, nor do the earlier novels juxtapose the forces of right and wrong as *Mansfield Park* does. This juxtaposition, which is central to the theatrical episode and the novel as a whole, and was at the heart of Austen's purpose, reveals a moral outlook that was not Aristotelian, Shaftesburyian and monistic but dualistic and Puritanical.

Countless examples could be drawn from Evangelical writings to demonstrate the importance of moral choice and to indicate an underlying dualism. For the Evangelical, as for his Puritan predecessor, whose theology he shared in many ways, making the right moral decisions was a matter of the greatest urgency. Looking at just one work, Wilberforce's *Practical View*, one finds a clear separation between right and wrong and constant appeals to the reader to choose the former and reject the latter. Drawing from the tradition of Puritanism, Wilberforce stressed self-denial and called idleness an 'acknowledged sin'. Men of the world, yielding to the lures of vanity and display, selfishly wasted themselves in 'parade, and dress, and equipage', rather than giving themselves to the more solid and noble virtues of 'moderation and sobriety'. To Wilberforce the world was filled with temptations that continually beckoned to those without firm principles and solid values. Those who were most easily led astray were those to whom he was addressing himself: people of means, the members of polite society. It was time, in his opinion, for the person of rank and fortune to mend his ways.

Beside focusing attention on moral choice the theatrical episode conveyed a hard political message. Elizabeth Inchbald, the English translator of *Lovers' Vows*, was part of a radical literary circle that included Thomas Holcroft, Robert Bage and Charlotte Smith. She also wrote sentimental, Rousseauistic novels, *Nature and Art* being the best known, that argued for the natural goodness of man. This was not a new idea, and was not necessarily revolutionary. It became revolutionary, however, when Rousseau said that man had fallen from his natural state because of vicious social and political institutions. Obscure as Jean-Jacques' political views often were, they came to be regarded as an attack on monarchical government and effete, decadent aristocracies. *Lovers' Vows* appeared to be an example of this revolutionary philosophy, as seen in Count Cassel's trying to force himself upon the innocent Amelia, and in the debauchery of Agathe by Baron Wildenhaim. That these aristocrats took cruel advantage of their privileged position put their entire class in an unfavourable light, or so contemporaries felt about this play and similar German plays that for a time enjoyed a considerable popularity. And it is important to realise that those who favoured and those who opposed German theatre both saw *Lovers' Vows* as politically radical. Hazlitt, representing the former, said 'German tragedy is a good thing . . . It embodies . . . the extreme opinions which are floating in our times; . . . we are all partisans of a political system, and devotees to some theory of moral sentiment.' Cobbett, representing the latter, felt that it was 'the universal aim of German authors of the present day to exhibit the brightest examples of virtue among the lower classes of society; while the lower orders by their folly and profligacy, are held up to contempt and detestation'. Those who favoured the *Lovers' Vows* project were giving their support to an enterprise that implied a radical social and political critique.

Obviously the various guests at Mansfield Park had no business giving the play. In Fleishman's interpretation, Austen was not just criticising the various members of the gentry who were gathered together at Mansfield Park, but also a certain segment of the aristocracy that dabbled in the radical culture of the French Revolution. Yates was a representative of that class. He had been present at Ecclesford, the landed estate of Lord Ravenshaw, where it had been necessary to abandon a production of *Lovers' Vows* because of a death in his host's family. When Yates brought the idea of *Lovers' Vows* to Mansfield Park he was spreading an infection that began with a certain segment of the aristocracy. For Fleishman the theatrical episode represents a criticism by the Tory gentry of the Whig aristocracy's irresponsible flirtation with the fasionable radical ideas spawned by the French Revolution.

As convincing as this interpretation is, it is too narrow, stressing social and political factors to the exclusion of the religious factor. Arguing that no Evangelical or Puritan attitudes 'can be pointed out in the novel during the debate about the performance', Fleishman concludes that the significance of the episode must lie elsewhere. Yet, the Evangelicals specifically denounced private theatricals, and as in *Mansfield Park* because of the familiarity they encouraged between the two sexes. Moreover, when Fleishman sees only a criticism of the upper classes for their dalliance with a radical ideology he overlooks one obvious point: the Evangelicals were saying exactly the same thing, and indeed this was central to what they were saying. Austen criticised the upper classes in much the same way as Wilberforce and the various members of his party, and she revealed a sternness and moral dualism that was consistent with Evangelicalism. On one level the private theatrical describes the irresponsibility of dandified young men such as Yates and Tom Bertram, but on another it reveals a dualistic moral world and the forces of right and wrong locked in a relentless struggle.

Austen did not view that struggle from a position of detachment. Rather, it was something that she knew personally and felt keenly, having herself been subject to wrong influences, or so she had come to believe. *Mansfield Park* can be viewed as a record of Austen's reflecting over certain parts of her life that made her uncomfortable and with which she wanted to come to terms. One way to trace the course of her reflections is through Mary Crawford, behind whom the spectre of Eliza de Feuillide can be seen.

Mary's using the private theatrical as an opportunity for flirtation sounds exactly like Eliza. In 1787 Eliza tried to urge her cousin Philadelphia Walter to come to Steventon during the Christmas season to participate in a production of *Which is the Man* and *Bon Ton*. 'I assure you we shall have a most brilliant company and frequent balls. You cannot possibly resist so many temptations, especially when I tell you your old friend James is returned from France and is to be at the acting party.'[21] Philadelphia Walter chose not to accept the invitation, nor did she do so when Eliza wrote her a second time. One of her reasons for declining might well have been a disapproval of Eliza. In a letter to her brother, James Walter, written in September 1787, two months before the first invitation, Philadelphia described a recent visit with her aristocratic cousin. What she experienced during the ten-day period was a 'gayer life' than she had ever seen and a 'dissipated life that led and put me in mind that every woman is at heart a rake'. This view of Eliza is confirmed by Eliza herself. In a letter of April 1787, she wrote to Philadelphia that 'I have been for some time the greatest rake imaginable', and in another of August 1788, she described her 'gallant' cousins, James and Henry Austen, the latter of whom she regarded as attractive, 'with his hair powdered and dressed in a very tonish style'. In August 1791, Eliza wrote Philadelphia that she was looking forward to a trip to Bath, 'a journey from which I promise myself much pleasure, as I have a notion it is a place quite after my own heart'.

Philadelphia Walter found it difficult to understand why a married woman and mother should dance until two in the morning while her husband was in France, even though she admitted no longer loving him. Recognising Eliza's interest in men, Philadelphia could hardly have misunderstood the nature of her appeal when she urged her to come to Steventon and participate in the private theatrical because her 'old friend' James Austen would be there as part of 'the acting company'. The opportunity for flirtation that Eliza held before Philadelphia seems not to have been an attraction but a deterrent; she chose not to go to Steventon and become party to the private theatrical.

Austen was twelve at the time, and must have followed the rehearsals and watched the final performance with considerable interest. It is impossible to know exactly how Eliza conducted herself, or what Austen saw, but given Eliza's well-established record of flirtation and her appeal to Philadelphia Walter to take female advantage of James Austen's participation in the enterprise, it is by no means difficult to imagine the scene. The theatrical episode in *Mansfield Park* would describe a similar opportunity for flirtation, with Mary Crawford playing the type of role that Eliza must have taken. ·

Eliza did not abandon her flirtatious ways even after marrying Henry Austen in 1797. Describing life at the militia camp of her new husband in 1798, she said:

I have not yet given you any account of my brother officers of whom I wish you could judge in person for there are some with whom I think you would not dislike a flirtation. I have *of course entirely left off trade* but I can however discover that Captn Tilson is remarkably handsome and that Mess^r. Perrot and Edwards may be chatted with very satisfactorily, but as to my Colonel Charles Spencer, if I was married to my third husband instead of my second I should still be in love with him . . . but alas! he is married as well as myself.

She then said that she had 'an aversion to the word *husband* and never make use of it'. Her decision to be free of marital constraints was apparent again, when she explained that it would be her pleasure to have 'my own way in everything for Henry well knows that I have not been much accustomed to control and should probably behave rather awkwardly under it, and therefore like a wise man he has no will but mine'.

It is no accident that the seductive Mary Crawford bears a definite resemblance to Austen's cousin. Looking back at the role that Eliza played in her own life and that of her brother, Austen incorporated certain of her responses into *Mansfield Park*. Not only did she do so in the theatrical episode, which echoes the private theatricals in Steventon, but also in the Sotherton episode, in which Mary Crawford told Edmund that 'a clergyman is nothing'. (MP,92) For Mary the church was no place for anyone who wanted to distinguish himself, by which she meant that a man in that profession could not maintain a respected and fashionable position in the world. This was how Eliza felt in 1797, when she wrote that Henry had just been appointed to the rank of captain. 'He is a very lucky young man and bids fair to possess a considerable share of riches and honours. I believe he has now given up all thoughts of the Church, and he is right for he certainly is not fit for a parson as a soldier.'

Having come under the influence of Evangelicalism when she wrote *Mansfield Park*, Austen must have found it disturbing that her cousin—and close friend—had helped dissuade her brother from entering the clergy. She recalled Eliza's flirting with Henry at the Austen's private theatricals, even though she was married, and connected those occasions to their later marriage. The sense of menace that is attached to Mary Crawford must be seen against this background. In time, Edmund saw into Mary's actual nature, concluding that she had 'no feminine—shall I say? No modest loathings.' (MP,455) Behind that passage lay Austen's self-loathing.

derived in part from Eliza's earlier influence over her. Eliza had played a key role in the formation of one of the two Jane Austens, the one who was ironic and iconoclastic. One result of those tendencies was Austen's irreverence, as seen in her treating serious subjects lightly in her youthful writings; another was her flirtatiousness, of which the letters give clear indications.

So Austen became displeased over the type of girl that she had been. The parson's daughter now found these memories unpleasant and burdensome. They caused a sensation of guilt. There is a sense of both guilt and sin in *Mansfield Park*, as Austen was clearly aware in the last chapter when she said 'Let other pens dwell on guilt and misery.' (MP,461) In fact, the language of *Mansfield Park* conveys a new, more sober and even dark atmosphere; there is more 'shade' than in the previous novel. And Fanny is completely at one with this aspect of *Mansfield Park*, not light, bright, vital, active, witty and clever, but quiet, passive, pensive, obedient and sickly. Above all, Fanny was serious. All of these characteristics put her, as Robert Colby has argued, in a certain moral tradition, that of the Christian heroine.[22] Thus, even though Fanny is not shown on her knees in prayer or even in Church, she embodied a set of ideals that very distinctively are Christian. There was a definite relationship between these ideals and those represented by Mary Crawford. Fanny was Mary's opposite, her anti-type.

Fanny looks behind the eighteenth century to an earlier Christian tradition, just as she looks forward to the more earnest, serious, disciplined, pious and religious nineteenth century. It has been well demonstrated that Austen's values, habits of mind, and spiritual qualities were shaped by the eighteenth-century world into which she was born. The classical dimension of her thought, the ironic mode of perception, the satirical bent, the detachment, the monistic system of morality, the control, the balance, the lightness of touch, the precision and the combination of verbal refinement and solidity all reflect the eighteenth century whose influence she came under as a girl. But during her lifetime the stable culture of the eighteenth century broke down under the impact of new forces. The serious-ness, earnestness and piety that became widespread did not harmonise with the dominant characteristics of eighteenth-century culture, nor did the Puritanical dualism that surfaced in the Evangelical movement mesh with established moral attitudes that were rooted in the thought of such writers as Shaftesbury. One culture broke down as a new one struggled to take its place. Out of this conflict came a new cluster of attitudes, a different set of values and, in the largest sense, a social re-orientation. The stress came to be on duty and responsibility, not individual freedom and happiness; inner worth, not outer display; seriousness of mind, not the perfection of taste; overcoming one's lower tendencies, not urbanely viewing those tendencies as natural. Much of this shift can be seen in *Mansfield Park*, a novel that uniquely reveals the stresses and strains in English society and shows the new configuration of attitudes and ideals that would become dominant during the Victorian period.

Mansfield Park, then, is a record of Austen's response to social change. But it is more than that. It is a record also of Austen's own, individual change. In fact, the two were closely connected, so much so that one can hardly be separated from the other. The type of person that Austen might have become between the age of twenty-five and thirty-five if the course of her life had unfolded two or three decades earlier cannot be imagined. What can be said is that living when she did and experiencing what she did she became deeply uneasy with herself, uneasy over the hard and brittle qualities of her mind and the cutting ironies and outcroppings of verbal malice to which she was sometimes given. She had a tendency to mock and ridicule the people who appeared on the stage of life, the friends, neighbours and relatives whose aberrant ways she ruthlessly exposed in her letters. Also, she came to be disturbed over the role that Eliza de Feuillide had played in her adolescent life and in the life of her brother, Henry. When she wrote *Mansfield Park* she was reacting against certain of her own characteristics, she was recalling and responding to some discomforting memories, and she was looking back over her past through eyes that had been influenced by Evangelicalism.

Austen never attempted anything like *Mansfield Park* again; never again would her moralising be as stern, never again would the hue of her palette be so dark, and never again would religion occupy such an important position. Mr. Elton and Charles Hayter, the clergymen in *Emma* and *Persuasion*, are conventional comic types, treated in Austen's usual satirical way. Unlike Edmund Bertram, these clergymen did not discuss topics such as residency and sermons, making it appear that after *Mansfield Park* Austen again drew a curtain between her religion and her fiction. However different her purposes may have been, the presence of Evangelicalism can still be felt in the last two novels.

Mark Schorer has shown that certain words crop up in *Emma* as 'buried metaphors', that their function is to take various measurements, and that their cumulative effect is to invest the novel with a feeling of Austen's world. 'The language itself defines for us, and defines most clearly, that area of available experience and value from which this novel takes its rise, and on which the novel itself must place the seal of its value.'[23] I would like to suggest that Austen's vocabulary in *Emma*, as in *Mansfield Park*, reflects an Evangelical influence. This is not the accepted view. Both Schorer and Norman Page, to mention but two critics, stress the abstract quality of Austen's language, which they say is rooted in the hard, firm and stable world of the eighteenth-century moralists. Page argues that Austen, drawing from the tradition of *The Tatler, The Spectator*, Cowper and Burney, chose words that conveyed an unambiguous meaning based on a social usage that was both subtle and fixed.[24] In his opinion, the key to Austen's ethical standards was social and moral rather than religious. But what does one do with phrases like 'she did not repent what she had done', (E,65) or 'his grave looks shewed that she was not forgiven', (E,69) both of which appear early in the novel? That Emma would not repent indicates the further errors that she would commit, and that she was not forgiven explains Knightley's ability to see into her mind and perceive its erroneous designs. The relationship between Emma and Knightley could take its final turn only when she did repent, which led to his forgiving her. This did not happen in a religious context. Yet, as in the theatrical episode in *Mansfield Park*, there were, in theological terms, appropriate occasions for sin. Emma persisted in her mistaken ways until she became aware of herself and her motives. When she realised that 'She had often been remiss, her conscience told her so,' (E,377) she could 'hope to be forgiven'. The words repent and forgiven not only suggest a theological analogy but also condition the novel's atmosphere, charging it with a religious sense.

These words serve as buried metaphors, much as those analysed by Schorer do, and contribute to the novel's feeling and ambience, just as 'vain spirit', 'serious spirit', 'conscience', 'penance', 'mortification' and 'true contrition' also do. Phrases such as 'strict adherence to truth and principle' and 'strict rule of right' have the same effect. Also noteworthy is the word 'evil,' which appears often in *Emma* and suggests a theological framework that was behind the social one and to which the above buried metaphors can be connected. So while God is not present in *Emma*, as Page says, a religious influence is present. The influence of Evangelicalism carried over from *Mansfield Park* to *Emma*, contributing to the vocabulary and atmosphere of both novels.

It might also be said that when Emma achieved a 'knowledge of herself' she was realising a goal that, while consistent with classical, eighteenth-century values, was also commensurate with the Christian idea of self-inspection. The reader becomes involved with the heroine because of her repeated errors; realising how she persists in going astray one wants her to mend her ways, but realises that she can do so only if she understands herself. One reason for Austen's way of treating the self-inspection theme was her own experience, her own inner conflict, her awareness of her two sides, and the long self-analysis that resulted from that awareness. This aspect of Austen's experience was connected to the religious conditions that influenced her thought and led to an internal change that, in a sense, was a conversion. The buried metaphors in *Emma* can be seen against this part of her life, just as Emma's self-inspection can be related to Austen's own examination of herself.

The reader enters into Anne Elliot's interior life in a completely different way than with Emma Woodhouse, not through the heroine's mistakes, but through her suffering. What the reader realises, and this in part is what makes Anne Elliot one of Austen's supreme creations, is that she grew morally through her trying and difficult experience. Completely unlike the other members of her family, and more than any one else in the novel, she had an immense capacity to sympathise with the difficulties of others. Also, her self-control and internal resources set her apart from shallow types such as Louisa Musgrove.

Mrs. Smith is another character who revealed the inner deepening that resulted from hardship and personal anguish. She was very different from Anne, both before and after the reversals that cast her from a position in the fashionable world to a dreary building in Bath, where she was confined to a 'noisy parlour, and a dark bedroom behind'. Her health was gone and her husband was dead. 'She had been used to affluence,—it was gone.' (P,154) Without a 'child to connect her with life and happiness' and with 'no relations to assist in the arrangement of perplexed affairs' she was isolated and thrown on to her severely limited resources. The strain had almost been more than she could bear. 'There had been a time, Mrs. Smith told [Anne], when her spirits had nearly failed.' (P,154) But somehow she managed to get a firm grip on herself, survive the crisis, and settle into her present mode of life. In doing so she obviously gave up a great deal, but also received compensations that helped offset the losses. Before, she 'had lived very much in the world', (P,153) belonging to a 'thoughtless, gay set, without any strict rules of conduct'. (P,201) Her goal in life had been to live for 'enjoyment'; the reality was a life of 'dissipation'.

As Mrs. Smith described her former life Anne sensed that, difficult as her present circumstances were in the external, material, physical sense, her world was by no means desolate. In adjusting to a loss of husband, wealth and social position she had to develop internally and was the beneficiary for having done so.

> Anne had reason to believe that she had moments only of languor and depression, to hours of occupation and enjoyment. How could it be?—She watched—observed—reflected—and finally determined that this was not a case of fortitude or of resignation only.—A submissive spirit might be patient, a strong understanding would supply resolution, but here was something more; here was that elasticity of mind, that disposition to be comforted, that power of turning readily from evil to good, and of finding employment which carried her out of herself, which was from Nature alone. (P,154)

At this point in the text Austen did something very interesting. After saying that Mrs. Smith's ability to overcome her difficulties came 'from Nature alone' she wrote in the next sentence that 'It was the choicest gift of Heaven'. To say that Mrs. Smith's elasticity and resourcefulness came from 'Nature alone' was one explanation; to say that 'It was the choicest gift of Heaven' was a very different one. Austen portrayed a woman who underwent some trying moments, nearly broke under the weight of hardship, but managed to adjust to her circumstances. There was nothing specifically religious about such an experience; yet Austen seems to have viewed this woman's response to her problems in a way that, at some level, was religious. First, she described her capacity to accept her condition and even, by 'finding employment which carried her out of herself', to benefit from the effort. Then she explained the matter differently, religiously. She did so by saying first that 'It was the choicest gift of Heaven', and then that 'Anne viewed her friend as one of those instances in which, by a merciful appointment, it seems designed to counterbalance almost every other want.'

So there are two explanations for Mrs. Smith. In one she overcame her difficulties through 'fortitude', 'resignation', and 'resolution'; in the other 'by a merciful appointment' and as 'the choicest gift of Heaven'. The latter reason is obviously religious, while the former is apparently human and secular. In fact, even those parts of the passage stressing Mrs. Smith's 'strong understanding' and ability to face adversity are not without a religious dimension. What Austen reveals in her description of this unfortunate woman, who turned 'evil to good', was an orientation that was rooted in one of the most fundamental of Christian traditions. In that tradition life is seen as a spiritual struggle, with one's two sides, the higher and lower, staking its claims on the individual who could hope to find victory even in defeat. The fallen, the stricken, those cut down from their high stations, could emerge as winners. Defeat at the hands of the world could be spiritual salvation.

Behind Mrs. Smith and, to an extent Anne Elliot, lay the dualistic tradition of Paul, Augustine, Jerome and Erasmus, not the monistic morality of Aristotle and Shaftesbury. This is not to say that Austen was uninfluenced by the latter tradition. Undoubtedly she was. It might well be that a Shaftesburyian morality was dominant in the Juvenilia and early novels, but in time new tendencies began to appear, tendencies that led to such a character as Mrs. Smith, who turned 'evil into good' through a 'fortitude' and 'resignation' that 'carried her out of herself'. This woman, who had suffered so much, was sounder in her present state than she had been before, when she lived in the world and belonged to a 'thoughtless, gay set, without any strict rules of conduct'. As she said, 'We lived for enjoyment. I think differently now; time and sickness, and sorrow, have given me other notions.' (P,201)

This reveals the impact on Austen of the new religious currents that passed through her age. The above passage, describing Mrs. Smith's former, dissipated way of life and her subsequent correction, does not sound unlike Wilberforce and Hannah More. Moreover, the idea of internal conflict and moral choice echoes sentiments that were commonplace in Evangelical writings of the time. What Austen demonstrates in *Persuasion*, just as she had in *Mansfield Park* and *Emma*, is a new frame of mind, a different orientation, way of viewing life and system of morality. Religiously, Austen's last three novels are of a piece.

The first three novels indicate Austen's state of mind and outlook before she came under the influence of Evangelicalism. The world of those novels is that of the eighteenth century; it is occupied by clergymen who lived a civilised existence away from their congregations or were pious in a way that made them offensive. This world was disrupted by the French Revolution. Fearful of Jacobinism, Evangelicals tried to bring about reform as a way to avoid ruin, thereby introducing a wave of solemnity into English life. Austen, being Austen, having the particular ironic tendencies that gave her mind such a distinctive cast, moving within a moral framework that was monistic and Shaftesburyian, and suspicious of excessive displays of feeling and exhibitions of zeal, was uneasy over the new religious views. At the same time, or perhaps it should be said with time, she was attracted to Evangelicalism. She went through an emotional and spiritual crisis herself as she became distressed over certain of her own tendencies. This led to a new reflectiveness, self-awareness, and in a sense, conversion.

A record of that change can be found in the last three novels. While *Mansfield Park* is the most visibly religious of those novels, the vocabulary, themes and characters of *Emma* and *Persuasion* reveal Evangelicalism's continuing influence on Austen. One particularly interesting way to see that influence is in a passage in *Persuasion*, when Anne Elliot became aware of the 'bad habits' of her cousin, Mr. William Walter Elliot. For this careless young man 'Sunday travelling had been a common thing . . . there had been a period of his life (and probably not a short one) when he had been, at least, careless on all serious matters.' (P,161) That Catherine Morland, or any of the early heroines, would have felt this way about travelling on Sunday is unimaginable. But they lived in a different world than Anne Elliot. As one historian has said, 'Jacobinism, which abolished the Christian calendar in France, helped to establish the Victorian Sabbath in England.'[25] He correctly cites the above passage in *Persuasion* as evidence of this change. To read Austen's last three novels is to enter into the life of a society that was becoming Victorian long before Victoria became queen, and long before the term Victorian came into use. It was a society that believed that a choice between reform and ruin was necessary, and chose to reform.

4 Women and the Family

Just as Jane Austen's creative life, the period stretching from the Juvenilia to the last, unfinished novel, was an era of political upheaval, military conflict and religious ferment, so too was it an important epoch in the history of feminism. That a heated debate over the position of women began in the 1790s was no accident; rather, it was a logical outcome of short and long-term developments that came together at this time. Slowly but surely a feminist movement began to unfold in the eighteenth century, as it was argued that woman was not the intellectual inferior of man, that the Bible did not decree her unequal, that her sphere should not be confined to the home and its attendant duties, and that her position as wife should not make her the subordinate of her husband.[1] While these views were dutifully and ably set forth, they did not have a terribly large impact.[2] But with the publication in 1792 of Mary Wollstonecraft's *A Vindication of the Rights of Woman* the feminist movement quickly gained strength and found new adherents. What made this book so timely was its obvious relevance to the larger ideological questions that were being discussed as a result of the French Revolution. The surge of interest in the position of women led to a heated debate; what would be decisive in determining its outcome was the inevitable connection in many minds between the feminist cause and political radicalism, which also opposed traditional relationships, stood for sweeping social change and took the side of oppressed groups.

Eventually, those favouring the rights of the individual and the socially oppressed and supporting a revolutionary ideology were overwhelmed by the conservative opposition; so too were those who wanted to redefine the position of women. The same forces that gave rise to a new and ideologically conservative Tory party, that made the upper and middle classes, in one of the key terms of the time, more responsible, that made the lower classes more tractable, and that made Methodism and Evangelicalism such powerful influences on English life also relegated woman to a conventional sphere, that of wife and mother. Victorian woman was born, so to speak, during the time of the French Revolution and Napoleonic Wars, and she appeared in part in response to feminist arguments that threatened the accepted relationship between men and women. The short-term result of the feminist effort was to narrow woman's role and underline her traditional position. All of this happened while Jane Austen was writing her novels. That Austen was concerned with woman's position is clear to any reader of the novels. What form that concern took will be the subject of this chapter.

There is not one reference to Wollstonecraft in Austen's writings, either her fiction or correspondence. Since most of Austen's letters have been lost or were destroyed it is entirely possible that she did comment on this controversial author; if so, her remarks undoubtedly expressed censure or disapproval. As the daughter of a Tory country parson, Austen did not favour the new, radical ideas that were so much in the air. Writing to Cassandra in 1801, she made an oblique but clearly negative reference to William Godwin,[3] one of the leading radicals of the day, a key figure in a circle that had included Wollstonecraft, and at the end of Wollstonecraft's life was her husband.

Like any well-read and reasonably informed person of her time, Austen would have associated Wollstonecraft with the republican cause. A year before writing *A Vindication of the Rights of Woman*, Wollstonecraft wrote *A Vindication of the Rights of Man*, in reply to Burke's *Reflections on the French Revolution*, and in support of her friend, Richard Price. Taking a firm stand in favour of the democratic and humanitarian principles of the Revolution, Wollstonecraft argued for the rights of all people and denounced such abuses as the slave trade and the economic domination of the landlord class. In championing the rights of man she was working towards the position that she would take in *A Vindication of the Rights of Woman*. Just as she believed that men had inalienable rights, so did women; just as she opposed social inequality, so did she oppose sexual inequality. Already dissatisfied with the position of women before 1789, Wollstonecraft, in the first, idealistic years of the Revolution, applied its democratic, libertarian concepts to her own sex.[4]

This is why Austen would have disapproved *A Vindication of the Rights of Woman*, not because she disagreed with Wollstonecraft's feminist views. In fact, on one point after another Austen's fiction takes a similar position to Wollstonecraft, commenting unfavourably on girl's boarding schools, female accomplishments, the triviality of female values, the female practice of coming out, the legal position of women and the manifold abuses that were related to marriage.[5]

One of Wollstonecraft's main concerns was middle-class women, those belonging or hoping to belong to genteel society. As the daughter of a silk weaver, Wollstonecraft at most grew up on the fringe of that society. Through acquaintances with several middle-class families, and even more as a companion of one woman employer and governess for another, she did know the world of female gentility that she criticised. But she knew it as an outsider. In criticising that same world Austen did so as an insider, as a member and participant, as someone who observed the rituals and ceremonies of her class and as a female who internalised many of its values. With Oxford University connections on both sides of her family, she grew up in an atmosphere of respectability. All of her brothers found decent stations in life and one inherited two estates of considerable size.[6] As a young man this brother went on the Grand Tour. The Austen family vactioned at one of the most modish of spots, Bath, which is where Jane, Cassandra and her parents moved at the time of her father's retirement. The Austens gave private theatricals, an activity confined to 'better' circles. A prominent figure at some of the theatricals was Eliza de Feuillide, who undoubtedly played a major role in transmitting genteel values to Austen. Eliza's letters reveal a woman who was greatly interested in fashions, seems especially to have been in her element at parties or while entertaining, and obviously enjoyed the company of men, whose attention she considered herself fully capable of winning with her arsenal of female skills. The influence on Austen of this stylish, ambitious, fun-loving, energetic, vivacious and aristocratic woman was considerable. Discussing the two Austen sisters in a letter written in 1792, when Jane was seventeen, Eliza said, 'still my heart gives the preference to Jane, whose kind partiality to me requires a return of the same nature.'[7]

Both Austen daughters went to boarding schools, and both were great novel readers. While the sons, at least James and Henry, received a classical education, Jane and Cassandra read the modern literature that in the genteel code was appropriate to their sex. Austen was definite in stating that she did not know classical literature.[8] During her lifetime female writers were under certain social pressures to remain anonymous, which Austen herself did until her brother Henry revealed her identity to a friend, after which she wrote under her own name. Throughout her novels she avoided politics, in compliance with the manners of the time. In many obvious, outer ways Austen is very much in the pattern of female novelists whose heroines occupied the centre of the stage but lived highly circumscribed lives.[9] These heroines made no effort to leave their proper female sphere but spent their time visiting neighbours, attending dances, going to Bath, and generally observing the rituals that were appropriate to their class and sex.

As a girl Austen went regularly to Assembly Hall dances at Basingstoke and Bath, as well as in Kent, while visiting her brother Edward. At those dances she saw the genteel females of her class in full plumage; she also poured a full measure of time, money and effort into preparing herself for them. As a girl of twenty she said, in the context of a ball, that 'all my money is spent buying white gloves and silk persian'. (L,3) Later in the same year she wrote that 'I have had my new gown made up, and it really makes a very superb surplice. I am sorry to say that my new coloured gown is very much washed out, though I charged everybody to take great care of it.' (L,9) A letter written in 1798 indicates unhappiness over her clothes. '*I* am determined to buy a handsome (gown) whenever I can, and I am so tired and ashamed of half my present stock, that I even blush at the sight of the wardrobe which contains them.' (L,44)

Liking to think of herself as fashionable, she wrote that she had 'a very good supper, and the greenhouse was illuminated in a very elegant manner'. (L,2) She regularly described her evenings to Cassandra, and looked forward to news of her sister's balls, the details of which she sometimes predicted. The letters are filled with information about suppers, visiting neighbours, exchanging civilities, vacationing at watering places, working for some charitable cause, sewing, drawing or practising the piano—in other words, doing the very things that were usual for genteel females. On one occasion, after having 'a very gay evening', she returned home 'by Moonlight' with 'everything quite in Stile'. (L,13) Her family was properly protective; when she wanted to travel to London by stage her brother Frank made arrangements for a private coach. Austen clearly had certain of the expectations that were usual in middle-class society. When an acquaintance married a husband whose economic position forbade her from keeping a servant she remarked: 'What a prodigious innate love of virtue she must have, to marry under the circumstances!' (L,26) She found life at Steventon threadbare compared to the much finer surroundings of Godmersham, her brother's estate in Kent. 'People get so horribly poor & economical in this part of the World, that I have no patience with them.—Kent is the only place for happiness, Everybody is rich there.' (L,41)

The first extant letter described an 'exceeding good ball' (L,1) that she had attended the night before. After saying that she had gone in her brother's carriage, she mentioned the various young men that she had danced with, and discussed 'a very gentlemanlike, good-looking, pleasant young man' that she seemed to care for especially, with whom she had danced 'at the three last balls', and expected to see at another ball 'next Friday'. (L,2) Such descriptions are common. Later in the same month she wrote, 'Our party to Ashe to-morrow night will consist of Edward Cooper, James (for a ball is nothing without *him*), Buller, who is now staying with us, and I look forward with great impatience to it, as I rather expect to receive an offer from my friend in the course of the evening.' (L,5) In September, 1796, she wrote to Cassandra that 'I shall be extremely anxious to hear the Event of your Ball', adding that '*We* were at a Ball on Saturday I assure you.' (L,11) These are the remarks of a young woman aged twenty-one who obviously considered local dances important social occasions, and attended them for the typical reasons: to be among friends, to show off her newest articles of clothing, to dance, which she clearly enjoyed, and to meet young men, whose offers she awaited as anxiously as the next female.

A somewhat different tone crept into Austen's letters in 1798, when she wrote that 'I expect a very stupid Ball, there will be nobody worth dancing with, & nobody worth talking to but Catherine.' (L,40) As it turned out, she enjoyed herself more than she expected, as indicated in a letter written six days later, in which she described the dance as 'thin but not unpleasant':

There were twenty dances, and I danced them all, and without any fatigue. I was glad to find myself capable of dancing so much, and with so much satisfaction as I did; from my slender enjoyment of the Ashford balls (as assemblies for dancing) I had not thought myself equal to it, but in cold weather and with few couples I fancy I could just as well dance for a week together as for half an hour. (L,44)

Of the eight young men at the dance she had to entice one, a Mr. Calland, on to the floor.

> [He] appeared as usual with his hat in his hand, and stood behind Catherine and me to be talked to and abused for not dancing. We teased him, however, into it at last. I was very glad to see him after so long a separation, and he was altogether rather the genius and flirt of the evening. (L,43)

She was less fortunate at another ball a few weeks later:

> I do not think I was very much in request. People were apt not to ask me till they could not help it; one's consequence, you know, varies so much at times without any particular reason. There was one gentleman, an officer of the Cheshire, a very good-looking young man, who, I was told, wanted very much to be introduced to me; but as he did not want it quite enough to take much trouble in effecting it, we never could bring it about. (L,51–2)

Later in the same month she danced with an 'odd set of partners', none of whom appear to have been interesting. While 'I had a very pleasant evening . . . you will probably find out that there was no particular reason for it; but I do not think it worth while to wait for enjoyment until there is some real opportunity for it.' (L,56) Austen did not always accept an unsuccessful dance with this type of resignation. In November, 1800—she was now twenty-four—she described an evening at which 'There were only twelve dances, of which I danced nine, & was merely prevented from dancing the rest for want of a partner.' (L,91) After listing the names of her partners, the last of whom, a Mr. Matthew, 'I liked the best of my little stock', (L,91) she gave vent to irritation in one of the most extraordinary passages in all her correspondence. This was the letter that described women with broad faces, fat necks and protruding stomachs, husbands who were pink, fat, ugly and goutish, and girls that did not look well, had large noses, bad breath and white necks that made them resemble queer animals.[10]

In trying to understand this eruption of ill-feeling it should be noted that previous letters indicated that young men had scarcely sought her out at dances. How she fared at the age of twenty-four or twenty-five as compared to a few years earlier is conjectural, but the fact is that her letters reveal a quite different perception. As a twenty-year-old she saw herself as a successful participant in these social rituals, whereas later letters evidence a definite sense of being neglected or even rejected. It is entirely possible that her letters over this five-year period do reflect the actual circumstances of her position. A twenty-five-year-old woman would not, under ordinary circumstances, have had as much hope on the marriage market as a girl of twenty. That outcroppings of hostility occurred as she described an unsuccessful ball could well indicate her reading certain signals only too clearly.

She did not direct her criticism just at individuals, but at the rituals themselves. The rounds, activities and ceremonies that had served as a reasonable and acceptable outlet for her time and energy came to be unsatisfactory. When she dressed herself for a ball in 1801 it would seem that she was not expecting to be admired, and hardly went for that reason. Her description of the party indicates that she went not to participate, to exchange repartees or seek out fashionable, attractive young people but to observe the occasion from a distance, with detachment, and as if she expected it to be tedious. 'Before tea, it was rather a dull affair, but then the before tea did not last long, for there was only one dance, danced by four couple.—Think of four couple surrounded by about one hundred people, dancing in the upper Rooms at Bath! After tea we *cheered up*.' (L,127) To occupy herself she followed the movements of 'an Adultress' who 'has the same defect of baldness as her sister's', and watched a woman who 'thought herself obliged . . . to run around the room after her drunken Husband'. (L,128) Continuing the same letter, but writing on the next day, she described 'Another stupid party last night', in which she brutally caricatured the guests. This is the letter that says 'I cannot anyhow continue to find people agreeable' and mentioned a Miss Langley, who was 'like any other short girl with a broad nose & wide mouth, fashionable dress, & exposed bosom', and Admiral Stanhope, 'a gentlemanlike Man, but then his legs are too short, & his tail too long'. (L,129)

By 1801 the letters reveal an irritation and depression that undoubtedly reflected the unhappiness that Austen felt living in Bath. One result was a sense of boredom that accompanied the ordinary happenings of daily life, as after a visit to some friends:

> We spend our time here as quietly as usual. One long morning visit is what generally occurs, & such a one took place yesterday. We went to Baugherst. The place is not so pretty as I

expected . . . The house seemed to have all the comforts of little Children, dirt & litter. Mr. Dyson as usual looked wild, & Mrs. Dyson as usual looked big.—Mr. Bramston called here the morning before,—et voila tout. (L,121)

A few months later, in May, 1801, she described some recent events, sometimes appearing weary with the activities and sometimes weary if not cross with herself.

My adventures since I wrote last, have not been very numerous; but such as they are, they are much at your service.—We met not a creature at Mrs. Lillingstone's & yet were not so very stupid as I expected, which I attribute to my wearing my new bonnet & being in good looks. (L,126–7)

She attended a party a few days later that 'was not quite so stupid as the two preceding parties here'. (L,131) A 'grand walk' which had been postponed was finally 'fixed for Yesterday, & was accomplished in a very striking manner'. Everyone but a certain friend backed out, so she and the friend went alone. This person, a Mrs. Chamberlayne, was a vigorous walker, but 'As to Agreeableness, she is much like other people.' That evening two 'civil, and not too genteel' female acquaintances paid a visit. While it was 'the fashion to think them both very detestable . . . I cannot utterly abhor them, especially as Miss Holder owns that she has no taste for Music'. (L,132) Her one saving grace, it seems, was that she was not accomplished. Looking forward to the next evening, Austen said 'We are to have a tiny party here . . . I hate tiny parties.' (L,132)

There might have been a measure of self-dislike in Austen's feelings toward people whose ways must have reminded her of herself. Had she not moved within the genteel world, accepted many of its conventions and values, and above all wanted to achieve the type of female success that was normally sought she would hardly have reacted so strongly. What we see, then, in letters written after 1800, as Austen moved into her mid and late twenties, is the transformation of an 'insider', meaning a person with the outlook of her class, into an 'outsider', a person who, at least in certain respects, became a critic of genteel female society and its typical rituals and ceremonies.

In turning to Austen's criticism of female gentility in her fiction I shall first treat that fiction as a whole, rather than examine differences in her position from novel to novel. My purpose, at this point, is to show that from the earliest work to the latest Austen found fault with certain facets of female life in her own middle-class society.

Already in 'Catharine' Austen attacked one of the bastions of gentility, the female accomplishments. One of the characters, Camilla Stanley, had been 'attended by the most capital masters' for twelve years, from age six to the previous spring. While this girl was 'not deficient in Abilities' and her 'temper was by Nature good' she had never, thanks to her education, developed her mind:

> those Years which ought to have been spent in the attainment of useful knowledge and Mental Improvement, had been all bestowed in learning Drawing, Italian and Music, more especially the latter, and she now united to these Accomplishments, an Understanding unimproved by reading and a Mind totally devoid either of Taste or Judgement. (MW,198)

Austen was not saying that any of these accomplishments—drawing, Italian or music—was wrong, or that any of the other accomplishments were either. Heroines in her novels played the piano, sang, drew, did needlework, and danced. What Austen criticised was not the accomplishments themselves but the female attitudes that, owing to the context in which they were acquired, were too often present. Girls were not taught these skills to develop their intellect; as female education was not regarded as intrinsically valuable it produced girls whose minds were ill-formed and whose values were shallow.

In *Emma* Austen described a female boarding school and showed the type of girl it could produce. Mrs. Goddard's school was 'a real, honest, old-fashioned Boarding-school', not the type that combined 'new principles and new systems—and where young ladies for enormous pay might be screwed out of health and into vanity'. (E,21) In this modest school, run by 'a plain, motherly kind of woman, who had worked hard in her youth', there were few of the pretensions of the more ambitious establishments. It was a place where 'a reasonable quantity of accomplishments were sold at a reasonable price, and where girls might be sent to be out of the way and scramble themselves into a little education, without any danger of coming back prodigies'. (E,21-2) As plain and home-spun as Mrs. Goddard's school was, it was a boarding school: for a certain price female accomplishments could be acquired, girls were temporarily out of their parents' way, and they picked up a little bit of learning, but not too much. The idea was to put girls in these schools to be rid of them and take them back with enough accomplishments to be respectable, but not to give them a solid education or develop independence of mind.

Another aspect of the genteel, female life that Austen criticised was the importance given to clothes. Her treatment of this theme is related to that of female education; the false values that accompanied the female accomplishment encouraged girls—indeed, taught them—to stress appearances. Camilla Stanley, the girl in 'Catharine' whose accomplishments we have already seen, is a fine example. After describing the unfortunate effects of her accomplishments Austen said that her mind was shallow and that 'All her ideas were towards the Elegance of her appearance, the fashion of her dress, and the Admiration she wished them to excite. She professed a love of Books without Reading, was Lively without Wit, and generally good humoured without Merit.' (MW,198) The connection between this girl's interest in clothes and her indifference to books—in other words to her defective education—became apparent when Catherine asked her, in the next minute, if she had read Charlotte Smith's novels. After making a few inept, superficial comments Camilla abruptly changed the topic of conversation, announcing that 'We are going to the Lakes this Autumn, and I am quite Mad with Joy.' (MW,199) Now she was able to discuss a subject that was more to her taste. 'I assure you that I have done nothing for this last month but plan what clothes I should take with me, and I have at last determined to take very few indeed besides my travelling dress . . . for I intend in case we should fall in with any races, or stopt at Matlock or Scarborough, to have something made for the occasion.' (MW,199) What a fine touch it was to have this girl, who thought so much about clothes, decide to travel lightly—so that, if she were to appear at certain fashionable spots during the journey, she could have some new ones 'made for the occasion'.

Mrs. Allen in *Northanger Abbey* is an example of a middle-aged woman who was empty-headed and overly concerned with appearances. She had 'the air of a gentlewoman, a great deal of quiet, inactive good temper, and a trifling turn of mind . . . Dress was her passion.' (NA,20) Another, and wiser middle-aged woman in the same novel was Catherine's aunt, who told her that 'Dress is at all times a frivolous distinction, and excessive solicitude about it often destroys its own aim.' (NA,73) Catherine was unable to follow this advice, lying awake at night thinking about a new gown. As if to drive home her point about clothes, Austen said that perhaps a man's advice, such as that of Catherine's brother, would have been more successful, 'for man only can be aware of the insensibility of man towards a new gown'. (NA,74) What this sentence reveals is Austen's view that females' main reason for concerning themselves so much with clothes was to please men, and that they were mistaken in doing so. Men scarcely noticed or cared; women would be mortified if they knew 'how little the heart of man is affected by what is costly or new in their attire'. (NA,74)

Austen clearly felt that genteel females cared too much about appearances and clothes, making them their own worst enemies, and she objected to the countless influences and pressures placed on girls to make attracting men their main goal in life. From beginning to end her novels are filled with flirtatious females, all of whom are flawed for that reason. Typically, they are vain, shallow, selfish and calculating. As well-known as the errors of such females as Isabella Thorpe, Lucy Steele, Lydia Bennet, Mary Crawford and Louisa Musgrove are, it will be useful to look at one of Austen's characters, Caroline Bingley, whom we shall observe in just one scene, when Elizabeth Bennet went to Netherfield to see after her ailing sister, Jane. After dinner Elizabeth and Jane joined Caroline and Mrs. Hurst in the drawing room, where they had an hour of conversation. Before Bingley and Darcy arrived, Caroline's and Mrs. Hurst's

> powers of conversation were considerable. They could describe an entertainment with accuracy, relate an anecdote with humour, and laugh at their acquaintance with spirit.
>
> But when the gentlemen entered, Jane was no longer the first object. Miss Bingley's eyes were instantly turned towards Darcy . . . (PP,54)

When Darcy started to read, Caroline picked out a book, but her 'attention was quite as much engaged in watching [his] progress through *his* book, as in reading her own'. (PP,55) Unable to strike up a conversation and bored with her book, she declared that there 'was no enjoyment like reading', hoping to catch Darcy's attention. The ruse failed, so she turned to her brother and brought up the question of the ball that he had been discussing. Darcy kept reading, so Caroline decided on another strategy. She got up, started walking about the room, and invited Elizabeth to join her, which she did. When 'Mr. Darcy looked up' Caroline asked him to join their promenade. After he declined, a discussion between Caroline and Elizabeth followed that perfectly revealed the chasm that separated these two women. By turns Caroline was coy and mentally helpless, professing to be unable, or unable, to understand one of Darcy's remarks. When Darcy himself explained the meaning Caroline said, in her archly female way, 'Oh! shocking! . . . I never heard anything so abominable. How shall we punish him for such a speech?' (PP, 56–7) When Elizabeth suggested to Caroline that she punish him by teasing him this genteel—and designing—young lady tried her female best to achieve her goal through flattery. 'But upon my honour I do *not* [think Darcy should be teased]. I do assure you that my intimacy has not yet taught me *that*. Teaze calmness of temper and presence of mind! No, no—I feel he may defy us there, and as to laughter, we will not expose ourselves, if you please, by attempting to laugh without a subject.' (PP,57) This speech was the capstone of Caroline Bingley's strategy. All evening long her goal had been to win Darcy's attention. Ever resourceful, she discovered an expedient, after several failures, that worked. Finally she was able to use her female skill, which she did in telling Elizabeth that she had achieved a certain measure of intimacy with Darcy, but not so much that she could make light of him. At this point her ploy was to imply to Darcy that they were on close terms; having done this she played on what she thought were his male susceptibilities, saying that he was no man to be trifled with, with his calm temper and presence of mind. He could not be laughed at, she said, because there was nothing laughable about him—and besides, any such efforts might arouse his defiance.

Accomplished young ladies whose main goal was to please men with their skills and catch their attention with clothes did not develop their minds. Superficial and without mental resources, they were fated, once they achieved their objective of marriage, to a life of emptiness. Lacking independent interests, they were typically pathetic and often unpleasant, as if resentful and defensive over their situation but without understanding why. In *Sense and Sensibility* Lady Middleton's principal role was to humour her children, so much so that 'these were [her] only resources'. (SS,32) Unable to exchange ideas in conversation, or uninterested in doing so, she always took one of her sons to the Dashwoods, 'by way of provision for discourse'. This meant that whoever was present had to 'inquire his name and age, admire his beauty, and ask him questions which his mother answered for him', or 'determine whether the boy were most like his father or mother'. (SS,31) Lady Middleton did not care for the Dashwood girls, 'Because they neither flattered herself nor her children . . . and because they were fond of reading, she fancied them satirical.' (SS,246) The very fact that Elinor and Marianne had minds of their own made her nervous and uneasy and suspect that they were critical of her idleness. She was, in fact, 'ashamed of doing nothing before them'. (SS, 247) Mrs. Grant in *Mansfield Park* was another woman whose life was hollow for lack of interests, and whose genteel occupations failed to fill her void. Her plight was that of the married woman who had no children. 'Mrs. Grant having by this time run through the usual resources of ladies residing in the country without a family of children; having more than filled her favourite sitting-room with pretty furniture, and made a choice collection of plants and poultry, was very much in want of some variety at home.' (MP,41)

Mrs. Elton in *Emma* was an accomplished young lady who was just settling into married life. Anxious to appear fashionable, she wanted to enter into all of the social activities of Highbury: 'I see what a life I am to lead among you. Upon my word we shall be absolutely dissipated. We really seem quite the fashion. If this is living in the country, it is nothing very formidable. From next Monday to Saturday, I assure you we have not a disengaged day!' (E,290) Considering herself fully able to meet the rigorous demands of her new life, she remarked that: 'A woman with fewer resources than I have, need not have been at a loss.' The reality was that this ambitious, presumptuous and affected woman was sorely deficient in resources and was bound to neglect her accomplishments, as had happended with her sister, Selina. In describing her sister and some female friends she was indicating the direction that her future was certain to take. 'Married women', she said, are a 'sad story', for 'They are but too apt to give up music.' While she felt that there was 'no danger, surely', that she would follow their example, she trembled when she thought about the others. Selina had given up music completely, as had her other friends who had married. 'Upon my word, it is enough to put one in a fright. I used to be quite angry with Selina . . .' (E,277) Then, as if to justify her neglect of the piano, and in fact indicating how she would follow her sister's and friends' pattern, she remarked that 'a married woman has many

things to call to her attention. I believe I was half an hour this
morning shut with my housekeeper.' (E,278) Emma, accurately
reading the message, understood that Mrs. Elton was 'determined
upon neglecting her music'. (E,278) With no solid, independent
interests and anxious always to strike the right pose, cultivate the
right people, and observe all the genteel civilities, her married life
was bound to be as frivolous and empty as her previous life had
been. In fact, one was the ideal preparation for the other, with its
superficial education in the female accomplishments, its disregard
the serious mental occupations, and its false values.

As vain and shallow as Mrs. Elton was, she had achieved her
great goal in life when she married Mr. Elton. In discussing the
marriage Emma and Harriet Smith looked at it first from the side of
the husband and then the wife:

> 'I am not at all surprized [said Harriet] that he should have
> fallen in love.'
> 'Oh! no—there is nothing to surprize one at all.—A pretty
> fortune; and she came in his way.'
> 'I dare say,' returned Harriet, sighing again, 'I dare say she
> was very much attached to him.'
> 'Perhaps she might; but it is not every man's fate to marry the
> woman who loves him best. Miss Hawkins perhaps wanted a
> home, and thought this the best offer she was likely to have.'
> (E,271)

What this dialogue reveals is the hard, material and grim business
of the marriage market. Throughout Austen's novels girls were
educated, trained, and conditioned socially and psychologically to
make a favourable impression on the young men they met at places
such as the Pump Room at Bath or the Netherfield Ball.[11] The
elegant, well-turned out girl had to perform in her female role with
the greatest skill, demonstrating the necessary degree of ease and
deference, as she went through such rituals as the dance, smiling in
her most beguiling way, bowing demurely to her partner, and
between numbers finding the apt, correct words over tea. Not to
succeed, not to be captivating, was to fail in the most urgent of
female missions. Winning a husband was essential if a girl wished to
occupy a fully respectable social position and, in the overwhelming
majority of cases, to enjoy the material benefits of her class. Not to be
married—to be a spinster—was to face a certain degree of social

opprobium, it was to live, in most instances, with one's family under conditions that were bound to cause discomfort, and it was to forfeit the economic advantages that went to the woman who became a wife. The marriage market was an active, thriving place of business where interested parties continually met to display their wares, enter into negotiations, and move towards, or be deflected from, the final, contractual stage. Beneath the glitter, refinement, and stylised movement of the Assembly Hall dance was the underlying reality of young men and women determining their economic future as, literally and figuratively, they went through their various steps.

This view of courting does not agree, at least in some respects, with a narrative pattern that runs through all of Austen's novels. None of the heroines entered into the state of matrimony for mercenary reasons, but all of them improved their material position through marriage, and most did so considerably. The point is that, complicated as the business of courting was with the heroes and heroines, it was conducted on a quite different level than was usual among other male and female characters. All of the novels end with the hero and heroine uniting in what would appear to have been perfect bliss. What is interesting is the contrast between the Cinderella endings of the novels and the courting that took place in other quarters. Also striking is the life of marital happiness that opened—or seemed to open—before the heroes and heroines, as the novels ended, and the unsatisfactory if not deeply unhappy marriages that tend to be the norm. This contrast makes one wonder about Austen's view of marriage.

There can be no question that as a young woman, say through her early twenties, she looked forward to and enjoyed the various ceremonies where she met men, whose attention she clearly sought. Years later, Mrs. Mitford said that she was 'the prettiest, silliest, most affected, husband-hunting butterfly that she ever remembers'. While Mrs. Mitford had left the neighbourhood by the time Austen was old enough to 'hunt' husbands, she did have friends there, whom she might well have visited and from whom she could have received this type of information. In any event, Austen had several romances and received one marriage proposal. Describing one of her love affairs she wrote, at the age of twenty, that 'At length the day is come on which I am to flirt my last with Tom Lefroy, and when you receive this it will be over. My tears flow . . . at the melancholy idea.' (L,6) Later in the same year, 1796, she said: 'We went by Bifrons, & I contemplated with a melancholy pleasure, the abode of Him, on whom I once fondly doated.' (L,14) Apparently she was referring to one of the five sons of the Rev. Taylor, but nothing is known about the matter beyond this one sentence. In 1798 a friend of Mrs. Lefroy who had been courting Jane wrote that he hoped to see the Austen family again, with whom he wished to create a 'nearer interest', but was unable to so at the time. Austen interpreted his remarks to mean that the affair was over. 'This is rational enough; there is less love and more sense in it than sometimes appeared before, and I am very well satisfied. It will all go on exceedingly well, and decline away in a reasonable manner.' (L,28) According to the *Memoir*, at some unspecified time Austen met a gentleman at a 'seaside place' who was capable of winning her love:

> When they parted, he expressed his intention of soon seeing them again; and Cassandra [on whose authority the incident was described] felt no doubt as to his motives. But they never met again. Within a short time they heard of his sudden death. I believe that, if Jane ever loved, it was this unnamed gentleman.

Caroline Austen said that a Harris Bigg-Wither, the son of a neighbouring farmer and a young man of twenty-one, proposed to her in 1802, that she accepted, but that she changed her mind the next day. She would have been twenty-seven, and six years older than he. Judging from her letters one wonders if she wanted to marry. Indeed, there are reasons to suspect that she did not.

As we have seen she had every opportunity to meet young men of comparable social background and there were a number of romances, but only one engagement, which lasted less than twenty-four hours. One admirer died, but there is no evidence that the relationship was heading toward marriage. As early as 1796 Mrs. Austen, anticipating Cassandra's marriage, wrote to a friend: 'I look forward to you as a real comfort to me in my old age, when Cassandra is gone into Shropshire, & Jane—the Lord knows where.' These are the remarks of a mother who had anxieties about her twenty-one-year-old daughter in connection with marriage. Later Mrs. Austen would say that Jane and Cassandra 'were wedded to each other'.

Austen was conscious of the danger of being married. She wrote in 1798 that 'I believe I never told you that Mrs. Coulthard and Anne, late of Manydown, are both dead, and both died in childbed.' (L,29) As her sister-in-law, Mary, was pregnant at the time 'We have not regaled [her] with this news.' (L,29) The following month, after Mary's child was born, Austen said: 'Mary does not manage matters in such a way as to make me want to lay in myself.' (L,35) In 1801 she wrote: 'I must now pause to make some observation on Mrs. Heathcote's having got a little Boy; I wish her well to wear it out—& shall proceed.' (L,135) When an acquaintance, Mrs. Tilson, had a child in 1808 Austen said 'poor Woman! how can she be honestly breeding again?' (L,210) She wrote about her niece, Anna, that she was a 'Poor Animal, she will be worn out before she is thirty.—I am very sorry for her.' (L,488) After a Mrs. Deedes had another child she remarked: 'Good Mrs. Deedes!— I . . . w^d recommend to her & Mr. D. the simple regimen of separate rooms.' (L,480)

How striking the contrast was between the attention that young men lavished on young women at dances and dinners as they observed the conventions of courting that preceded offers of marriage, and the reality of marriage itself, with the risk of having children, the debilitating effects of delivery, the confinement of laying in and, then, the nuisance and noise of children, upon which Austen did remark. It was a prospect that she did not find appealing, and that made her sympathetic to the position of women. As girls they were courted in a way that she found objectionable; if they chose not to marry they were relegated to the unfortunate position of spinsterhood; if they did marry they could look forward to the multiple burdens of having children and living under their husband's authority. In 1813, when the Prince and Princess of Wales were at the height of their marital difficulties, Austen wrote: 'Poor woman, I shall support her as long as I can, because she *is* a Woman, & because I hate her Husband—but I can hardly forgive her for calling herself "attached & affectionate" to a Man whom she must detest . . .' (L,504)

In the England of 1800 the pressures to marry were enormous. In describing those pressures Austen looked at the problem primarily from the woman's point of view. One way of doing so was by revealing the attitudes and feelings of women as they considered marriage. In depicting those attitudes and feelings Austen focused attention on two particular problems: the plight of the woman who had reached an age at which she no longer considered herself a moveable commodity on the marriage market, and the competition between females for male favour. That competition was sometimes ruthless and always pathetic.

The Watsons begins with two sisters, Emma and Elizabeth Watson, riding towards a party that the former was to attend. She was nineteen and had just returned home, after spending the last fourteen years with a wealthy aunt and uncle. The uncle had died and the aunt remarried, necessitating Emma's departure. Emma's family assumed that her uncle would include her in his will, which he had not, leaving her in the same position as her sisters: her future would depend on the man she married. Elizabeth, who was twenty-eight, felt this keenly, and offered Emma advice that she hoped would help her in her search. Emma should be particularly careful of Tom Musgrave, whom she would meet at an upcoming party. 'He generally pays attention to every new girl but he is a great flirt & never means anything serious.' (MW,315) After saying that Musgrave was a 'universal favourite' and that most of the girls had been in love with him, she explained that she was the only one to escape 'with a whole heart', even though he had paid attention to her first. The reason, she continued, was that she had preferred a young man by the name of Purvis. They had been in love and every one thought a marriage was imminent, but her own sister, Penelope, whom she had trusted, 'set him against me, with a view of gaining him herself, & it ended in his discontinuing his visits & soon after marrying somebody else'. (MW,316) The result was 'the ruin of my happiness. I shall never love any man as I loved Purvis.' In spite of her bitterness Elizabeth wished that her sister was married, not to a bad man and out of spite, and not to be rid of her, but because 'we must marry'. (MW,317) As to herself, she was content with 'A little Company, & a pleasant Ball now & then', but one was not young forever, and 'my Father cannot provide for us, & it is very bad to grow old & be poor & laughed at'. (MW,317) This could be her own fate as well as that of her sisters Penelope and Margaret, both of whom had tried unsuccessfully to catch Tom Musgrave. After Penelope's failure on that front she had launched another campaign, apparently directed at an elderly asthmatic, Dr. Harding, but she maintained such secrecy that her plans were unclear.

Emma—at nineteen—was sorry about Penelope's anxieties over marriage, and did not like 'her plans or her opinions . . . To be so bent on Marriage—to pursue a Man merely for the sake of situation—is a sort of thing that shocks me.' She found her sister's views difficult to understand. While poverty was unfortunate it could not be the greatest evil to 'a woman of Education & feeling . . . I would rather be teacher at a school [and I can think of nothing worse] than marry a Man I did not like'. For her part, Elizabeth 'would rather do anything than be a teacher at a school . . . I have been at school, Emma, & know what a life they lead; *you* never have.—I should not like marrying a disagreeable man any more than yourself,—but I do not think there *are* many very disagreeable men; I think I could like any good humoured man with a comfortable income.' (MW,318) Pathetic as this woman of twenty-eight was, convinced in her quiet desperation that not many men were 'very disagreeable', and willing to settle for any good-humoured husband with a decent income, she was not the hard, ruthless competitor that Penelope was. On the contrary, resigned to her lot, she was anxious to see Emma go to the ball at the Edwardes, and was staying home to watch her ailing father in order that she could. Even as they were approaching their destination Emma tried to persuade Elizabeth to go in her place, offering to stay home with her father. 'No [said Elizabeth] . . . I would not be the means of keeping you from being seen.—You are very pretty, & it would be very hard that you should not have as fair a chance as we have all had, to make your fortune.' (MW,320) Then, after Elizabeth gave further tactical advice, and once again commented on the marriage fortunes of her sisters, the coach arrived at the Edwardes' residence. It was now time for Emma to have her turn. Perhaps she would have better luck and, if so, be in a position to assist the less fortunate members of her family, as Emma herself recognised. 'The Luck of one member of a Family is Luck to all', (MW,321) she said, fully grasping the economic importance of courtship and marriage, and not just for young women but their entire families.

Charlotte Lucas, in *Pride and Prejudice*, was another woman who had reached an age—twenty-seven—that dimmed her marital chances. She responded to her position by scaling down her expectations, which she did through rationalising a view of marriage that would enable her to accept almost any one. She felt that happiness in marriage was 'entirely a matter of chance', and that however well husband and wife knew one another at the beginning they were bound to 'grow sufficiently unlike afterwards to have their share of vexation'. That being the case, it was 'better to know as little as possible of the defects of the person with whom you are to pass your life'. (PP,23) Elizabeth Bennet's response was to say 'You make me laugh, Charlotte; but it is not sound. You know it is not sound, and that you would never act in this way yourself.' (PP,23) But she did act exactly in that way. With such a view of marriage she was prepared—unflinchingly ready—for Mr. Collins. The hard reality was that she was motivated by a 'pure and disinterested desire of an establishment . . .'. (PP,122) Her family's response to the engagement indicates the intense pressure that she was under to marry. Lady Lucas immediately thought about the economic consequences of her daughter's moving into Longbourne. Her husband, Sir William, decided that when that day came he and his wife should make an appearance at St. James's, the younger girls thought it meant that they could come out a year or two earlier than they might have otherwise, and 'the boys were relieved from their apprehension of Charlotte's dying an old maid'. (PP,122) Once Charlotte had time to think over her decision she was 'tolerably composed'. True, Mr. Collins was irksome and his attachment to her was 'imaginary', but 'still he would be her husband.—Without thinking highly of men or matrimony, marriage had always been her object.' For a 'well-educated young woman of small fortune' it was the only 'honourable provision' and it was a 'preservative from want'.

The pressures to marry that Charlotte Lucas felt from her family were not unusual. In all of Austen's novels older parties, whether parents, relatives, or friends—marriage brokers, one might call them—made girls feel the urgency of finding a husband and 'helped' them to do so. Sir John Dashwood was concerned for his two sisters only when he became interested in their marital chances. After meeting Colonel Brandon he wanted to know, in a conversation with Elinor, if he was a 'man of fortune'. Upon learning that he had a 'very good property in Dorsetshire' he went straight to the point, without even bothering to inquire about his sister's feelings.

> 'I think, Elinor, I may congratulate you in the prospect of a very respectable establishment in life.'
> 'Me, brother! what do you mean?'
> 'He likes you. I observed him narrowly, and am convinced of it. What is the amount of his fortune?'
> 'I believe about two thousand a-year.'
> 'Two thousand a-year;' and then working himself up to a pitch of enthusiastic generosity, he added, 'Elinor, I wish, with all my heart, it were *twice* as much for your sake.' (SS,223)

Elinor's explaining that Brandon had no wish of marrying her had no effect on the mercenary brother. 'A very little trouble on your side secures him . . . some of those little attentions and encouragements which ladies can so easily give, will fix him, in spite of himself.' (SS,223) His hopes for Marianne, whose illness left her physically altered, were less high. When he saw her in a weakened condition his response was to say, 'I am sorry for that. At her time of life, any thing of an illness destroys the bloom for ever!' (SS,227) Before, her 'style of beauty' was particularly attractive to men; now, considering her appearance in strictly economic terms, he doubted that her looks would allow her to 'marry a man worth more than five or six hundred a-year, at the utmost . . .'. (SS,227)

A different type of marriage broker was Mrs. Bennet in *Pride and Prejudice*, who still had a house full of unmarried daughters. Having heard that 'a young man of large fortune' (PP,3) had let Netherfield Park, she began 'thinking of his marrying' (PP,4) one of her daughters, and proceeded to take steps that would further her design. That she did so was completely in character: 'The business of her life was to get her daughters married.' (PP,5) It can be inferred that Mrs. Bennet's main goal as a girl had been to make romantic attachments and land a husband. In an interesting comment about her two youngest daughters, Catherine and Lydia, she remembered that as a girl she had been much as they were. Just as they could talk of nothing but officers, so too did she 'remember the time when I liked a red coat myself very well—and indeed so I do still at heart'. (PP,29) Here is a woman who did not mature fully, at least in the sense that she never completely overcame deeply engrained female habits, habits that made her frivolous and foolish and overly interested in men, not for herself but for her daughters, and in a way that made her irresponsible. When Lydia ran off with Wickham, Mrs. Bennet was delighted, in spite of everything. 'To know that her daughter would be married was enough.' Knowing full well that Lydia was living with a man out of wedlock, and believing that the marriage was to take place because her brother had made a settlement with Wickham, she said, 'This is delightful indeed!—She will be married! . . . How I long to see her! . . . and to see dear Wickham too! But the clothes, the wedding clothes!' (PP,306)

That the two youngest Bennet girls were overly concerned with men and overly anxious to marry is not surprising; they were just as their mother had encouraged them to be, and much as she must have been. One can well imagine these girls, years later and with daughters of marriageable age, becoming brokers on the marriage market and repeating the same dreary pattern.

Given the pressures that girls were under to find husbands, it is not surprising that their marriages were often unsuccessful. I will not examine all of the unhappy marriages in Austen's novels, but limit myself to two, both of which reveal a distinctive type of problem. While Mrs. Jennings in *Sense and Sensibility* took pride in her matchmaking, the results for her daughter, Charlotte, were anything but pleasant. It was true that her efforts helped this daughter to land a husband of considerable property and some political influence, but the marriage was miserable. When Charlotte's husband, Mr. Palmer, first appeared, his wife introduced him to Elinor and Marianne, and said that he must 'persuade the Miss Dashwoods to go to town this winter'. (SS,110) His response, which was typical of his way of relating to his wife, was to ignore her and her suggestion. He 'made no answer; and after slightly bowing to the ladies, began complaining of the weather'. That complaint led to others, all of which revealed impoliteness. Whenever his wife would make a comment he corrected her in abrupt, savage sentences that led him at one point to say that his mother-in-law was 'ill-bred'. Mrs. Jennings replied by saying that abuse her as he would, he had taken her daughter off her hands, and could not give her back. At that, 'Charlotte laughed heartily to think that her husband could not get rid of her . . . The studied indifference, insolence, and discontent of her husband gave her no pain: and when he scolded or abused her, she was highly diverted.' (SS,112) Elinor realised that Mr. Palmer's ill-treatment of his wife resulted partly from his having married a 'very silly woman' who happened to have been good-looking, but she knew that this was a 'common blunder', too much so to be the reason for his impoliteness. Mr. Palmer's harsh treatment of his wife resulted largely from his 'desire of appearing superior to other people'; (SS,112) he mistreated her to gratify his pride. Such was the position of the unfortunate Mrs. Palmer, who had been raised by a silly mother, was silly herself in a female way, and had to put up with the ill use of a husband who treated her with open contempt. Passive creature that she was, she simply took his abuse, trying to pretend that it made no difference. After all, she did have a husband.

Mr. Bennet is another husband who was stuck with a shallow, superficial wife, whose interest in men she was now indulging by trying to find husbands for her daughters. Having been captivated by 'youth and beauty', having married a girl of 'weak understanding', he soon lost all affection for his partner. 'Respect, esteem, and confidence, had vanished for ever; and all his views of domestic happiness were overthrown.' (PP,236) Long weary with such a wife, this discerning, rational man found solace in the country and in his books. Like Mr. Palmer, he abused his wife, although much less ruthlessly. His way was to amuse himself at her expense. 'To his wife he was very little otherwise indebted, than as her ignorance and folly had contributed to his amusement.' (PP,320) Eventually, Elizabeth, the one daughter that Mr. Bennet respected, had to feel that her father had been incorrect in 'exposing his wife to the contempt of her own children . . . she had never felt so strongly . . . the disadvantages of so unsuitable a marriage'. (PP,236)

Once it can be agreed that Austen was not merely reflecting the manners of the time in describing female life as she did, both before marriage and in marriage, but addressing herself to problems related to the position of women, there can be little doubt as to her taking a feminist position. And this is precisely what I believe she did. She found fault with educational practices because of their effect on girls, the sad and pathetic results of which she illustrated through one character after another. Trivial, clothes-conscious females were clearly viewed critically; Austen obviously considered the female penchant for fashions misdirected. In authorial asides she indicated that girls were deceiving themselves when they fretted about their new gowns because the men whose favour they sought scarcely noticed what they wore. That females poured so much of their time and energy into courting favour with men brought forth some of Austen's sharpest satire; what fed that satire was a definite feeling that the members of her sex who did so were demeaning themselves, not merely through their pitiable attempts to flatter the male ego but through the system of values that led them to do such a thing. These females had not developed their minds, they were shallow and superficial, and sometimes, in their pursuit of men, ruthless. And why?—because of the pressures of the marriage market. Beneath the refinement, the cultivated manners, the rituals and ceremonies that brought the opposite sexes together, was the fact that young ladies had to make successful matches. The most obvious pressures to marry came from parents, brothers and sisters, but also from 'marriage brokers' of various types as well as from the countless small and subtle influences that girls could not avoid, that were a normal part of their life and that indicated the orientation—and organisation—of society. These influences led to compromises by desperate women who would do anything for a husband, and they led to unhappy marriages. But women did have their revenge—by inflicting themselves in all of their triviality upon their husbands. Unfortunately this was a form of revenge that they were little able to enjoy. The plain truth was that women who did not develop their minds and become independent before marriage were unable to fulfill themselves in marriage; they moved in a world that was limited by their own shallowness, sometimes unaware of their folly, sometimes dimly aware of their position, at least sufficiently so to become defensive when faced with women of a different, more independent type. A novelist who presented female life in this way, and at times commented on it in the third person, was not just reflecting contemporary life and manners; she was thoughtfully and critically examining a social pattern that as a woman she found unsatisfactory.

Another way to see Austen's feminist point of view is through two of her heriones, Catherine Morland and Elizabeth Bennet, and through their relationship to the young men who courted and eventually married them. Both of these heroines have been seen as anti-Evelina types, although in a completely different sense.[12] Catherine is a burlesque of the innocent girl who enters the world, not just unaware of society's ways as Burney's heroine was but also 'her mind [was] about as ignorant and uninformed as the female mind at seventeen usually is'. (NA,18) In creating such an anti-heroine, Austen made her the intellectual inferior of the hero, Henry Tilney. Throughout the novel Henry was the voice of reason, and he understood and corrected Catherine's errors. Intelligent and well-informed as Henry was, and superior in understanding to Catherine, he could be as mistaken as she; in correcting her errors, and those of his sister, he committed his own. Further, he did so condescendingly, as a male who looked down upon mentally deficient females.

When Catherine, Henry and Elinor Tilney went for a walk outside Bath, Catherine found it difficult to follow a conversation on the picturesque, which made her 'heartily ashamed'. It was argued that her shame was misplaced. 'Where people wish to attach, they should always be ignorant . . . A woman especially, if she have the misfortune of knowing any thing, should conceal it as well as she can.' (NA,110–11) In mock serious language Austen continued her disquisition on the advantages of female ignorance. She first said that a 'sister author' had argued in favour of a beautiful girl's 'natural folly.' Then Austen explained that in fairness to men it must be admitted that while most of them find female imbecility agreeable, some, those who were 'reasonable' and 'well informed' preferred women to be—'ignorant'.

And this is how Henry, in a certain sense, did treat Catherine. Of course the passage does not read as if he were doing so deliberately, but up to a point this is what happened. Ostensibly the conversation connects with the theme with which the novel began, that of the young lady's introduction to the world. Catherine was the female innocent and Henry the sophisticated young man who pointed out her various mistakes and contributed to her 'education'. Not realising the advantages that a 'good-looking girl, with an affectionate heart and a very ignorant mind' had in 'attracting' a young man, 'she confessed that she lamented her want of knowledge' (NA,111) This led to a lecture on the picturesque, which Catherine, a hopeful scholar, followed with the closest attention. Anxious to demonstrate her understanding, she 'voluntarily rejected the whole city of Bath, as unworthy to make part of a landscape', a further sign of her ignorance. At this point, 'Delighted with her progress, and fearful of wearying her with too much wisdom at once', Henry changed the subject, moving by a series of shifts through a number of topics that led him inadvertently and accidently to politics. In avoiding politics Henry was observing the manners of the time, as defined in certain quarters. But also, he was apparently justified in doing so: Catherine's innocence, and ignorance, rendered her unfit to discuss such a subject.

When Henry arrived at politics Catherine ended the silence when she said that 'something very shocking indeed, will soon come out in London'. (NA,112) Having already examined the discussion that followed this remark there is no point in going through the passage again; my present concern is that Henry was mistaken in explaining that there was no riot in London. What made his error all the more serious was the finality and—as it were, male ruthlessness—with which he put down Elinor: 'my stupid sister has mistaken all your clearest expressions . . . Forgive her stupidity. The fears of the sister have added to the weakness of the woman; but she is by no means a simpleton in general.' (NA,113) So while females might be occupied with trivia and they might be the intellectual inferiors of men, as they outwardly appeared in this and the previous passage, men were by no means universally right, even when discussing weighty topics, such as politics, that they reserved for themselves. In this case female ignorance was matched by male error, which was accompanied by arrogance.

Elizabeth Bennet is an anti-Evelina type in a completely different sense than Catherine Morland, not a burlesque of the 'young girl who enters the world' but the opposite of Burney's shy, bashful, uncertain heroine. Austen revealed a feminist point of view in *Pride and Prejudice* not by commenting ironically on the 'advantages' of female ignorance and then exposing male ignorance, but through a positive, independent heroine.

We have seen that Elizabeth completely disagreed with Charlotte Lucas's view of marriage. For her to have married a man like Mr. Collins, to have made the compromise that her friend did, would have been unthinkable. Of all Austen's heroines she was the most energetic, vital, strong-willed and self-assured. She did not have the white skin that was expected of a lady in genteel society, but was well-tanned. On one of her long walks she crossed 'field after field at a quick pace, jumping over stiles and springing over puddles with impatient activity', arriving at her destination with 'a face glowing with the warmth of exercise'. (PP,32) In conversation her lucid mind and quick tongue kept her firmly in control. Her repartees with Bingley, when he was discussing the possibility of leaving Netherfield, showed her verbal agility and willingness to let her sentences cup as deep as they might.

> 'You begin to comprehend me, do you?' cried he, turning towards her.
> Oh! yes—I understand you perfectly.'
> 'I wish I might take this for a compliment; but to be so easily seen through I am afraid is pitiful.'
> 'That is as it happens. It does not necessarily follow that a deep, intricate character is more or less estimable than such a one as yours.' (PP,42)

Darcy, who was present at the time, and also matched wits with Elizabeth, found such a young woman as this interesting. The next day, when Miss Bingley and Miss Hurst played some songs, Darcy asked Elizabeth to dance. She smiled but did not answer, which forced him to repeat the question.

> 'Oh!' said she, 'I heard you before; but I could not immediately

determine what to say in reply. You wanted me, I know, to say "Yes", that you might have the pleasure of despising my taste; but I always delight in overthrowing those kind of schemes, and cheating a person of their premeditated contempt. I have therefore made up my mind to tell you, that I do not want to dance a reel at all.—and now despise me if you dare. (PP,52)

The result of Elizabeth's remarks was that 'Darcy had never been so bewitched by any woman as he was by her.' It should be noted that this was not her objective; Elizabeth was not trying to beguile Darcy with cleverness. Having decided that 'She liked him too little to care for his approbation', (PP,51) she chose to amuse herself at his expense.

Elizabeth's disregard of the genteel code is seen in the cut and thrust of her conversation, her scorn for the marriage market, and disinterest in the accomplishments. The usual civilities she found boring, and chose either to ignore or ridicule them. Darcy viewed the genteel, female code much as Elizabeth did. He was critical of the female accomplishments, which he considered much less important than the improvement of the mind that resulted from extensive reading, and he had no use for the ploys that women used to attract men. 'There is meanness in *all* the arts which ladies sometimes condescend to employ for captivation. Whatever bears affinity to cunning is despicable.' (PP,40) He criticised unmarried girls for thinking too much about marriage: 'A lady's imagination is very rapid; it jumps from admiration to love, from love to matrimony in a moment.' (PP,27) Unlike Caroline Bingley, he did not consider tan skin unattractive in a woman. And he fell in love with the one female who shared his views on all these subjects, who was independent, had a mind of her own, and possessed great energy. In fact, he was attracted to Elizabeth, at least in part, because she was unorthodox, not genteel in the usual way, and ridiculed people and conventions that he also held in low regard: 'her manners were not those of the fashionable world [and] he was caught by their easy playfulness'. (PP,23)

Finally, Austen commented on female gentility and took a feminist position by having Mr. Collins read from Fordyce's sermons after tea and in the presence of the Bennet family. He did so by choice and after rejecting a novel that had been handed him. Dr. Fordyce's *Sermons to Young Women* appeared in 1766 and became one of the more popular courtesy books, running to eleven editions by

1798 and fourteen by 1814. It contained typical genteel advice: the feminine ideal was one of modesty, 'bashful beauty', 'shamefaced-ness', 'sedate manners', and attentiveness to husbands. 'Sprightli-ness' and a 'love of shining' led to dissipation. Wit was inappropriate to the gentle sex. Needle-work was an ideal pastime, and drawing was recommended because it promoted elegance and grace.[13] And so on. This was a book that indeed appealed to Mr. Collins, whose view of women seems to have agreed with that of Dr. Fordyce. When he proposed to Elizabeth he refused to accept her negative decision, assuming that she was going through the usual motions of young ladies who 'reject the addresses of the man whom they secretly mean to accept, when he first applies for their favour'. (PP,107) Repeated reassurances by Elizabeth that her refusal was genuine had little effect. 'I know it to be the established custom of your sex to reject a man on the first application, and perhaps you have even now said as much to encourage my suit as would be consistent with the true delicacy of the female character.' (PP,108) His view of the female character and his acceptance of the genteel code was exactly what Austen was satirising—and ridiculing. Again, Elizabeth was the positive ideal, speaking directly and with a mind completely her own: 'Can I speak plainer? Do not consider me now as an elegant female intending to plague you, but as a rational creature speaking the truth from her heart.' (PP,109) These remarks exactly agreed with the views of Mary Wollstonecraft.

Having looked at Austen's feminism as if it were one segment of her thought and a unified whole, I will approach the topic differently by examining a change that began in *Mansfield Park* and continued through *Emma* and *Persuasion*. In the last three novels, as before, Austen commented adversely on female gentility and represented female life negatively. She did so by criticising the female accomplishments and boarding schools, and depicting women such as Mrs. Grant and Isabella Knightley whose adult lives were empty because they did not have independent interests or a life of their own.[14] As in the first three novels, Austen exposed the evils of the marriage market, most pointedly through Jane Fairfax, but also in other instances. Miss Bates was a pathetic example of a woman who had not married and had to suffer the indignity and material strain of her single, spinsterly condition. Females were typically flawed: Mrs. Norris, the Bertram sisters, Mary Crawford, Lady

Bertram, all the younger Musgrove females, Elizabeth Elliot and others. And they had the usual defects: vanity, selfishness, superficiality and false values. Yet, while the general pattern of female life in the last three novels is in many ways the same as in the first three, Austen's point of view on the woman question underwent a definite change. In *Mansfield Park* Austen showed clear signs of moving away from her earlier position. *Emma* and *Persuasion* indicate a continuation of that direction.

When Austen wrote her last three novels the anti-feminist reaction was in full swing. Three editions of Wollstonecraft's *Vindication* appeared between 1792 and 1796. This work established a reputation for Wollstonecraft that guaranteed a market for anything she wrote. The sequel that she promised did not follow immediately; rather, she published her *Letters written during a short residence in Sweden, Norway and Denmark* in 1796, in which she alluded to her relationship with Imlay and their illegitimate child. Godwin published her final work, *The Wrongs of Women; or Maria. A Fragment*, in a posthumous 1798 edition that also included the *Vindication*. In the meantime Wollstonecraft's friend Mary Hays published the *Memoirs of Emma Courtenay* (1796), in which contemporary readers incorrectly saw a plea for greater sexual freedom. It is not difficult to understand the hostility toward both Wollstonecraft and Hays. While Wollstonecraft supported the family and felt that a woman's maternal responsibilities came first, she sometimes struck a different chord, as when she argued that 'women of a superior cast' should not be 'called to fulfil the duties of wives and mothers', but should be able to 'pursue more extensive plans of usefulness and independence'. In her own life, the details of which became known, she appeared as the emancipated woman, living with one man out of wedlock and bearing his child, and then living with another whom she married only after becoming pregnant. Godwin and Wollstonecraft recognised one another's independence, more at his preference than hers. It was not a conventional marriage. They maintained separate rooms and went out alone in mixed society, a clear and conscious rejection of the accepted code. So while Wollstonecraft defended marriage in her writings, she also argued that some women should be allowed to follow a different path, and even though she married it was to a man who opposed the institution of marriage. That marriage struck most contemporaries as a mockery of the marital ideal.

Wollstonecraft would have made far less impact and stirred far less hostility had she advanced her feminist arguments and lived an unconventional life in a different political climate. As a friend of Paine and Priestley, as the author of the *Vindication*, and as the wife of Godwin, she identified herself with the cause of the French Revolution and English 'Jacobinism'. To contemporaries her radical feminism was of a piece with her political radicalism, making it appear all the more subversive. So when the conservative reaction came it came with a vengeance. One adversary referred to Godwin's *Memoirs* of Wollstonecraft as his *History of the Intrigues of his Own Wife*. Another found the circumstances of her death singularly appropriate, as this woman who claimed sexual equality died in childbed. *The Anti-Jacobin* savagely attacked Wollstonecraft, Hays and anyone or anything it connected to them, from Rousseau to contemporary German drama.[15] Other journals joined the assault. The *Critical Review* wrote in 1804 that Wollstonecraft applied 'modern infidelity and absurd paradoxes to her own sex'.[16] In 1799 the *Lady's Monthly Museum* published a case history demonstrating the harmful effects on one family of reading the *Vindication*. To Horace Walpole, Wollstonecraft was a 'hyena in petticoats'. Wollstonecraft appeared in thinly disguised fictional form in Edgeworth's *Belinda* (1801). Her name was Mrs. Freke and in a chapter titled 'Rights of Woman' she seemed like a revolutionist in the French mould. 'This is just the way you spoil women, by talking to them of the *delicacy of their sex* and such stuff . . . I hate slavery! vive la liberté!'[17] Interestingly, Mrs. Freke was not part of Edgeworth's initial conception, but was added late in the writing, perhaps as a foil to protect her in her attack on the attitudes towards women of Thomas Day.[18] By 1801 Wollstonecraft was so notorious that an author who criticised the traditional female role found safety in doing so by ridiculing her.

This is not to say that Edgeworth did not disagree with Wollstonecraft. She admired Elizabeth Hamilton's *Memoirs of Modern Philosophers* (1800), which satirised novels of the school of Godwin and Wollstonecraft.[19] Hamilton was but one of many novelists who attacked that school. Others were Jane West, George Walker, Charles Lucas, Isaac d'Israeli, Charles Lloyd, Robert Bisset and Amelia Opie.[20] One of the character types in this fiction was the emancipated girl who demanded a right to pre-marital sexual intercourse. An example is the heroine in Mrs. Opie's *Adeline Mowbray*, or *Mother and Daughter* (1804), who fell in love with a philosopher who opposed marriage on principle, lived with him out

of wedlock, and came to a pitiful end after he died, unable to face a
society whose standards she had rejected. Interestingly, Mrs. Opie
had been a friend of Godwin in the 1790s, an indication of the
conservative reaction that spread through English society and left
such a vivid mark on novels. Out of this reaction came a large
number of family manuals and guidebooks, such as Mrs. Taylor's
Practical Solicitude for a Daughter's best Interests (1814) and *Practical
Hints to young Females, on the Duties of a Wife, a Mother, and a Mistress of
a Family* (1815).

Probably the most influential anti-feminist was Hannah More,
whose *Cheap Repository* tracts, begun in 1795 at the request of Bishop
Porteus, made her one of the most widely read writers of the time. At
first the avowed objective of these didactic stories was to counteract
the influence of Paine, whose revolutionary views appeared to be
spreading among the lower classes. Soon they went beyond
arguments against Paine, showing the lower classes how to regulate
their lives. She worked hand-in-hand with Wilberforce, and was a
leading figure in the Sunday School movement. The rapid growth
of the Sunday School movement in the 1790s reflects the success of
the conservative reaction, and indicates the close connection
between that reaction and Evangelicalism.

As a political conservative and Evangelical, More's anti-
feminism was inevitable. Evangelicalism stood for order, stability,
permanence, continuity, retention of traditional institutions, respect for established authority and, on the level of individual
morality, self-denial and a sense of duty. With such an orientation,
Evangelicals waged a campaign against a political ideology
stressing the rights of man, and a related ideology stressing the rights
of woman. More wrote to Horace Walpole that she refused even to
read Wollstonecraft:

> I have been pestered to read *Rights of Women*, but I am invincibly
> resolved not to do it. Of all jargon, I hate metaphysical jargon;
> besides there is something fanatic and absurd in the very title.
> How many ways there are of being ridiculous! . . . So many
> women are fond of government, I suppose, because they are not
> fit for it. To be unstable and capricious, I really think, is but too
> characteristic of our sex; and there is perhaps no animal so
> indebted to subordination for its good behaviour as woman.

Had More read the *Vindication* she would have discovered many views that agreed with her own. In fact, staunch anti-feminist that More was, she was a feminist of sorts, perhaps it should be said an unconscious feminist.[21] Her views on the education of women agreed substantially with those of Wollstonecraft. In the introduction to her *Strictures on the Modern System of Female Education* (1799), she said it was 'a singular injustice . . . towards women, first to give them a very defective education and then to expect from them the most undeviating purity of conduct; to train them in such manner as shall lay them open to the most dangerous faults and then to censure them for not proving faultless'. Like Wollstonecraft, More criticised boarding schools, and she too attacked one of the foundations of female gentility, the accomplishments. 'This frenzy of accomplishments unhappily is no longer restricted within the usual limits of rank and fortune; the middle orders have caught the contagion, and it rages downward with unceasing and destructive violence, from the elegantly dressed but slenderly proportioned curate's daughter to the equally fashioned daughter of the little tradesman, and of the more opulent but not more judicious farmer.'[22] The result of the 'contagion' was women who were frivolous, indolent, and unfit for the duties of life. Girls ran 'to snatch a few of these showy acquirements' for two reasons, 'to make their fortunes by marriage, or if that fail, to qualify them to be teachers of others: hence the abundant multiplication of superficial wives, and of incompetent and illiterate governesses'. Wollstonecraft could hardly have put the case against accomplishments more effectively. Just as More felt that the domestic role was most appropriate to women, so did Wollstonecraft. Both attached great importance to the proper raising of children. More felt that a wife should not be an ornament who could 'paint, and play, and sing, and draw, and dress, and dance', but one who could 'reason, and reflect, and feel and judge, and discourse and discriminate . . .'. The leading feminist and leading anti-feminist were in basic agreement in attacking the code of female gentility and standing for an ideal emphasising the development of the mind.

More and Wollstonecraft differed on two fundamental points. While the charge against Wollstonecraft of atheism was groundless, it is true that as she poured her time and energy into feminism her religious convictions lost some of their force, and as her personal life became difficult her faith yielded to disillusionment. Even when she lost hope in a God who intervened on behalf of individual humans she believed in a deity and a 'grand plan of the Universe'. These views did not find expression in the *Vindication* but in the later *Letters Written . . . in Sweden*. Even if Wollstonecraft's critics were unfamiliar with this work they would have regarded her as an infidel, if only through guilt by association. In all probability many of her critics, like More, did not read the *Vindication*; they did know that she was a friend of Paine and Godwin, both of whom were identified with a rationalistic philosophy and whom conservative Christians regarded as heretics.

The other area of disagreement between More and Wollstonecraft concerned the nature of the two sexes. At times they sounded almost alike, calling for well-educated women who would develop their rational faculties, but while Wollstonecraft saw reason as a basis for equality, More did not. One of Wollstonecraft's guides was the philosophe Helvétius, who wrote that 'man is indeed but the product of his education'.[23] Believing this doctrine to apply to woman as well as to man, Wollstonecraft regarded it as a basis for equality. Also believing that education was the key to improving the lot of women, More moved within a different set of assumptions. For her women were different from men by nature, and central to her ideal was 'Christian meekness' and 'Christian self-denial'. Women should be taught that 'this world is not a stage for the display of superficial or even of shining talent, but for the strict and sober exercise of fortitude, temperance, meekness, faith, diligence, and self-denial . . . Life is not a splendid romance . . . [but] a true history, many pages of which will be dull, obscure, and uninteresting.' Firmly denying the principle of sexual equality, More felt the position of woman to be subordinate to that of man. While she agreed with Wollstonecraft that woman's position was in the home, she defined it differently. For More the husband was the dominant figure; remaining within the Pauline, Christian tradition, she emphasised modesty and sobriety and felt that woman should not try to usurp the authority of man.

In many respects Austen's feminism in the first three novels was similar to that of Hannah More. Yet in those novels, at certain points, she went beyond More. Such a heroine as Elizabeth Bennet did not agree with More's ideal of the modest female, nor did she accept a subordinate marital role. More was suspicious of wit and irony, the very qualities that made Elizabeth so attractive to Darcy. Elizabeth possessed the judgement and discrimination that More called for, but not the 'Christian meekness' or 'self-denial', which is not to say that she was anything but Christian. But in conversation with men Elizabeth more than held her own, and when treated by Mr. Collins as a delicate female she insisted that she was a rational person. So while in some ways Austen's feminism was like that of More, in others it simply did not fit in to her mould.

When Austen wrote to Cassandra on 4 February, 1813, that *Pride and Prejudice* was 'rather too light, and bright, and sparkling; it wants shade . . .', (L,299) she was nearing completion of *Mansfield Park*, which she finished four months later, in June. The new novel was much less light and bright, and did contain more shade. Its heroine, Fanny Price, was the opposite of Elizabeth Bennet, not vital, energetic and witty as her predecessor, but shy, modest, bashful, self-effacing and weak. As a girl Fanny 'was small of her age, with no glow of complexion'; (MP,12) in manner she was 'timid', 'shy', 'quiet', and 'passive', and 'her feelings were very acute'. When her aunt Norris told her that she would have to live with her she replied 'with a faltering voice'. (MP,25) She thought she could 'never be important to any one', (MP,26) and that she was foolish and awkward. With this type of self-view it is understandable that she lacked the verbal agility, presence of mind and conversational brilliance of Elizabeth Bennet.

As a Christian heroine, Fanny resembled the heroines that were beginning to appear in novels that bore the stamp of Evangelicalism, such as More's *Cœlebs*.[24] The heroine of that novel, Lucilla Stanley, did not like levity, especially when serious subjects were under discussion. 'All the light things he uttered, and which he meant for wit, so far from raising a smile, increased her gravity.'[25] In *Mansfield Park*, when Mary Crawford expressed amusement over female members of the Rushworth family attending chapel, Fanny 'coloured and looked at Edmund, but felt too angry for speech'. (MP,87) Lucilla Stanley was indifferent to 'those pleasures which are usually thought to constitute the sole happiness of young women of a certain rank', and maintained 'sober habits of life', just as Fanny Price did. Lucilla was the type of female who passed through life honoured and respected in her own small unimportant sphere, approved by the husband she served, giving no occasion for gossip, and producing 'much happiness at home'. Fanny, too, had no desire to make herself known, to bring herself to the attention of others with clever, amusing remarks, choosing instead to remain in the background. Like More's heroine, she blushed easily and as a wife would have retained the good opinion of her husband. Not only was Fanny 'formed for domestic life' (MP,473) but also she was careful not to oppose Edmund. When Edmund solicited Fanny's opinion on his decision to participate in the theatrical she was stunned but unable to voice her disapproval, beyond saying that Sir Thomas would not approve the project.[26] As the conversation unfolded, Edmund moved from rationalisation to rationalisation, as Fanny either agreed to arguments that were beside the point or remained noncommittal. In other words, throughout the discussion she remained steadfast but without challenging Edmund. This is the type of female that Hannah More held up as the ideal wife, morally sound, sensible, prudent, consistent and reserved.

Obviously, Fanny Price would be a very different type of wife from Elizabeth Bennet. I will now try to show that the contrast between these heroines is part of a larger development in Austen's view of women and their position in marriage. My way of proceeding will be to examine one facet of her fiction: the type of relationship that evolved between the hero and heroine as her stories proceeded to their marital conclusion. Rather than limiting the discussion to *Pride and Prejudice* and *Mansfield Park* I will look at all of the novels. My objective will be to explain the relationship, in the context of my chosen theme, between *Mansfield Park* and the rest of the novels, to show how Austen viewed women and their position in marriage before this novel and how she viewed it afterwards.

In *Northanger Abbey* Henry Tilney amused himself at Catherine Morland's expense, spoke down to her, and in his superior wisdom corrected her errors. Moreover, 'his affection originated in nothing better than gratitude, or, in other words . . . a persuasion of her partiality for him had been the only cause of giving her a serious thought'. (NA,243) He offered his hand in marriage, in part, as a man of honour. It had been his father's idea to ask Catherine to Northanger Abbey, thinking that she was a wealthy heiress. Once General Tilney learned otherwise he abruptly sent her home, under circumstances that showed a complete breach of civility. This breach prodded Henry into acting as he thought necessary. His father had invited Catherine to his estate so that Henry could marry her for her money; thinking that she was poor he brutally dismissed her. Under these circumstances Henry 'felt himself bound as much in honour as in affection to Miss Morland', and made a proposal of marriage.

Northanger Abbey is not a romance as much as an anti-romance. Austen described a hero and heroine who fell in love, but also deflated the conventions of falling in love. In concluding the novel

she explained that Henry's affection for Catherine, having originated in gratitude, was a 'new circumstance I acknowledge, and
dreadfully derogatory of an heroine's dignity'. (NA,243) In another
authorial intrusion that poked fun at the lovers, Austen said, 'I fear,
to the bosom of my readers, who will see in the tell-tale compression
of the pages before them, that we are all hastening together to
perfect felicity.' (NA,250) Language was inflated for the same
purpose, to amuse the reader, who is reminded of stock passages in
romantic fiction. 'Catherine, wrapt in the contemplation of her own
unutterable happiness scarcely opened her lips, dismissed them to
the extasies of another tête-à-tête.'(NA,243) In the fiction that
Austen burlesqued the hero and heroine had to overcome various
obstacles while courting and before they could marry. Austen
parodied both situations by creating machinery that she set before
the hero and heroine and then, at the appropriate moment,
removing it. Her interest was not in tracing the development of a
relationship that would lead to marriage, as much as parodying the
conventions of courting. To the extent that she did describe the
relationship between the hero and heroine, it hardly appeared as an
ideal preparation for marriage, at least from the female point of
view. The hero's affection resulted from a pride that he felt over the
heroine's partiality, his way of treating her reflected the superiority
that he clearly assumed, and he married her from a sense of honour
as well as for love.

Both of the marriages that took place at the end of *Sense and
Sensibility* present certain problems. That the impassioned, romantic
Marianne Dashwood should accept a husband as different from
herself as Colonel Brandon makes one wonder about the basis of the
union. What adds to the difficulty is that she accepted Brandon
while still feeling the effects of Willoughby's rejection. When she
returned to Barton Cottage memories of the romance rushed back,
bringing an inevitable pain that she resolved to regulate, 'by
religion, by reason, by constant employment'. (SS,347) Without
this suffering, and the subsequent sense of resignation, she would not
have married Brandon. This seventeen-year-old girl (or nineteen;
the text is inconsistent) married a man of thirty-six only after the
trauma of an unsuccessful love affair and at the urging of her
mother, sister and brother-in-law. 'With such a confederacy against
her . . . what could she do?' (SS,378) So Marianne, her spirits
dampened by romantic misfortune, married a man she had
considered old enough to be her father. Elinor's marriage to

Edward Ferrars seems, at least on the surface, to have been the happy union of a couple who had long been in love and finally overcame the obstacles that kept them apart. Nevertheless, there are questions about this marriage too. Edward, while good and virtuous, lacked spirit and resolution. Elinor, defending him, claimed that 'his mind is well-informed, his enjoyment of books exceedingly great [and] his imagination lively'. (SS,20) But little that he said or did supported this opinion. True, his 'coldness and reserve' when he visited Barton Cottage could be explained, as events later seemed to indicate, by his entanglement with Lucy Steele. Yet Edward continued to be shy and diffident. Elinor was far more energetic and resourceful. It was she who, 'as usual, broke through the first positive resolution of not marrying till every thing was ready . . .'. (SS,374) Given the husbands that the two heroines chose, one has to wonder about the supposedly happy marriages with which the novel ends. It seems that Austen arranged matters arbitrarily and unconvincingly. One critic has said that Marianne dwindled into marriage with a vengeance and that Austen's brusque manipulation of the plot makes one suspect that the ending was a last, bitter irony.[27]

Marriage took place in *Pride and Prejudice* after the typical removing of obstacles. In this instance, the main impediment was Elizabeth Bennet's misunderstanding of Darcy. His pride was the cause of her prejudice; upon realising her mistake her feelings changed until, by the time of the second proposal, she was prepared to accept. All of this Austen did with great skill. When Darcy, in his most tactful way, again raised the question of marriage, Elizabeth, for once, lost her poise. Conscious of the 'awkwardness and anxiety of his situation' she had to force herself to speak, 'immediately, though not very fluently' (PP,366) giving her consent. When he told her of his feelings his affection became 'every moment more valuable'. In their happiness they 'walked on, without knowing in what direction. There was too much to be thought, and felt, and said, for attention to any other objects.' (PP,366–7) Passages of such warmth one does not find in the first two novels, nor does one find previous heroines saying, as Elizabeth did with tears in her eyes: 'I do, I do like him . . . I love him.' (PP,376) Here is an emotionally deep, credible romance. As touching as it might be to see Elizabeth lose her composure amidst the welter of her feelings, such a response is not exactly what one might expect of this poised heroine. And upon moving into Pemberley, as Darcy's wife, Elizabeth resumed her former, energetic, strong-willed ways, taking 'liberties' with her husband, talking to him in her usual 'lively, sportive manner', and making him the 'object of open pleasantry'. (PP,388)

The heroine of *Mansfield Park* is completely different from that of *Pride and Prejudice*; so too is her relationship with the hero. By the same token, her marriage would rest upon different foundations. As a wife Elizabeth Bennet amused herself at Darcy's expense, much as she had when single. Fanny would be a new type of partner, not playful and certainly not taking liberties, but quiet, dutiful and responsible, making every possible effort, one can well imagine, to support her clerical husband in word and deed. Just as Elizabeth's and Darcy's marriage was bound to be lively, thanks to Elizabeth's energy, Fanny's and Edmund's was certain to be calm and stable, owing to Fanny's evenness and prudence.

Austen's way of working towards the marital conclusion in *Mansfield Park* reinforced other themes in this novel. The world of *Mansfield Park* was threatened, both internally and externally. In helping to deflect Henry and Mary Crawford, Fanny responded to one problem, and by marrying Edmund she dealt positively with another, bringing to Mansfield Park her moral judgement, rectitude, sense of duty and responsibility, respect for religion and tradition, and domesticity. As Edmund's wife, and the mother of his children, she would not only be a vital link in the family unit but also strengthen the community as a whole and help further the cause of social continuity. In *Mansfield Park* Austen viewed the family as an institution whose function was to transmit values and traditions from generation to generation. And it was all the more important for the Bertram family, standing at the head of the community, to be internally sound and capable of setting the right example. Had Edmund married Mary Crawford the results would have been unfortunate for himself, his children, the Mansfield estate and the community whose well-being would be influenced by his leadership. Austen's view of the family in this novel was inextricably connected with a social view that stressed continuity, emphasised the importance of organic relationships, and was inherently conservative.

Emma, too, stressed the importance of social continuity and the community, and related these themes to marriage. It did so by demonstrating from the very beginning the necessity for the heroine's reform, without which she could not have assumed a positive role in Highbury. One of Austen's great achievements in this novel was exposing Emma's faults in a way that clearly put her in an unfavourable light, but at the same time making the reader like her anyway.[28] One might become irritated with her, and is probably encouraged to as she committed one mistake after another, refusing persistently, stubbornly, to understand others, to understand herself, and to recognise the reality of social and intellectual gradations. Because one likes Emma one wants her to change, to overcome her shortcomings. These shortcomings made her a threat to the social order, and in that sense a subversive. By encouraging the reader to wish for Emma's reform Austen involves him—or her—in a set of concerns that transcend the problems of the heroine and relate to the right and proper ordering of society. This is how a fictional technique served as a persuasive device, helping advance a conservative social argument.

One of the reasons for Emma's errors was that she was spoiled. Her mother, who died when she was a child, was the one person who could have coped with her and kept her, as a girl, in the needed state of 'subjection'. Her weak, indulgent father was unable to exercise a parent's proper authority, and her governess, Miss Taylor, was like a sister and friend. As a result, Emma had things 'rather too much her own way'. (E,5) As Knightley understood, Emma had dominated Miss Taylor. She was accustomed to exercising her authority over others; she did so because she enjoyed it; and she wanted to continue doing so. That was one of the reasons, and probably the main one, for her deciding not to marry.

The one person who saw through Emma and was the instrument of her correction was to become her husband. The 'humiliation' of Emma after the Box Hill incident, and the subsequent self-understanding that she achieved as a result, was a necessary prelude to her realising that she alone could marry Knightley. What must be stressed is that Knightley, the man who told Emma what was necessary, had the inner strength and force of personality to win her over and bring about her correction, unlike the more feeble Frank Churchill, to whom Emma was initially attracted. Before Churchill arrived, Emma gathered that he was 'well-bred and aggreeable' and predicted that he would be the 'sensation' of Donwell and Highbury, while the more sagacious Knightley understood better. To Knightley, Churchill was a 'chattering coxcombe'; Emma's idea was that he could 'adapt his conversation to the taste of every body, and has the power as well as the wish of being universally agreeable'. (E,150) If so, that much the worse as far as Knightley was concerned. Emma, in fact, accurately described Churchill, who was socially adept but without a fixed centre, an actor on the stage of life, nowhere in his element more than playing games, which he liked to organise. By contrast, Knightley was stable, responsible and serious. When at home he read or worked on his accounts. With another farmer he talked about 'business, shows of cattle, or new drills . . .'. (E,473) Public minded, he was a magistrate. At the party in the Crown, Knightley did not dance, but was conspicuous with his 'tall, firm, upright figure'. (E,326) Manly, decisive and resolute, he found everything about Churchill disagreeable, even his handwriting, which he said was 'like a woman's writing'. (E,297) In his opinion, Churchill was 'a disgrace to the name of man', (E,426) a clear expression of the male standards that he considered important. Another such expression was his belief that 'A man would always wish to give a woman a better home than the one he takes her from.' (E,428) Quiet in manner, unassuming, graceful and dignified, Knightley was also a person of great authority, to whom others in the village looked up for leadership. Unlike Churchill, he commanded respect.

Having heard about Churchill's engagement to Jane Fairfax, and aware of his various ruses, Emma said, 'I cannot say how it has sunk him in my opinion. So unlike what a man should be!—None of that upright integrity, that strict adherence to truth and principle, that disdain of trick and littleness, which a man should display in every transaction of his life.' (E,397) While Emma did not yet realise that she was in love with Knightley, she was on the verge of doing so, and in this comment described the exact ideal that he represented. The key to her falling in love was Knightley's reprimanding her over her unkind comments to Miss Bates, in the course of which he necessarily set himself up as a higher authority, pointing out item-by-item how she had acted wrongly. How strikingly this man's rectitude and resolution differed from the smugness and indulgence of Emma's father is clear from a conversation that followed Emma's visit to Miss Bates to make an apology. Knightley had correctly pointed out that Miss Bates had known and been kind to her since she was an infant, when 'her notice was an honour . . .'. (E,375) Now, when her circumstances were so much lowered, to 'laugh at her, humble her . . . and before others . . . is not pleasant to you . . . and it is very far from pleasant to me . . .'. (E,375) Angry and mortified with herself, Emma decided to make amends, and did so with a feeling of shame and penitence. Upon returning home, her father said, in Knightley's presence, 'Well, my dear, and did you get there safely?—And how did you find my worthy old friend and her daughter?—I dare say they must have been very much obliged to you for coming. Dear Emma has been to call on Mrs. and Miss Bates . . . She is always so attentive to them.' (E,385) As Emma blushed at her father's embarrassing comment her eye moved toward Knightley, whose expression indicated that he understood the purpose of her mission. In this moment she wanted the approval of a man who was completely different from her father, whose criticism had won her admiration—and more. 'He looked at her with a glow of regard. She was warmly gratified—and in another moment still more so, by a little movement of more than common friendliness on his part.— He took her hand.' (E,385-6) Just as Knightley's just criticism gave him an ascendancy over Emma, so too did her soft, expressive glance have a telling effect upon him. So the story proceeds towards its conclusion, with Knightley assuming an ever more important role, casting his shadow over the woman that he was to marry and whose transformation he had effected. By the end of the story her position had changed, her importance diminished, as she was assimilated by Knightley. This happened in 'a kind of decrescendo into social twilight',[29] in a drawn-out ending that gave Emma time to prepare herself for the new world, that of marriage, which she was about to enter.

Interestingly, the novel's atmosphere and texture reflect this shift. In the early parts words are used that stressed freedom and independence, but this changed in the last chapters as the focus came to be on dependence.[30] Emma, thanks to the man that she was to marry, was a changed person. No longer a meddler and 'imaginist', she was prepared to accept a new station in life. Because of her reflections she became more open, more transparent, the very kind of woman that Knightley wanted as a wife. She would call her husband 'Mr. Knightley', except for the one occasion when she would address him by his first name.

In *Persuasion*, the heroine's relationship to the hero is completely different. Although Anne Elliot loved Wentworth, she had turned down his offer of marriage, which disappointed him, hurt his pride and made him bitter. 'She had used him ill; deserted and disappointed him; and worse, she had shown a feebleness of character in doing so, which his own decided, confident temper could not endure.' (P,61) This had been eight years earlier, but so great was Wentworth's sense of ill use that 'he had no desire of meeting [Anne] again'. When he did see her, he found her 'altered beyond his knowledge', which further damaged any chances that she might have had. Returning from the war, 'It was now his object to marry', but Anne did not appear as a possibility. 'Her power with him was gone for ever.' Rather, 'He had a heart for either of the Musgroves . . . [or] any pleasing young woman who came in his way, except Anne Elliot.' As Wentworth explained to his sister, he had been at sea so long that he was 'quite ready to make a foolish match. Any body between fifteen and thirty may have me for the asking. A little beauty, and a few smiles, and a few compliments to the navy, and I am a lost man.' (P,62) This was not exactly true, as he indicated by concluding, on a more serious note, that he should like a wife with 'A strong mind, and sweetness of manner . . .' Even as he said these words 'Anne Elliot was not out of his thoughts'.

This conversation helped set the stage for what was to follow. In a light-hearted moment Wentworth described one type of woman, the outwardly attractive female who deliberately flattered the male ego, and in a more sober, reflective mood he pictured a different type, serious, deep and gentle. Louisa Musgrove agreed with the former ideal, Anne Elliot with the latter. Initially, Louisa gained the ascendancy, only to lose it as Wentworth began to appreciate Anne's steadiness and goodness, and was attracted to her thoughtful, feminine way. The incident on the Cobb was important in bringing about the shift, revealing as it did the contrast between the two rivals. When the party came to the stile leading to the lower Cobb, Louisa wanted to jump into Wentworth's hands, as she always did while walking with him, rather than climbing down step-by-step. She jumped once, and then, in spite of his advising against it, insisted on a second time. He felt that the pavement was too hard and that if he should fail to catch her she could be hurt. 'She smiled and said, "I am determined I will."' (P,109) What this passage brings out is the superficiality of Louisa's 'determination'. While playing a piquant, female game that brought her into close, seductive positions, she affected fixity of purpose. Anne's quiet, unassuming, able assistance after the accident brought out her resourcefulness and much deeper firmness of character. While the other members of the party lost their composure, Anne retained her self-control, acting with a 'strength and zeal' that, in the moment of crisis, put her in a position of leadership. She had to tell the others, Wentworth included, what to do. Her very real fortitude could hardly have contrasted more sharply with Louisa's superficial individualism.

The very qualities in Anne that Wentworth was beginning to appreciate, and would soon tip the scales in her favour, were connected to the same qualities that earlier caused her to turn down his proposal. In rejecting the offer she was following Mrs. Russell's advice, because she was persuaded that it was right, even though she loved Wentworth and wanted to marry him. She had the necessary resolution to do what she believed best, even though her individual preference was otherwise; she sacrificed her wishes to her sense of duty. Unable to appreciate Anne's reasons, Wentworth felt that her refusal was a sign of weakness and that it revealed a lack of character. The truth is that she had always been strong. This is what, at the age of twenty, Wentworth had not been able to understand.

In doing as Mrs. Russell recommended Anne recognised the higher understanding of a woman who was her elder and had been close to her since her mother's death. As a woman who had seen more of life than Anne—and Wentworth—and their generation, Mrs. Russell appreciated the advantages of waiting until conditions were more favourable. Her advice was that of an older person, it was prudent, it meant acting against a momentary preference for the sake of what was best over the long term, and of course it was conservative. Other novelists, such as Jane West, Mary Wollstone-craft, Charlotte Smith, Mary Brunton, Maria Edgeworth, Eliza Parsons and Mary Hays also treated the 'persuasion' theme, some siding with youth, others with their elders.[31] This was a theme that had great interest for Austen's contemporaries, partly because writers of the 'romantic-revolutionary school' brought the problem into such sharp focus by stressing the rights of the individual. Godwin wrote in *Political Justice* (1973) that 'there is but one power, to which I can yield a heart-felt obedience, the dictate of my own conscience. The decrees of any other power, especially if I have a firm and independent mind, I shall obey with reluctance and adversion.' Predictably, female writers who moved in Godwin's radical circle, such as Mary Hays, incorporated this view into their fiction. Also, novels such as Wollstonecraft's *Mary: A Fiction* and Smith's *Emmeline* had already taken the side of youth in the 1780s. So there was a long, running debate between romantic-revolutionary and conservative novelists over the 'persuasion' theme. This same debate also pitted feminists against anti-feminists, as the former came down on the side of youth, the latter on the side of elders and parents. The argument moved simultaneously on several levels, with youth, the rights of the individual, and the freedom of female choice representing one position, while the opposite position gave preference to the older generation, the importance of responsibility, and limits on female choice.

Wentworth, wanting to marry in spite of Mrs. Russell's objections, and feeling resentful towards Anne, was on the side of the romantic-revolutionaries. Given his youth, ardour and self-confidence this was not surprising. Instinctively, however, he was undoubtedly conservative, as one might expect of someone of his profession, and as his quiet, forceful behaviour indicated at the time of his appearance. One incident perfectly illustrates the discipline and sense of place and limit that Wentworth felt and was prepared to enforce. He, Charles Hayter, Anne, and the older of the Musgrove children, Charles, happened to be together in the drawing room at Uppercross Cottage. Charles was ill, and Anne was watching after him as he lay on the sofa. Presently the younger brother, Walter, made a 'determined appearance among them, and went straight to the sofa to see what was going on, and put in his claim to any thing good that might be giving away'. (P,79) After trying unsuccessfully to find something to eat, he began to tease his brother and climb over his aunt, who was unable to shake him off, busy as she was tending to Charles. After ordering, entreating and insisting that he leave, and even shoving him, Anne had to say, 'I am very angry with you'. This prompted Charles Hayter to ask Walter why he did not do as his aunt had bid, and to ask him to 'Come to me'. The boy did not stir. In the next moment Anne found herself free, as Walter's hands were removed from her neck and 'he was resolutely borne away' (P,80) by Wentworth, who acted without speaking a word.

Charles Hayter was the uncle of Walter Musgrove, the boy who had just made such a nuisance of himself. Properly, he should have been the one to have done what Wentworth did, which he understood and which made him resentful. What added to his resentment was his suspicion that Wentworth was his rival for Henrietta's attention. Having recently arrived at Uppercross, Hayter sensed a change in the atmosphere, which he correctly attributed to Wentworth's presence. Mary Musgrove, Anne's sister, had just been discussing Charles Hayter and Wentworth, saying that she hoped the latter would win Henrietta over, as she suspected he already had. She did have to admit, however, that 'Charles is positive!' The truth was that Charles' weakness and inability to be firm with children suited him for life at Uppercross. Mary said earlier that her husband 'spoils the children so that I cannot get them into any order'. (P,44) In fact, she was an indifferent and irresponsible parent, who did little beyond complaining about how unmanageable her children were becoming. Her husband, in turn, complained that he could manage them if it were not for his wife's interference. The 'little social commonwealth' (P,43) of the Musgrove family lacked order; Wentworth's removing young Walter shows the type of authority that was needed.

Wentworth clearly was not suited for Louisa. With her schooling at Exeter, her accomplishments, modern mind and modern manners she kept up with all the latest fashions. Her 'individualism' was of the new, superficial type and made her affected in a coy, female way; it was part of her manners, not directed by inner principle and rooted in morals. She certainly did not have the strength of mind and sweetness of manner that Wentworth wanted in a wife. Anne's solid mental qualities and depth of feeling are revealed in a conversation with Harville, in which she discussed the role and nature of her sex. 'We live at home, quiet, confined, and our feelings prey upon us. You have always a profession, pursuits, business of some sort or other, to take you back into the world immediately, and continual occupation and change . . .' (P,232) Not only did women live more quietly in their domestic world, but did so naturally, as if formed for such a life. She was willing to concede that 'Man is more robust than woman', and that 'Your feelings may be the strongest', but 'ours are the most tender'. Thus, the two sexes have their own, separate 'attachments'.

> 'You have difficulties, and privations, and dangers enough to struggle with. You are always labouring and toiling, exposed to every risk and hardship. Your home, country, friends, all quitted. Neither time, nor health, nor life, to be called your own. It would be too hard, indeed,' (with a faltering voice) 'if woman's feelings were to be added to all this.' (P,233)

Harville had argued that men were more constant than women, and cited as evidence their sense of loss when separated from wives and children and the deep emotions that accompanied a reunion. Anne responded by saying:

I should deserve utter contempt if I dared to suppose that true attachment and constancy were known only by woman. No, I believe you capable of every thing great and good in your married lives. I believe you equal to every important exertion, and to every domestic forbearance, so long as—if I may be allowed the expression, so long as you have an object. I mean, while the woman you love lives, and lives for you. All the privilege I claim for my sex (it is not a very enviable one, you need not covet it) is that of loving longest, when existence or when hope is gone. (P,235)

When Anne Elliot said that she and others of her sex lived at home and that men constantly toiled and laboured in their business or profession, she echoed the views of Hannah More.[32] Wollstonecraft said the same thing, but she also offered some women other possibilities. What clearly separated More and Wollstonecraft was their view of the female nature and its impact on domestic relationships. Wollstonecraft argued that women were not 'formed for softness', and that it was insulting to regard them as 'gentle, domestic brutes', winning their husband's affection by obeying. For More, woman belonged in the home because of her emotional makeup, because she was a creature of feeling. This is where she and Austen agreed, as seen in Anne Elliot's remarks. While men were busy at their jobs and exposed to risks and hardships, women lived at home, their feelings preying upon them. Anne was willing to concede that man's feelings were the strongest, but those of women were most tender. The logical result was different roles, each having its own 'attachments'. Man, with his exertions and dangers, could not have a woman's feelings. The one claim she made for her sex was loving longest, which men need not envy. The feelings that went so deep in women were unique to them and made them the loving wives they were fitted to be. Anne would be the ideal wife and mother. It should be noted that Charles and Walter Musgrove respected their Aunt Anne more than their own mother. Everything about Anne's care for the two boys indicates her maternal instincts, in which their mother was deficient. As a tender, gentle, inwardly strong woman she was the perfect complement to the man she was to marry.

So while Austen continued in some respects to represent female life in the last three novels much as she had in the first three, in other ways she struck off in a new direction. Her stories moved toward their marital conclusion more positively, without the former ambivalence and uneasiness. Austen came under the influence of the larger forces that were at work in English society, those stressing order, stability, continuity, and individual duty and responsibility. Out of these changes came a different view of marriage. Related to that view was a new type of heroine, more reserved, modest and gentle. Fanny Price was shy and given to blushing, and Anne Elliot was tender, kind and thoughtful. Emma was initially headstrong, but as she changed she became more tactful, unassuming, and like Fanny and Anne willing and ready to assume a proper wifely role. Just as Austen created a new type of heroine, so did she create a new type of hero, more masculine, forceful, and decisive. Knightley was contemptuous of Churchill, who did not measure up to his male standards and whom he regarded as effeminate. This direct, forthright hero established his authority over the misdirected heroine and won her admiration and love in doing so. As a father his children would undoubtedly know their place, much as Wentworth's would.

Lines of authority are firmer in Austen's late novels. I believe this indicates that she grappled with some of the most difficult problems of the age—an age that had to make hard and painful emotional adjustments to historical forces that issued from an age of Revolution. The relaxed, permissive ways of the eighteenth century became anachronistic in the stressful period after 1789; it was necessary to tighten society, to emphasise the individual's duties rather than rights, and to stand behind the father. So English society emerged from this crisis more conservative, more serious, oriented more toward tradition than change. Austen was not isolated from this pattern; on the contrary she felt it keenly and responded to it in her writing. The novels show that Austen initially leaned toward female independence, but eventually shifted her position by emphasising differences in male and female roles and depicting new types of heroine. Fanny Price can be regarded as the Christian heroine, sickly and delicate of constitution but internally strong and sound of moral judgement. She was a necessary instrument in the 'salvation' of Edmund. Weak as she was physically, she was resolute in her convictions. Here was one ideal type of wife. Emma Woodhouse can be seen as the victim of a permissive upbringing. Accustomed to too much freedom and independence, she went astray, until Knightley guided her onto the right track. Having been 'humiliated', she was ready to occupy the wifely role that she had decided against. Anne Elliot is in many ways the most interesting of these three heroines, representing Austen's exploration of the female mind and temperament. Throughout the novel, but most pointedly in the conversation with Harville in the next-to-last chapter, Anne was soft, gentle, kind and loving. She was feminine in the deepest recesses of her nature, and argued that this was woman's finest attribute. The only privilege that she claimed for her sex was 'that of loving longest'.

While Wentworth had turned against her she had not done so against him. Tender as she was and deep as her feelings ran, she was not pliable when principle was at stake. As she said, she had been right in submitting to the authority of Mrs. Russell; in her opinion, 'a strong sense of duty is no bad part of a woman's portion'. (P,246) This comment reveals that Austen's heroine was by no means the shy, shamefaced, delicate female that eighteenth-century moralists such as Fordyce and Gregory held forth as their ideal. She did have some of the qualities that they prescribed, but also and more importantly she possessed interior resources that would be unimaginable in the type of female that they had in mind. As different as Anne Elliot was from Elizabeth Bennet she shared her strength of character. Her individualism was rooted in self-control and inner discipline, and it commanded respect. Here is a heroine who at once was deeply feminine and firm, resolute, and prepared to subordinate her own wishes to moral principle. She would be the ideal wife and mother and, with her sense of continuity and tradition, an agent through whom lasting, enduring values could be transmitted.

Conclusion

In trying to understand how the French Revolution affected Austen's thinking and writing, it is useful to divide her life into three periods. First is the 1790s. When the people of Paris stormed the Bastille, Austen had already begun the Juvenilia. These youthful pieces are a clear indication of how much her language, values, outlook and habits of mind were rooted in the world of the eighteenth century. More particularly, the Juvenilia reflects the milieu of Austen's family and social class; her world was that of the eighteenth century, but as defined in a certain way. It was the world of the English gentry, the southern counties and the local village, with its Rectory and Church; it was the genteel world in which girls went to boarding schools, picked up the usual accomplishments, read novels, attended assembly hall dances in their best finery, met young men, and got on with the business of finding a husband; it was an insular world, especially for women, whose conversation could move only within carefully circumscribed boundaries and for whom independent careers were precluded by the prevailing code.

The quiet and stability of this world was shaken by the French Revolution. Through Eliza de Feuillide Austen knew about the Reign of Terror in Paris, which claimed the life of a man whose fate had become a matter of concern to the entire Austen family. Austen's sailor brothers, Francis and Charles, made her aware of the naval struggle between England and France, and through her brother Henry, an officer in the Oxfordshire militia, she was conscious of England's attempt to build a stronger army. Exactly how she learned about the Revolution's impact on English society is less easy to determine; what is clear is that she knew about the repressiveness and climate of fear that gripped the country during the 1790s. That she did so is evident from two passages in *Northanger Abbey*, one of which alluded to the spectre of violence and the other to the abridgement of hallowed English liberties and the use of spies in the campaign against internal Jacobinism.

Those passages are a key to Austen's way of responding to the troubled conditions of this difficult decade. She did not comment on those conditions directly but referred to them indirectly, ironically and, in a way, comically. Throughout *Northanger Abbey* Austen used literary devices as a way to reach behind illusion and reveal the real world. The 'riot' and 'spies' passages are consistent with this larger aspect of the novel; what is interesting is how little Austen chose to show of the reality that they exposed. Aside from these passages there is no indication that she was aware of or affected by the conditions to which they alluded. She did not work out her responses to violence and repression in a way that was central to this novel and its narrative scheme, but inserted passages here and there without integrating them into a larger framework. Obviously the disturbances of the 1790s was a subject that she did not wish to treat in any extended way. To have done so would have gone completely against her view of herself as a novelist; moreover, it would have violated the code that not only determined the type of fiction she wrote but how she related to her world. As a creature of her sex and class, there was nothing else for her to do, at this stage of her life, but stand apart from the great events of the day. What the 'riot' and 'spies' passages reveal is that she did know about those events; the stresses and strains of the Revolutionary era did enter the rural recesses of Steventon and were part of Austen's experience.

During the 1790s Austen was conservative, but not in the ideological sense. Her conservatism was a matter of temperament and a result of her background; it was not the Burkean conservatism that would have such a deep influence on her later thinking and writing. The conditions that made Austen conservative by temperament might well have worked against her becoming politically aware. That conservatism was a function of the insularity of her world, a natural outgrowth of her social experience before the stresses of the Revolution were felt. Historians are correct in saying that parts of English society were not deeply touched by the great events of the Revolutionary and Napoleonic period. This was probably most true of Austen's class, and it was probably most true in the southern counties. The society that was most insular, whose collective outlook and habits of mind most conformed with the civilised security of eighteenth-century life, was the very society from which Austen came and, just as this narrowness made adjustments to the Revolutionary age difficult for others, so did it have a similar effect on her.

From 1800 to 1808 Austen wrote only the unfinished fragment,

The Watsons. As unproductive as this period of her life was, she emerged from it a much altered person and ready for the remarkable achievements of her last years. In 1800, she was twenty-five and still single. Her father retired in 1801, and with her parents and sister she moved to Bath. Her letters reveal the depression of these years, indeed the personal crisis that she underwent. Uprooted from Steventon and faced with the grim prospect of spinsterhood, she found little satisfaction in her life, with its hollow rituals and ceremonies, and she took little pleasure in the people she saw. Parties and dances particularly irritated her and led to eruptions of ill feeling, as indicated by the brutal ironies and grotesque descriptions that stand out so strikingly in her correspondence. These outbursts made her uneasy with herself, and made her wish to change her ways, as in time she did.

The crisis in Austen's life took place when English society was undergoing deep internal change. Fearful of Jacobinism, reformers argued that only through moral and religious improvement would their country be safe. There is no question that Austen came under the influence of the reform movement. Her two clerical brothers were Evangelical, and her sister encouraged her to read authors such as Gisborne and Hannah More. Austen did read the books that Cassandra recommended; her response indicates that she was ambivalent, which other remarks also suggest. That the Evangelicals made her uneasy should not come as a surprise. Austen belonged very much to the eighteenth-century world that they were denouncing. In all probability she had been the type of 'husband hunting butterfly' they censured; her mind had a brittleness and ironic and satiric bent, the very tendencies that they criticised. As a girl she watched private theatricals in the Steventon barn; the reformers said private theatricals were wrong. Through Eliza she had been attracted to French culture; the Evangelicals regarded France and its culture as wicked and depraved. She had parodied a sermon and commented ironically and satirically on clerical relatives and acquaintances; they decried levity and irreverence.

Exactly when and how Austen's personal crisis became intertwined with the collective crisis in English life cannot be determined, but it seems to have happened as she became uneasy with herself over eruptions of ill feeling that resulted from the move to Bath and from the emotional strain of entering spinsterhood. While she could have felt this uneasiness in some other historical moment, the conditions that were peculiar to this period heightened it and contributed to an ensuing change of outlook. That she liked Gisborne's *Enquiry* in 1805 is significant not only because it indicates a positive response to an Evangelical publication, but because it helps to explain a self-awareness and reflectiveness that is so pronounced in her letters at this time. When she said in 1807 that looking back at her childhood made her 'all astonishment and shame', she was viewing her past through eyes that were influenced by Evangelicalism. She was unhappy over the type of girl that she had been and she was uncomfortable over her earlier life, when she had lived in the world that the reformers were trying to change.

There is no question that in Austen's final period, 1808–17, she was disturbed over past memories. The evidence of her being so is in *Mansfield Park*, the first of Austen's novels that fully reveals her new state of mind and outlook, just as it was the first to have been conceived and written in the nineteenth century, during the Revolutionary era. Its autobiographical references indicate a retrospective view, a looking back at the past and its eighteenth-century levity and self indulgence, its entertainments and amusements. In those references there is a clear element of censure, a disapproval and sense of guilt. The social argument in *Mansfield Park* continues that of the two previous novels, but presents it in a way that is new. Austen did not work that argument into an eighteenth-century framework, but placed it in the unstable world of the nineteenth century. The Bertram estate was divided, made up of sound and weak parts. Into its midst came the Crawfords and Fanny Price, responding differently to questions that, private as they might seem, stood for issues that were public. This novel could have had 'reform or ruin' as its motto, and precisely in the way that Evangelicals regarded that question; reform was necessary publicly and politically as well as individually and spiritually. *Mansfield Park* is not just about the ordination of Edmund Bertram but the ordination of society. And one of its subjects is the improvement of society, in the Burkean sense.

So what one finds in *Mansfield Park* is a novel that represents a major departure from Austen's earlier fiction. While she introduced a Burkean argument into *Sense and Sensibility* and *Pride and Prejudice*, she developed it more fully in *Mansfield Park* and tested it in ways that were possible only within the type of narrative framework that it provided. And this is the first novel to reveal the influence of Evangelicalism on Austen's thinking and writing, just as it is the first to carry an imprint of her wartime experience and her new way of viewing the family. Between all of these parts of *Mansfield Park* there were logical connections. Together, they were part of an integrated whole, a cluster of ideas, values and commitments that took shape as a common response to the French Revolution and Napoleonic Wars.

In the final two novels and *Sanditon* Austen continued to work out her conservative views. Her ideology was less visible in these works, but she treated some of the same topics. Her way of doing so reflected the shifting conditions of the last years of the Napoleonic Wars and the first years of the post-war period. While the themes of community and continuity continued to be important, they were treated differently, as Austen became more apprehensive over conditions that threatened the gentry's chances of survival. The traditional social order had been shaken and appeared incapable of adjusting to the new state of affairs. Indeed, judging from *Sanditon* Austen found a willingness among the propertied classes to identify with and support the very changes that were most menacing to the old society. After *Mansfield Park* Austen continued to develop themes that were consistent with and influenced by Evangelicalism and that reveal a deep sense of national awareness and indeed patriotism. The last two novels also show a continued retreat from the feminism of the early novels, depicting in Emma Woodhouse a heroine whose independent, wilful ways had to be corrected and in Anne Elliot a woman whose feelings suited her for the quiet and confinement of the home. Finally, there is a sense of order, a structure of authority, in the last two novels that connects them to *Mansfield Park*. Just as the theatrical episode indicated the importance of authority, so did the outcome of the Box Hill incident in *Emma* and the scene in *Persuasion* when Wentworth carried off a troublesome child. When Knightley told Emma how mistaken she had been he gained an ascendancy that was the necessary condition of their marriage. The masterful way of this hero was matched by that of Wentworth, whose achievements as a sailor gave him a presence and inner strength that won the begrudging respect of the smug, complacent Elliots.

How different the heroes and heroines of the late novels are from those of the early novels. As a non-resident clergyman who was fully acquainted with the urbane ways of Bath, Henry Tilney was at one with the eighteenth century. So too, in a very different way, was Edward Ferrars, who was content to live a life of leisure until Brandon gave him a curacy. That Austen would have created such heroes after *Mansfield Park* is all but unimaginable. By the time she wrote that novel she lived fully in the nineteenth century; by that time her thinking and writing had been deeply affected by the sea change that swept over England as a result of the French Revolution. So the heroes of the late novels are not urbane or ineffectual but serious, principled, socially responsible, publicly active and instruments of national salvation. By the same token the heroines of the late novels had different characteristics, or did so after being corrected. Just as Emma Woodhouse mended her ways, so was the world of Austen's late novels reformed. It was a world whose sense of order, atmosphere and underlying value structure at once represented the profound change in English life during the Revolutionary Age and the personal change that gave Austen a new awareness of herself and her society. It was a world that anticipated the coming of the Victorian age.

Notes

Introduction

1. Frank Bradbrook, *Jane Austen and her Predecesors* (Cambridge, 1967).
2. *My Aunt Jane Austen, A Memoir* (London, 1952), 9.
3. 'Sanditon – The Seventh Novel', in *Jane Austen's Achievement*, ed. Juliet McMaster (London, 1976), 1–26.
4. *The Reign of George III, 1760–1815* (Oxford, 1960), 538.
5. *England in 1815* (New York, 1961: 1st French ed., 1913), 514.
6. *British History in The Nineteenth Century and After, 1782–1919* (New York, 1966; 1st ed., 1922), 129.
7. *An Introduction to the English Novel*, vol. 1 (London, 1967; 1st ed., 1951), 25.
8. *The Social History of Art*, vol. 4 (New York, n.d.; 1st German ed., 1953), 120.
9. *Sincerity and Authenticity* (Cambridge, U.S.A., 1973), 76.
10. 'Mansfield Park', in *The Opposing Self* (New York, 1959; 1st ed., 1955), 206–30.
11. 'Emma', in *Encounter*, vol. VIII (June, 1957), 49–59.
12. *A Reading of Mansfield Park: An Essay in Critical Synthesis* (Baltimore, 1970).
13. *The Improvement of The Estate: A Study of Jane Austen's Novels* (Baltimore, 1971).
14. *Jane Austen and The War of Ideas* (Oxford, 1975).
15. 'Manners, Morals, and the Novel', in *The Liberal Imagination: Essays on Literature and Society* (New York, 1953), 200.

Chapter 1

1. *Northanger Abbey, The Novels of Jane Austen*, vol. 5, ed. R. W. Chapman (London, 1969). All subsequent references will be to the 6 vol. Chapman edition.
2. *Jane Austen's Letters*, ed. R. W. Chapman, 2nd ed. (London, 1952). All subsequent references will be to this edition.
3. *Persuasion, with a Memoir of Jane Austen*, ed. R. W. Harding (Harmondsworth, 1965), 282.
4. Ibid., 279.
5. *Life and Letters*, (New York, 1965), vii.
6. *Jane Austen* (New York, 1949), 37.
7. *My Aunt*, 9.
8. *The Double Life of Jane Austen* (London, 1952), 29.
9. 'Jane Austen and the Peerage', *Proceedings of the Modern Language Association*, vol. LXVIII (December, 1953), 1031.
10. 'The Education of Emma Woodhouse', in *Jane Austen: Emma: a Casebook*, ed. David Lodge (London, 1968), 188–94.

11. *A Reading*, 29.

12. For this discussion I have used Lewis Namier, *England in the Age of the American Revolution* (New York, 1930), 180–202, 'Country Gentlemen in Parliament, 1750–84', and 'Monarchy and the Party System', both in *Personalities and Powers* (New York, 1965; 1st ed., 1955), 59–77, 13–38; Keith Feiling, *The Second Tory Party, 1714–1832* (London, 1939); John Brooke, 'Party in the Eighteenth-Century', in *Silver Renaissance: Essays in Eighteenth-Century English History*, ed. Alex Natan (New York, 1961), 20–37; Ian B. Christie, 'Was There a "New Toryism" in the Earlier Part of George III's Reign?', in *Myth and Reality in Late-Eighteenth-Century British Politics and Other Papers* (Berkeley, 1970), 196–213; Richard Pares, *King George III and the Politicians* (London, 1967; 1st ed., 1953), 71–92; Archibald Foord, *His Majesty's Opposition, 1714—1830* (Oxford, 1964); Michael Roberts, *The Whig Party, 1807–12* (London, 1965); F. O'Gorman, *The Whig Party and The French Revolution* (New York, 1967).

13. For the impact of the French Revolution on England, see Hevda Ben-Israel, *English Historians on The French Revolution* (Cambridge, 1968), 3–9; R. R. Palmer, *The Age of Democratic Revolution, A Political History of Europe and America, The Struggle*, vol. 2 (Princeton, 1964), 459–505; Watson, *The Reign*, 356–77; Briggs, *The Making of Modern England, 1783–1867: The Age of Improvement* (New York, 1965; 1st ed., 1959), 129–83; P. A. Brown, *The French Revolution in English History* (London, 1918); W. E. H. Lecky, *A History of England in the Eighteenth Century*, vols. 6, 7 (London, 1877); George Stead Veitch, *The Genesis of Parliamentary Reform* (London, 1913), chs. 5–14; E. P. Thompson, *The Making of the English Working Class* (New York, 1966; 1st ed., 1964), 1–185; Alfred Cobban, *The Debate on the French Revolution* (London, 1950); Crane Brinton, *The Political Ideas of the English Romantics* (New York, 1962; 1st ed., 1926); and Carl Woodring, *Politics in English Romantic Poetry* (Cambridge, USA, 1970).

14. 'Regulated Hatred: An Aspect of the Work of Jane Austen', *Scrutiny*, vol. VIII (1940), 351.

15. *Life and Letters*, 42.

16. Ibid., 44.

17. Ibid.

18. *Jane Austen's Literary Manuscripts* (Oxford, 1964), 7.

19. A Walton Litz, *Jane Austen: A Study of Her Artistic Development*, (New York, 1965), 63–5; Alistair Duckworth, *The Improvement*, 96.

20. For the Gordon Riots see J. P. De Castro, *The Gordon Riots* (London, 1926) and Christopher Hibbert, *King Mob: The Story of Lord George Gordon and the London Riots of 1780* (London, 1958).

21. R. A. Austen-Leigh, *Austen Papers, 1704–1856* (London, 1942), 146.

22. There was a fear in 1797, the year before Austen began *Northanger Abbey*, that the Bank and Tower would fall into rebel hands. See Arthur Bryant, *The Years of Endurance, 1793–1802* (London, 1942), 69.

23. For a discussion of spies see Thompson, *The Making*, 82–3, 485–94, 582–3, 593–9, and Veitch, *Parliamentary Reform*, 335–7.

24. 'Regulated Hatred', 348. For a brilliant critique of the spies passage, and of the Harding article, see B. C. Southam, ' "Regulated Hatred", Revisited,' *Jane Austen: Northanger Abbey and Persuasion, a Casebook*, ed. B. C. Southam (London, 1976), 121–7, which I saw only after writing the present text. Southam assumes that Austen inserted the spies and riot passages while making revisions

in 1816. While there is no way to prove his case or mine, I do think that Austen's comments in the Advertisement about changes in English life in the last thirteen years, which might make parts of the novel seem obsolete, indicate that she did not introduce new elements with a contemporary frame of reference.

25. J. M. S. Tompkins, *The Popular Novel in England, 1770–1800* (London, 1961; 1st ed., 1932), 251. Marilyn Butler sees anti-Jacobin imaginings in the Gothic novels of the 1790s, suggesting that the similarities between fictional horror and the actual violence of the time was not entirely accidental, *Jane Austen*, 30–1, 114. The historian Georges Lefebvre says that the Revolution 'inflamed human passions, and its numerous and terrible vicissitudes affected a good many people who were to develop a morbid taste for the unstable and the horrible, as the success of Anne Radcliffe's novels aptly demonstrated', *Napoleon: From 18 Brumaire to Tilsit, 1799–1807*, trans. Henry F. Stockhold (London, 1969; 1st French ed., 1935), 13. W. L. Renwick, *English Literature, 1789–1815* (Oxford, 1963), 87, sees conscious comparisons between Radcliffe's Gothic horror and violence in contemporary France, and comments on Radcliffe's conversations with French *émigrés* in Germany.

26. 'Francophobia in *Emma*', *Studies in English Literature*, vol. v, no. 4 (Autumn, 1965), 607–17.

27. *Sincerity and Authenticity*, 57 ff.

28. *Strictures on the Modern System of Female Education* (London, 1799), 315.

29. *The Works of Hannah More* (New York, 1835), 2 vols. in 1, 435.

30. Ibid., 453.

31. See Tony Tanner, 'Jane Austen and the Quiet Thing', in *Critical Essays on Jane Austen*, ed. B. C. Southam (London, 1968), 136–61.

32. Gerald W. Chapman describes Burke as a 'Tory Whig', *Edmund Burke: The Practical Imagination* (Cambridge, U.S.A., 1967), 1.

33. R. R. Palmer, *The Age*, 308–17; Peter J. Stanlis, 'Edmund Burke and the Scientific Rationalism of the Enlightenment', in *Edmund Burke and the Modern World*, ed. Stanlis (Detroit, 1967).

34. Quoted in Alfred Cobban, *Edmund Burke and the Revolt Against The Eighteenth Century* (New York, 1929), 81–2. For my discussion of Burke I have also used Chapman, *Edmund Burke*; Carl Cone, *Burke and the Nature of Politics: The Age of the French Revolution*, vol. 2 (Kentucky, 1964); Gertrude Himmelfarb, *Victorian Minds* (New York, 1970), 3–31; Leslie Stephen, *History of English Thought in the Eighteenth Century*, 2 vols. (New York, 1962; 1st ed., 1876), vol. 2, 185–214; Robert A. Smith, 'Burke's Crusade Against the French Revolution: Principles and Prejudices', in *Edmund Burke and the Modern World*; C. E. Vaughan, *Studies in the History of Political Thought* (New York, 1960), 7–63; and Bernard M. Schilling, *Conservative England and the Case Against Voltaire* (New York, 1950), 165–77.

35. Litz believes that Austen completely re-saw *Pride and Prejudice*, which she had not done with *Sense and Sensibility*: *Jane Austen*, 97.

36. I would again like to express my indebtedness to Duckworth, on whom the following discussion leans heavily, *The Improvements*, 35–80. I have also used Fleishman, *An Introduction*, esp. 3–42; Litz, *Jane Austen*, 112–31; Kenneth Moler, *Jane Austen's Art of Illusion* (Lincoln, Nebraska, 1968), 109–54; David Lodge, 'The Vocabulary of Mansfield Park', in *Language of Fiction: Essays in*

Criticism and Verbal Analysis of the English Novel (London, 1966), 94–113; Charles Murrah, 'The Background of Mansfield Park', in *From Jane Austen to Joseph Conrad*, ed. Robert C. Rathburn and Martin Steinman, Jr. (Minneapolis, 1958), 23–34; Joseph W. Donahue, 'Ordination and the Divided House at Mansfield Park', *English Literary History*, vol. 32 (June, 1965), 169–78; Lionel Trilling, 'Mansfield Park'; Tony Tanner, introduction to the Penguin edition of *Mansfield Park* (Harmondsworth, 1966), 7–36, and 'The Quiet Thing'; Denis Donoghue, 'A View of "Mansfield Park"', in *Critical Essays*, 39–59; Stuart M. Tave, *Some Words of Jane Austen* (Chicago, 1973), 158–204; Joseph M. Duffy, Jr., 'Moral Integrity and Moral Anarchy in *Mansfield Park*', *ELH*, vol. xxii (March, 1956), 71–91; and Thomas R. Edwards, Jr., 'The Difficult Beauty of *Mansfield Park*', *Nineteenth-Century Fiction*, vol. xx (June, 1965), 51–67.

37. *Reflections on the Revolution in France* (Indianapolis, 1955), 97.
38. Ibid., 108.
39. For my discussion of *Emma* I have used Duckworth, *The Improvement*, 145–78; Litz, *Jane Austen*, 132–49; Butler, *Jane Austen*, 250–74; Trilling, 'Emma'; R. E. Hughes, 'The Education'; Edgar F. Shannon, Jr., 'Emma: Character and Construction', *PMLA*, vol. lxxi (Sept., 1956), 637–50; Mark Schorer, 'The Humiliation of Emma Woodhouse', *The Literary Review*, vol. ii, No. 4 (Summer, 1959), 547–63; Karl Kroeber, *Styles in Fictional Structure: The Art of Jane Austen, Charlotte Bronte, George Eliot* (Princeton, 1971), 18–78; Malcom Bradbury, 'Jane Austen's *Emma*', *Critical Quarterly* (Winter, 1962), 335–64; Arnold Kettle, *An Introduction*, 86–98; and Tave, *Some Words*, 205–55.
40. Mingay, *English Landed Society in the Eighteenth Century* (London, 1962), 89.
41. For my discussion of *Persuasion* I have used Duckworth, *The Improvement*, 180–208; Moler, *Art of Illusion*, 187–223; Butler, *Jane Austen*, 274–86; Tave, *Some Words*, 256–87; and Litz, *Jane Austen*, 150–64.
42. For *Sanditon* I have used Duckworth, *The Improvement*, 210–29 and Southam, *Jane Austen's Literary Manuscripts*, 100–35. Since this was written Southam's superb article has appeared, 'Sanditon: The Seventh Novel'. See note 3 to Introduction.
43. Harold Perkin, *The Origins of Modern English Society, 1780–1880* (London, 1969), 176–95.
44. Cobbett is the best guide to the former, *Rural Rides*, ed. George Woodcock (Harmondsworth, 1967). For the East Anglian riots and agricultural conditions generally see E. J. Hobsbawn and George Rudé, *Captain Swing* (New York, 1975; 1st ed., 1968), 13–93, and F. M. L. Thompson, *English Landed Society in the Nineteenth Century* (London, 1963), 231 ff. For a discussion of the 1811–12 riots see Frank Darvall, *Popular Disturbances and Public Order in Regency England* (New York, 1969; 1st ed., 1934).

Chapter 2

1. F. M. Pinion, *A Jane Austen Companion* (London, 1973), 24.
2. *Jane Austen: A Survey* (London, 1929), 281–2.
3. *George Meredith and English Comedy* (New York, 1969), 28.
4. *The Pelican Guide to English Literature: from Blake to Bryon*, vol. 5, ed. Boris Ford (Harmondsworth, 1957), 52.

5. *Jane Austen's Novels, a Study in Structure* (Harmondsworth, 1962; 1st ed., 1953), 26.

6. For my discussion of the war I have used David G. Chandler, *The Campaigns of Napoleon* (New York, 1966), 319–27, 593–660; Sir J. W. Fortescue, *A History of the British Army*, 10 vols. (1899–1920); Watson, *The Reign*, 356–434, 463–500; Briggs, *The Making*, 129–83; R. J. White, *The Age of George III* (Garden City, 1969), 217–29; Arthur Bryant, *The Years of Endurance*; Corelli Barnett, *Britain and her Army, 1509–1970: A Military, Political and Social Survey* (New York, 1970); Georges Lefebvre, *Napoleon*, vol. 1, 4–115, 162–231; *The New Cambridge Modern History, The Old Regime, 1713–63*, vol. 7, ed. J. A. Lindsay (Cambridge, 1957), 163–89, *The American and French Revolution, 1763–93*, vol. 8, ed. A. Goodwin (Cambridge, 1965), 174–217, and *War and Peace in an Age of Upheaval, 1793–1830*, vol. 9, ed. C. W. Crawley (Cambridge, 1965), 60–90; Carola Oman, *Britain Against Napoleon* (London, 1943); and J. R. Western, *The English Militia in The Eighteenth Century, The Story of a Political Issue, 1660–1802* (London, 1965).

7. Peter Paret, 'The History of War', in *Historical Studies Today*, ed. Felix Gilbert and Stephen R. Graubard (New York, 1972), 372–92.

8. John H. Glazley, 'Arthur Young and Nationalism', in *Nationalism and Internationalism, Essays, Inscribed to Carlton J. H. Hayes* (New York, 1950), 144–89.

9. See Lefebvre, *Napoleon: From Tilsit to Waterloo, 1807–1815*, vol. 2, trans. J. E. Anderson (New York, 1969; 1st French ed., 1935), 288–95; Norman Hampson, 'The French Revolution and the Nationalization of Honour', in *War and Society, Historical Essays in Memory of J. R. Western, 1928–1971*, ed. M. R. D. Frost (London, 1973), 199–212; Carlton J. H. Hayes, *The Historical Development of Modern Nationalism* (New York, 1931), 99 ff.; Hans Kohn, *The Idea of Nationalism, The First Era of Global History* (New York, 1944), 155–83, 458–64; and Boyd Shafer, *Faces of Nationalism, New Realities and Old Myths* (New York, 1972), 23–137.

10. *Critical Review*, vol. 28, (August, 1803), 465.

11. *Edinburgh*, vol. 20, (July, 1812), 215.

12. Ibid., vol. 23, (April, 1814), 2.

13. Ibid., 8.

14. *Practical View of the Religious System of Professed Christians Contrasted with Real Christians* (New York, 1856), 453.

15. *Edinburgh*, vol. 10, (April, 1807), 1.

16. Jan. 5, 1809.

17. *Edinburgh*, vol. 13, (October, 1809), 198.

18. From a review in *The Critical Review*, vol. 12, (October, 1795), 161–2.

19. Ibid., 162.

20. Ibid., vol. 29, (November, 1803), 350.

21. *Edinburgh*, vol. 23, (January, 1814), 303.

22. *Jane Austen's Sailor Brothers* (London, 1906).

23. See Notes for Letter 47.

24. For discussions of the invasion plans see William James, *The Naval History of Great Britain, from The Declaration of War by France in 1793 to the Accession of George IV*, 6 vols. (London, 1878), vol. 3, 212–33, vol. 4, 78–85; Chandler, *Campaigns*, 319–26; Capt. A. T. Mahan, *The Influence of Sea Power Upon The French Revolution and the Empire, 1793–1815*, 2 vols. (Boston, 1898), vol. 2, 101–97; *The*

Cambridge Modern History, vol. 9 (New York, 1907), ch. 8; Carola Oman, *Napoleon at The Channel* (Garden City, 1942), 139–97; and Watson, *The Reign*, 409–32.

25. Hubback, *Sailor Brothers*, 113.

26. *Letters*, 166.

27. Marvin Mudrick, *Jane Austen, Irony as Defense and Discovery* (Berkeley, 1968; 1st ed., 1952), 1.

28. J. H. Greene, 'Austen and The Peerage,' 1030–1.

29. *The Quarterly Review*, vol. 5, (1811), 404.

30. Ibid.

31. *The Military Policy and Institutions of the British Empire*, 5th ed. (London, 1914), 129.

32. See Sir Alan Burns, *A History of the British West Indies* (London, 1965), 564–97; Fleishman, *A Reading*, 136–9; and Lefebvre, *Napoleon*, vol. 1, 194–7.

33. Hubback, *Sailor Brothers*, 192.

34. Brigid Brophy thinks that the pun '*was* anatomically intended', 'Jane Austen and the Stuarts,' *Critical Essays*, ed. Southam, 25.

Chapter 3

1. *Reaction and Revolution, 1814–1832* (New York, 1934), 17.

2. *The Truthtellers, Jane Austen, George Eliot, D. H. Lawrence* (New York, 1967), 23–8.

3. *The Improvement*, 26.

4. 'Jane Austen and the Moralists', in *Critical Essays*, ed. Southam, 106–22.

5. *Persuasion with A Memoir of Jane Austen*, 338.

6. R. W. Chapman, *Jane Austen, Facts and Problems*, 3rd ed. (Oxford, 1950), 98.

7. *Remarks on the Speech of M. Dupont, made in the National Convention of France, on the Subjects of Religion and Education*, 2nd ed. (London, 1793), 7.

8. See V. G. Kiernan, 'Evangelicalism and the French Revolution', *Past and Present*, vol. 1 (February, 1952), 44–70; Ford K. Brown, *Fathers of the Victorians, The Age of Wilberforce* (Cambridge, 1961); W. R. Ward, *Religion and Society in England, 1790–1850* (New York, 1973), 1–69; Maurice Quinlan, *Victorian Prelude: a History of English Manners, 1700–1830* (Hamden, 1965), 68–100; Richard A. Soloway, *Prelates and People: Ecclesiastical Social Thought in England, 1732–1852*, 19–93; Soloway, 'Reform or Ruin: English Moral Thought During the First French Republic', *The Review of Politics*, vol. 25 (January, 1963), 110–28; Norman Sykes, *Church and State in the XVIIIth Century* (Cambridge, 1934); David Spring, 'Aristocracy, Social Structure and Religion in the Early Victorian Period', *Victorian Studies*, vol. 6 (March 1963), 263–80; Halévy, *England*, 389–485; Muriel Jaeger, *Before Victoria: Changing Standards and Behaviour, 1787–1837* (Harmondsworth, 1967; 1st ed., 1956); and R. W. Harris, *Romanticism and the Social Order, 1780–1830* (London, 1969), 126–40.

9. *An Enquiry into The Duties of the Female Sex* (Philadelphia, 1799), 69.

10. *Strictures*, 313.

11. *Edinburgh*, vol. 11 (January, 1808), 357.

12. Litz, '*The Loiterer*: a Reflection of Jane Austen's Early Environment', *Review of English Studies*, vol. XII (August, 1961), 251–61.

13. C. S. Lewis, 'A Note on Jane Austen', *Essays in Criticism*, vol. IV (October, 1954), 359–71.
14. Southam, *Jane Austen's Literary Manuscripts*, 45–52, J. A. Levine, 'Lady Susan: Jane Austen's Character of the Merry Widow', *Studies in English Literature 1500–1900*, vol. I, no. 4 (1961), 23–34.
15. Frank C. Bradbrook suggests that Laclos was Austen's model, *Jane Austen and Her Predecessors* (Cambridge, 1967), 123.
16. Fleishman, *A Reading*, 19.
17. See Max Weber, *The Protestant Ethic and The Spirit of Capitalism* (New York, 1958; 1st German ed., 1906); R. H. Tawney, *Religion and the Rise of Capitalism* (New York, 1958; 1st ed., 1926); Ernst Troeltsch, *The Social Teachings of the Christian Church* (New York, 1960; 1st German ed., 1911); David Little, *Religion, Order and Law, a Study in Pre-Revolutionary England* (New York, 1969); and H. R. Trevor-Roper, 'Religion, the Reformation and Social Change', in *The European Witch Craze of the Sixteenth Century, and Other Essays* (New York, 1969), 1–45.
18. '*Mansfield Park* and *Lovers' Vows*', *Rev. Eng. Stud*, vol. IX (1933), 451–56. Also see E. M. Butler, ' "Mansfield Park" and Kotzebue's "Lovers' Vows" ', *Modern Language Review,* vol. XXVIII (July, 1933), 326–37, and Sybil Rosenfeld, 'Jane Austen and Private Theatricals', *Essays and Studies*, vol. XV (1962), 40–51.
19. Lodge, 'A Question of Judgement, the Theatricals at Mansfield Park', *Nineteenth-Century Fiction*, vol. 17 (December, 1972), 275–82, and 'The Vocabulary', 94–113.
20. See Joel Weisenheimer, '*Mansfield Park*: Three Problems', *Nineteenth-Century Fiction*, vol. 29 (Sept., 1974), 185–205.
21. R. A. Austen-Leigh., *Austen Papers*, 127.
22. *Fiction with a Purpose: Major and Minor Nineteenth-Century Novels* (Bloomington and London, 1967), 66–104.
23. 'The Humiliation', 550.
24. *The Language of Jane Austen* (Oxford, 1972), 60–8.
25. Kiernan, 'Evangelicalism', 44.

Chapter 4

1. See Doris Stenton, *The English Woman in History* (London and New York, 1957), 183–349; W. Lyon Blease, *The Emancipation of English Women* (London, 1910), 3–79; Myra Reynolds, *The Learned Lady in England, 1650–1760* (Boston and New York, 1920); Jacob Bouten, *Mary Wollstonecraft: the Beginnings of Female Emancipation in France and England* (Amsterdam, 1922); and Gina Luria, *Mary Hays (1760–1843)*, doctoral dissertation (NYU, 1972). Professor Luria has edited a series of 44 works, published in 89 volumes under the title *The Feminist Controversy in England, 1788–1810*. This series makes available the key feminist and anti-feminist works of this period in facsimile editions, and includes valuable introductions and bibliographical sections. The other main source for the feminist controversy is the journals of the time, such as the *Edinburgh Review, Gentleman's Magazine, The Quarterly Review, The Anti-Jacobin Review, The Evangelical Review* and the *Critical Review*.
2. Reynolds, *Learned Lady*, 454–6.

3. *Letters*, 133.
4. Her immediate reason for writing the work was the issuance in France of a report, on 10 September, 1791, recommending free education but saying nothing about the education of women. Wollstonecraft wanted to promote the cause of womens' education both in France and England. See Eleanor Flexner, *Mary Wollstonecraft, A Biography* (Baltimore, 1973), 148–9.
5. For a discussion of eighteenth-century female life see Macaulay, *History of England, from the Accession of James II*, 4 vols. (London and New York), vol. 1, 296–7; G. E. and K. R. Fussell, *The English Countrywoman, a Farmhouse Social History, A.D. 1500–1900* (New York, 1971), 74–156; and Dorothy Gardiner, *Girlhood at School, a Study of Women's Education Through Twelve Centuries* (Oxford, 1929), 333–59.
6. Except, of course, the retarded brother, George.
7. *Austen Papers*, 148.
8. *Letters*, 443.
9. For a discussion of eighteenth-century female novelists and their way of depicting the female code see Tompkins, *Popular Novel*, 116–71; Philippe Séjourné, *Aspects généraux du roman féminin en Angleterre, de 1740 a 1800* (Aix-en-Provence, 1960); Robert Palfrey Utter and Gwendolyn Bridges Needham, *Pamela's Daughters* (New York, 1930); Joyce M. Horner, *The English Women Novelists and Their Connection with the Feminist Movement, 1687–1797* (Northampton, U.S.A., 1929–30); Muriel Masefield, *Woman Novelists, from Fanny Burney to George Eliot* (Freeport, 1967); G. B. McCarthy, *The Later Women Novelists, 1744–1818* (Oxford, 1947); and Joyce Hemlow, 'Fanny Burney and the Courtesy Books', *PMLA*, vol. LXV (1950), 1732–61.
10. See above, p. 115.
11. See David Daiches, 'Jane Austen, Karl Marx, and the Aristocratic Dance', *The American Scholar*, vol. XVII (Summer, 1948), 289–96; Utter and Needham, *Pamela's Daughters*, 30–5; Ian Watt, *The Rise of the Novel, Studies in Defoe, Richardson and Fielding* (Berkeley, 1967; 1st ed., 1957), 135–73; and J. F. G. Gornall, 'Marriage and Property in Jane Austen's Novels', *History Today*, Vol. XVII (December, 1967), 805–11.
12. Moler, *Jane Austen's Art*, 24–5, 85–6; Litz, *Jane Austen*, 62.
13. Fordyce, *Sermons to Young Women* (Philadelphia and New York, 1809), esp. pp. 3, 8, 12, 24, 38, 43, 47–8.
14. For Mrs. Grant see quote on p. 167 above. Isabella Knightley passed 'her life with those she doated on, full of their merits, blind to their faults, and always innocently busy (was) . . . a model of right feminine happiness', *Emma*, p. 140.
15. Tompkins, *Popular Novel*, 315–17.
16. Vol. II, (May, 1804), 457–8.
17. *Tales and Novels*, 9 vols. (New York, 1833), vol. 6, 221–2.
18. As Marilyn Butler very helpfully explained to me after reading this chapter.
19. Butler, *Maria Edgeworth: A Literary Biography* (Oxford, 1972), 109.
20. See Butler, *Jane Austen*, 117–23; Tompkins, *Popular Novel*, 318–28; and Allene Gregory, *The French Revolution and the English Novel* (New York, 1966; 1st ed., 1926), 139–52.
21. Bouten, *Wollstonecraft*, 3–8, 99–104.
22. *Strictures*, 323.

23. J. H. Randall, *The Making of the Modern Mind* (New York 1954; 1st ed., 1926), 317. For a discussion of Helvétius's influence on Wollstonecraft, see Bouten, *Wollstonecraft*, 150–51.

24. Colby, *Fiction with a Purpose*, 68–70.

25. More, *Complete Works*, 381.

26. More also disapproved of German plays in *Cœlebs*. See *Complete Works*, 432.

27. Tony Tanner, Introduction, *Sense and Sensibility* (Harmondsworth, 1969), 32.

28. Trilling, 'Emma', 43–4; Wayne C. Booth, 'Point of View and the Control of Distance in *Emma*', *Nineteenth-Century Fiction*, vol. 16 (September, 1961), 95–116.

29. Schorer, 'Humiliation', 109.

30. Krober, *Styles*, 19–21.

31. See Moler, *Art*, 187–223.

32. Lloyd W. Brown interprets the Anne Elliot–Harville conversation differently, 'Jane Austen and the Feminist Tradition', *Nineteenth-Century Fiction*, vol. 28 (December, 1973), 321–38, finding a 'skeptical reserve' (p. 325) in her 'understatements' that he regards as evidence of Austen's feminism. What strikes me about Anne's part of the conversation is the depth of her feeling, as indicated by her 'faltering voice' and inability, at the end, to 'have uttered another sentence; her heart was too full, her breath too much oppressed'. (P,235) Emotions such as these do not seem to me to be compatible with a 'skeptical reserve'. Nor do I agree with Brown's statement that Austen was 'little concerned with marriage as a socially sanctified and self-justifying good'. (p. 336) In fact, the conversation between Anne and Harville is evidence of the seriousness with which Austen, at this time of her life, regarded marriage. One of the reasons that Anne was so overcome by emotion as she discussed the male and female roles and how they related to marriage was that, a few moments before, a remark by Mrs. Croft about engagements led her instinctively to look at Wentworth, just as his eye moved toward her. Thinking about her marriage to Wentworth gave her a 'nervous thrill all over . . .'. (P,231) Brown's view of Austen in this article is consistent with that of his book, *Bits of Ivory: Narrative Techniques in Jane Austen's Fiction* (Baton Rouge, 1973), which sees the novelist as a representative of the eighteenth century.

Index